Making Media

Making Media

FOUNDATIONS OF SOUND AND IMAGE PRODUCTION

Second Edition

JAN ROBERTS-BRESLIN

Photography by JAN ROBERTS-BRESLIN
Illustrations by DANIEL BRESLIN

ELSEVIER

AMSTERDAM • BOSTON • HEIDELBERG • LONDON
NEW YORK • OXFORD • PARIS • SAN DIEGO
SAN FRANCISCO • SINGAPORE • SYDNEY • TOKYO

Focal Press is an imprint of Elsevier

Focal Press

Publisher: Elinor Actipis
Associate Acquisitions Editor: Cara Anderson
Publishing Services Manager: George Morrison
Senior Project Manager: Dawnmarie Simpson
Assistant Editor: Robin Weston
Marketing Manager: Marcel Koppes, Becky Pease
Cover Design: Alisa Andreola
Interior Design: Alisa Andreola

Focal Press is an imprint of Elsevier
30 Corporate Drive, Suite 400, Burlington, MA 01803, USA
Linacre House, Jordan Hill, Oxford OX2 8DP, UK

 Recognizing the importance of preserving what has been written, Elsevier prints its books on
acid-free paper whenever possible.

Library of Congress Cataloging-in-Publication Data
Roberts-Breslin, Jan.
  Making media : foundations of sound and image production / Jan Roberts-Breslin. – 2nd ed.
      p. cm.
  Includes bibliographical references and index.
  ISBN 978-0-240-80907-6 (pbk. : alk. paper) 1. Multimedia systems. 2. Sound–Recording and
reproducing. 3. Image processing–Digital techniques. I. Title.
  QA76.575.B74 2007
  006.7–dc22

                                                                        2007023245

British Library Cataloguing-in-Publication Data
A catalogue record for this book is available from the British Library.

ISBN: 978-0-240-80907-6

For information on all Focal Press publications
visit our website at www.books.elsevier.com

09 10 11 5 4 3 2
Printed in the United States of America

For Gene and Eleanor, who gave me my foundation.

CONTENTS

Acknowledgments   xi
Introduction   xiii

1 Content and Preproduction   1

The Primacy of Content   1
Developing Story Ideas   1
Preproduction Process   7
Ethical and Legal Responsibilities   15
Conclusion   19
Putting It Into Practice   21
Key Concepts   21

2 The Frame   23

Seeing the World Through a Frame   23
Controlling the Frame   24
Reproducing the Frame   39
The Frame Applied to Different Media   50
Conclusion   62
Putting It Into Practice   62
Key Concepts   63

3 Depth and Movement in the Frame   65

Media Illusions   65
Creating Visual Depth   66

Movement   69

Movement Considerations in Different Media   80

Animation and Motion Graphics   82

Conclusion   83

Putting It Into Practice   83

Key Concepts   84

4 Light   85

The Importance of Light   85

Understanding Light   86

Lighting Concerns of Different Media   107

Conclusion   113

Putting It Into Practice   113

Key Concepts   113

5 Sound   115

The Importance of Sound   115

Understanding Sound   116

Reproducing Sound   119

Sound Variations   129

Types of Audio Media   138

Conclusion   140

Putting It Into Practice   140

Key Concepts   141

6 Sound and Image   143

A + B = C   143

Sound Recording for Different Media   146

Conclusion   150

Putting It Into Practice   151

Key Concepts   151

7 Time   153

Time and Space   153

Sounds and Images Existing in Time   157

Conclusion   162
Putting It Into Practice   162
Key Concepts   163

8 The Theory of Linear Structure   165

Putting the Story Together   165
Approaches to Structuring Film and Video   168
Applications of Structure   182
Conclusion   186
Putting It Into Practice   186
Key Concepts   187

9 The Practice of Linear Structure   189

Sound and Image Transitions   189
Live Editing   191
Postproduction Editing   194
Digital Nonlinear Editing   208
Issues of Convergence and Compatibility   220
Conclusion   221
Putting It Into Practice   222
Key Concepts   222

10 Nonlinear Structure   225

Understanding Nonlinearity   225
Interactive Media   228
Software Applications   235
Putting the Pieces Together   239
Conclusion   242
Putting It Into Practice   243
Key Concepts   243

11 Approaches to Production, Exhibition,
and Distribution   245

Traditional and Convergent Trends and Predictions   245
Determining Your Approach   245

Distribution and Exhibition   253

The Future   255

Conclusion   256

Putting It Into Practice   256

Key Concepts   256

Glossary   257

Works Consulted   271

Index   273

With the second edition, the list grows of people whose contributions were integral to the completion of *Making Media*. I would first and foremost like to thank Daniel Breslin—for the illustrations, the original CD-ROM development (now moved to the web), and his ongoing help and support.

I am grateful to friends and colleagues who contributed examples of their creative work: Brooke Knight, Jeff Talman, Karla Berry, Roberto Carminati, Sanjeev Chatterjee, Michelle Citron, Christopher Outwin, Jean Stawarz, Robert Todd, Shun Liang, and Michael Petroff.

Thanks to James Sheldon and other Emerson faculty for their development of the course design on which this book is based and to Emerson College for many forms of support.

I would like also to thank those who contributed their feedback to this edition—David Kelleher, Heidi Mau, H. James Gilmore, Kelly Anderson, Susan Hogue, Cindy Stillwell, and Elizabeth McGraw—and students and friends who appeared in photographs or videos and helped with research—Manuel Abady, Sandy Prudencio, Kamil Can Akat, Kathryn Hall, Yael Bowman, Adam Catino, Gaia Chiesa, Joshua de la Fuente, Thomas Gallagher, Megan Hanceford, Eric Holland, Rashika Kaul, Shun Liang, Arlette McNeill, Edward Ryan, Wael Sayedalahl, Allyson Sherlock, Sharon Stafford, D. Rand Thomas, Takayuki Yukawa, and Ben Erlandson. A special thanks to Jack and Ellie Breslin who helped when asked and put up with my distraction.

Finally, thanks to those at Focal Press, including Elinor Actipis, Robin Weston, Alisa Marie Andreola, Dawnmarie Simpson, and especially Cara Anderson for her patience and much-needed nudging.

Introduction to Second Edition

There's an old saying that comes to mind as I complete the second edition of this book: "The more things change, the more they stay the same." Media making certainly changes. Since the first edition of this book was published just four years ago, high-definition video has gone from a very expensive cutting-edge medium to a format available in consumer-priced camcorders. Video on the web has progressed from small low-definition short videos that took forever to download to a common means of viewing television programming and a way of sharing content, allowing other users to reedit videos and repost them. Tapeless audio and video recorders are commonplace. The 4:3 shape of old television sets is quickly disappearing. All of these developments and more are covered in this edition. Interactive examples and activities that were included on a CD-Rom in the first edition are now available online at books.elsevier.com/companions/9780240809076.

Despite the changes, though, principles of visual and aural aesthetics are much the same. Framing, depth, movement, lighting, sound, time, and structure are all still important considerations in creating media that move us, entertain us, inform us. Learning to control these aesthetic elements allows us to reinforce the meaning of the stories we want to tell, the emotions we want to elicit, the beliefs we want to challenge. Styles of media change. Multicamera sitcoms with laugh tracks are being replaced by film-style comedies without. Galleries and museums are exhibiting more digital artworks and installations. Hollywood films are created in front of a green screen with virtual sets. Media are created, distributed, and consumed within a computer-based virtual society. But the passion of those who make the media is a constant. So learn the rules, break the rules, adapt to the changes, innovate, shock, inspire. Create tears, hilarity, and hope. Go make some media.

CHAPTER 1

Content and Preproduction

THE PRIMACY OF CONTENT

"I've got a great idea for a movie."
"I think other people would relate to my experience."
"The word needs to get out, and I want to say it."
"I want to make people laugh/cry/scream/care/change."

Do any of these statements sound familiar? Most of us become media makers because there are things we want to say and stories we want to tell. Figuring out what matters to you, what moves you, and what in turn will move others is the true starting point of making media.

This is not a book on writing. There are many good ones out there already. There are books about writing scripts for mainstream movies and television shows. There are ones that present an alternative approach and ones that emphasize the creative process and development of story ideas. This book is about the production process and the ways of realizing story ideas through sound and pictures. However, if we don't recognize the importance of content, the rest is in vain. All the virtuosity in the world when it comes to camera work, sound recording, lighting, and editing is not what brings us to the movie theater or causes us to turn on the TV, radio, or computer. We want information. We want to be entertained. We want to feel emotion or get a glimpse of life through another person's point of view. The techniques of media production are the tools that make telling your stories possible.

DEVELOPING STORY IDEAS

The term *story* is used here in the broadest sense. It refers to imagined events enacted by made-up characters. It also refers to information you want to teach or messages you want to share. I would even argue (though some would certainly disagree) that an emotional response elicited from abstract sounds and images tells a story of sorts. Sometimes production is a process of realizing your own story idea; sometimes it's a matter of interpreting an idea developed by someone else. Generating ideas is something that comes easy to some people; for others it's a challenge. There are many techniques for encouraging creativity. Keeping a dream journal and creating a scrapbook of intriguing news clippings are just

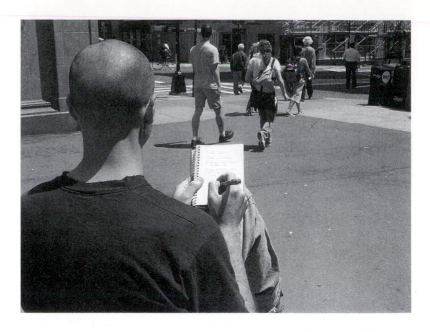

Figure 1.1 Careful observation of life around you is an important tool of story development.

a couple of ideas. Careful observation of everyday life helps you create fictional characters and situations that are believable (Figure 1.1). Keeping involved in the community and informed about social and political issues spurs the desire to inform and persuade others. Appreciation of other art forms, such as painting, sculpture, theater, live music, and dance, helps in making artful media. Ultimately, passion, keen observation, and perseverance mark good storytellers.

KNOWING YOUR AUDIENCE

Deciding what story you want to tell is just the first step. Next, you must decide to whom you want to tell it. There are a couple of ways to look at this. Do you want to produce your work and then try to find an audience that will respond to it? Or are you trying to target your message to a specific audience, be it large or small?

Media artists often fall into the first category. The creation of the work is satisfying in and of itself. Artists hope that others will appreciate the work too and that profit, or at least subsistence, will be forthcoming. As satisfying as self-expression can be, however, most artists are not satisfied to work in a vacuum. They want to contribute to the culture. Their work might be a critique of social values or an attempt to encourage debate or evoke a universal emotion. For that to happen, the work must find its audience.

Media activists and advertisers often fall into the second category. The work is created from and based on researched data or intuitive beliefs as to what will sway opinions and motivate action. The media activist might be promoting universal health care through a grassroots documentary to be shown at a community gathering. The advertiser might be trying to get everyone to buy a soft drink. Both are driven by how the audience responds.

For many makers of media, the audience relationship is somewhere in between. There is the desire to create high-quality work that fulfills the maker's drive for self-expression. But media makers must also face the realities of the marketplace and the need to make a living. In a capitalistic society, the value of a piece of work is judged, by many, in primarily economic terms. Sometimes the motivation to express one's creativity and the motivation to reach an audience are compatible; sometimes conflict arises between them. Sometimes that conflict exists within an individual maker; sometimes it is a conflict between different participants in a collaborative media project. The dynamics of self-expression and audience response, and the resulting tension between them, can make a better work.

MATCHING THE MEDIUM TO THE MESSAGE

You can categorize a work of audiovisual media in many different ways. You can consider the *type of programming*—fiction feature, sitcom, installation, documentary, etc. You can consider the *method of production* used to create the programming—film, video, audio recording, or digital imaging. You can also consider the *means of distribution*, the specific form of media on which the programming has been distributed. This could be a movie theater, radio broadcast, museum or gallery, cable TV, the Internet, or a DVD.

In the past, the relationship between the programming, the method of production, and the means of distribution has been much more straightforward than it is today. Movies were shot on film and seen in the theater. Television programming originated live and was broadcast to the TV set in your living room. Radio programming, also broadcast live, traveled through the air, via radio waves, and was heard in your house or car. Museums and galleries were for paintings, sculpture, and sometimes photography.

Now, the types of programming, the production methods, and the distribution means of media overlap much more. This is sometimes called **convergence** of the media. Movies can be in the theater, on DVD, streamed over the Internet, or downloaded to your iPod or cell phone. Movies are still mostly shot on film, but digital video and imaging techniques are increasingly being used in feature films. High-definition video is replacing film in many instances. Even if it is shot originally on film, footage is most likely transferred to video to be edited digitally, at least initially.

In the 1950s, television was almost exclusively live broadcast of video images and sound. By the 1960s, film became the prevalent production tool of prime-time television, and it is still widely used, along with digital video. Video is also used in interactive applications on DVD and on the Internet. Radio programming is often simultaneously broadcast via radio waves and streamed over the web. Such convergence is only expected to increase, but that doesn't mean the end of current combinations of programming, production methods, and means of distribution. It means new types and combinations of each. It means new opportunities for media artists to create new forms and explore challenging content (Figure 1.2).

Figure 1.2 One example of media convergence is the increasing use of video on iPods.

So many options do provide a challenge to the media maker. "I have a story to tell. Which is the best way to tell it? Should it be a two-hour film or an interactive story distributed on DVD? Should it be an audio documentary or a website?" These are not easy questions. Often the answer is driven by many factors. Audience becomes key to determining programming type and means of distribution. Who is your audience and what forms of media are they most likely to use? An entire sector of the media industry is dedicated to audience research to help answer these important questions. What programming type best communicates the message you want to send? Is the history of the civil rights movement in the United States told best by a dramatized reenactment or a factual website or perhaps by both? If you want to teach children about biology, is it better to create an entertaining TV show with a wacky scientist host or an interactive website that allows students to conduct virtual experiments and create digital habitats? The method of production is driven by the maker's talents and preferences, industry practice, and budget restrictions. The maker might prefer film to video, but the industry practice is to shoot talk shows on video. Industry practice might dictate that sitcoms are shot with multiple cameras in the studio, but a creator's vision and a budget to support it might allow a single-camera, location-based sitcom. If the audience likes it, there will be more, and it, too, will become an accepted way of doing things.

CLASSIFYING CONTENT

A basic premise of this book is that there are underlying concepts and concerns that apply to all types of media production, from Hollywood blockbusters to museum video installations. You will find as you make your way through this book that concepts such as frame, sound, time, and movement exist in all types of media. But you will also find that it becomes necessary or convenient at times to be able to classify works of media production, even though those classifications can overlap. One way of starting to organize the types of media production is to set up categories that apply to the relationship of the content to reality, or whether the content of the production is **fiction** or **nonfiction**.

Any time you start exploring the concepts of what is real or what is true, you're opening up a can of proverbial worms. Philosophers have been struggling with those questions for thousands of years. But for the sake of convenience and trying to provide some structure to the way we organize our thinking about the broad spectrum of media production, perhaps we can agree that *fiction* is based on an imagined event or series of events, often with made-up participants and locations. *Nonfiction*, then, portrays actual events or situations that exist in the material world. Common examples of fiction media include romantic comedy films, detective TV series, radio dramas, and simulated video or computer games. Generally, fiction media will involve actors playing roles, and plot and dialogue constructed by a writer. Nonfiction media range from historical documentaries, to video or webcam diaries, to reality TV, to live coverage of a football game. The events are often constructed into a story or **narrative** structure, but that narrative is based on real events. Participants or **subjects** represent themselves.

It doesn't take long, however, to start asking questions about these terms. As with many attempts to categorize and label, these terms are problematic or, at the very least, incomplete. What about a fictionalized account of actual people or events that really happened in which real and imagined characters interact? What about documentary subjects that stage events for the camera or behave only as they do because the camera is there? What about "mockumentaries" that are made to look like nonfiction but are completely scripted and cast with actors? What about a webcam diary that is made to look real but turns out to be someone playing a character? What about reality TV, where "real" events are later constructed into a narrative that does may not accurately represent the people or events? In our times, truth is often perceived as a subjective notion, and the media follow suit.

An equally tricky category to nail down is the common term **documentary**. Some would argue that any piece of media is a documentary—some document the physical world around us and some document our imaginations. More commonly, a documentary is considered a subcategory of nonfiction media—a narrative based on real people, places, and events. This definition assumes a maker with a point of view and a hand in structuring the narrative. It would not include the nonfiction media forms such as radio talk shows, game shows, testimonials, or coverage of a news event—though they may share some characteristics.

Another category of media production could be called **nonnarrative**. Works of mediated sound and/or image that don't tell a story in the conventional sense would fall into this group. Once again, some would argue with this thinking, saying that any media representation has a story or narrative of some kind, but I think we can agree that there are works of media art that defy our broadest definition of *story*. Nonnarrative works include art pieces found in a museum or gallery, such as a work of acoustic art comprised of ambient nature sounds or a video **installation** made up of abstract computer-generated images. It could also include a website that creates maps and gives driving directions or a video game where the player shoots animated clay pigeons. Nonnarrative media works may not tell a conventional story but can evoke meaning or emotion or give information.

Despite the arguments and contradictions, some forms of media are, by convention, associated with fictional stories and other forms or approaches are associated with nonfiction stories. Theatrical films, prime-time TV dramas, sitcoms, soap operas, and radio dramas are common forms of fiction. News features, historical and nature programs, reality TV shows, talk shows, and websites are generally considered to be nonfiction or based on "real" events and featuring "real" people. Because of these conventions the audience has expectations as to whether a production is fiction or nonfiction. Therefore, a prescripted reality show is perceived as "fixed" or somehow dishonest, and Hollywood feature films based on actual events are often perceived as more emotionally compelling than ones that are purely fiction.

Fiction or nonfiction, story is key. Much of what we know about presenting a good story was observed and recorded by the Greek philosopher Aristotle in the fourth century B.C. (Go to the Source—Aristotle's *Poetics*). *Plot*, or the building of events or actions, is vital. *Character* development, letting the audience know who your characters are and *why* they're doing what they're doing, enriches the plot. *Thought* (underlying meaning), *diction* (the quality of the writing), *song*, and *spectacle* (sets, special effects) all add to the power of the story.

Stories can be told in many ways. Say you want to tell the story of your grandmother's life. How many different types of stories could you tell? If she's still alive, you could record her oral history by asking her questions about her life experiences. You could interview people who know her and ask for anecdotes about her. You could take a particular event in her life or use her entire life to write a script and cast actors to dramatize it. You could collect photos, memorabilia, and songs that were popular when she was young and create a sound and image collage with no words at all. All of these could tell a different story of your grandmother. What's most important is that it is the story you want to tell and that it is told in such a way that others (your audience) will care, too.

LINEAR VS. NONLINEAR STORYTELLING

In media, we frequently use the distinction between linear and nonlinear to describe different aspects of a production such as the process by which we structure or put a piece together. Rerecording pieces of video from one machine to another in the order that you want them is **linear** video editing. Development or editing done on a computer is generally **nonlinear**, letting you jump easily from spot to spot and make changes

Go to the Source—
Aristotle's *Poetics*

The Greek philosopher Aristotle was born in 384 B.C. and died in 322 B.C. His thinking and writing in the areas of science, philosophy, art, literature, and logic were fundamental to the development of Western culture. His work titled *Poetics* was the first systematic study of dramatic or narrative form. Aristotle gave plot (mythos) the primary importance in a drama, a position still held by some literary theorists. He also presented concepts of complication (or conflict), climax, and denouement (or resolution) as part of plot development. Much of what we take for granted as part of a good story or narrative was initially recognized and explained by Aristotle.

that ripple through the whole piece. These processes will be covered in detail in Chapter 9.

Forms of media can be inherently linear or nonlinear, as well. A movie is meant to be watched from beginning to middle to end. The structure of the movie is a straight line, one shot following the next—a linear experience. An informational website or a video game can be experienced in many different sequences and in many different time frames. Such works of media can be visualized as a branching structure, instead of a straight line. Even the story itself can be linear or nonlinear. This is true whether the form of the medium is linear or not. A movie, which provides a linear viewing experience, can have a story that is quite chronological in which there is strong cause-and-effect relationship between one shot and the next (i.e., a linear story). A good linear story will give us the information we need to understand what is happening (**exposition**) and will lay out events in a logical manner, leading to a culmination or climax of events that seems believable, given what has come before. Elements of the climax have been **foreshadowed** or predicted, but an element of suspense keeps the audience waiting and engaged. These conventions of linear storytelling are effective in a current blockbuster action-adventure film, a documentary on the endangered rain forest, and also in the story of your grandmother. The chronology of the events is implied. Even if everything does not move in strict chronological order, the order of events is clear. Flashbacks are signaled and lapses of time are clearly indicated so there is no viewer confusion.

Some stories jump through time and space, where one event suggests another through emotional association. Think of how your memory works. You see (or hear or smell or taste) something in the present that triggers a memory. Something in that memory triggers another line of thought of another time or place. I walk into a room that reminds me of my grandmother. I realize that the tall, narrow windows in the room are like the ones upstairs in her farmhouse. I then remember looking out those windows, seeing my grandmother on her way back from collecting fresh eggs in the henhouse and then having the eggs with toast for breakfast. Toast reminds me of picking strawberries for homemade preserves. I'm back in the room with the narrow windows, and a bowl of strawberries is on the table (Figure 1.3). I pop one in my mouth. It is not a story in the classical sense, lacking Aristotle's primacy of action or plot. A nonlinear story freely defies time and place, concentrating on creating a sense of character or eliciting an emotional response, as opposed to the unfolding of events.

PREPRODUCTION PROCESS

The process of creating a media project is usually divided into the preproduction, production, and postproduction stages. The **preproduction** stage is everything leading up to the actual acquisition of sounds and images. **Production** is that acquisition stage, whether it is a 20-minute audio interview or two years spent filming a documentary. **Postproduction** is everything that needs to be done to that raw material (e.g., roll of film, videotape, digital files) to prepare it for exhibition or distribution.

Figure 1.3 Stories can be nonlinear, like memories.

Preproduction starts with the inception of the concept, the formation of that concept into a concrete expression or story, the identification of the audience, and the decision as to what media form is best suited to the material and the intended audience. Often at this point, a **proposal** is written that clearly and persuasively states those decisions for the purpose of obtaining the necessary cooperation such as funding, access to necessary people, and the participation of others you need to help you. A proposal often includes a treatment, or a brief narrative description of the story. The proposal may be sent to a client or your teacher or a funding organization or network executive. The format of the proposal may be prescribed or flexible. It may be verbal, such as a pitch, commonly made in the film and television industry. During a pitch, a producer meets with decision makers and tries to interest them enough in an idea that they ask for a script.

BUDGET, PERMISSIONS, AND INSURANCE

A **budget** is generally necessary at this point as well. Whether that budget is a few videotapes and food for people who are helping you for free or $10 million, an accurate estimate of the costs that will be incurred is important in determining the project's feasibility.

In addition, legal clearances need to be obtained, and insurance issues need to be considered. Do you have the rights to any copyright-protected material you want to use? (Issues of copyright are discussed later in this chapter.) Is your equipment insured for theft and damage? Are you covered by liability insurance if you damage property or inadvertently injure someone during your production? These questions of insurance are important to even the smallest productions. In large productions legal and insurance issues are numerous and complex.

PERSONNEL

Personnel must be selected or hired. Most media making is a collaborative process that requires a variety of personnel with differing expertise. For a low-budget production or personal media making, the maker might be the producer, director, writer, shooter, editor, caterer, and custodian. The larger the production, the more people tend to be involved. Performers need to be cast; crew members need to be secured. That's a big part of preproduction. The exact responsibilities of the different crew members vary by size of production and by the specific type. For instance, **producer** is a job title everyone has heard, but exactly what a producer does can vary tremendously. Generally, though, in feature film production, the *executive producer* is the one who is responsible for financing the film and has the ultimate responsibility for getting it made. She or he may have secured the script and director. Under the executive producer is a line of command that can include a producer, coproducers, and associate producers. These positions are all considered to be *above the line* in a budget, which means they are considered, along with the director and assistant director, to be involved in the creative management of the film. Line producers and unit production managers are considered, like the technical positions, to be *below the line*. They have responsibility for the physical production itself and are responsible for the budget and schedule. A low-budget film might have just one producer doing it all. Producer credits have also become a way of rewarding people for various contributions, even those not directly related to the outcome of the film. For that reason, the title of producer has, to some, lost some of its prestige and, certainly, its specificity.

In series television the executive producer is often the person who created the series and has say over ongoing story development. In the United States the term *show runner* is the producer on set who has day-to-day responsibility. Interactive or web projects are headed as well by a producer who provides the creative and financial leadership. The *project manger* (similar to a line producer) oversees all the designers and other team members and has final responsibility for getting the job done.

SCRIPT

The preproduction stage also includes the creation of a concrete plan to take into production. In many cases, that plan is a *script,* or written version of the text of a production. Some media projects lend themselves to prescripting. A dramatic fiction piece, a narrated educational documentary, and a situation comedy are just some of the program types that require a specific word-for-word script. However, many different types or formats of scripts are used for various types of programming. A **screenplay** format is used for fiction pieces, such as feature films, television dramas, and comedies (Figure 1.4). Typically a screenplay breaks the story down into scenes and includes location, time of day, dialogue, and action. Later a **shooting script**, which breaks the action down into specific shots and camera angles, is created from the original screenplay.

Prescripted documentaries, commercials, educational videos, or training media are usually written in column scripts. A prescripted radio

POWWOW HIGHWAY

WRITTEN BY JANET HEANEY AND JEAN STAWARZ

EXT. MAIN STREET — DAY

Philbert circles the street, showing off his junker.

> BUDDY
> Philbert, stop! Hey, Philbert!

The Buick BRAKES, grinding METAL on METAL.

HINGES SHRIEK as the door opens. Buddy lands on the seat beside an astonished Philbert.

> PHILBERT
> Buddy Red Bird...

> BUDDY
> Whose car is this?

Philbert gulps nervously.

> PHILBERT
> I made a trade, as of the days when
> men possessed nothing.

> BUDDY
> Huh? Whose car is this, man?

> PHILBERT
> This is Protector, the war pony.

> BUDDY
> But it's yours, right?

Philbert nods proudly.

> BUDDY
> (satisfied)
> That's good, because we have to go
> to Santa Fe.

> PHILBERT
> Santa Fe, New Mexico? You and me?

> BUDDY
> That's right.

> PHILBERT
> There's a powwow in Billings.

Figure 1.4 An example of standard screenplay format, used for single-camera fiction narratives on film and video, this is a page from the screenplay *Powwow Highway*. (Courtesy of screenwriter Jean Stawarz.)

program uses either a single-column script, including spoken lines, descriptions of music, and sound effects cues, or a two-column audio script format. One way to organize a two-column audio script is to have the left side indicate the speaker and dialogue and the right side contain engineering instructions, music, and sound effects (Figure 1.5).

Scripts for television or other video programs usually use a two-column script, though a one-column format exists. A two-column script has visual content on the left and audio on the right. A **fully scripted** program includes every word said and each shot seen. In radio and television, a run-down sheet is used in talk shows, for example, to time and describe the content of the show, without writing out what people will say. A **run-down sheet** allows for ad-libbed conversation and interviews, while still keeping tight control over the structure and timing of a show. A *semiscripted* program combines fully scripted segments with general descriptions of ad-libbed material. A good example of a semiscripted program is one that has scripted narration and a general outline of the parts of the show when interviews take place (Figure 1.6).

Scripts are generally written before production, laying out the plan for what follows. However, some types of projects cannot be prescripted. If you want to produce a documentary about a college basketball player in his first year, you might have an idea of what the story is going to be, but you're not going to know all the details. You may know the kind of footage you want to get—recruiters courting the player, the big move to campus, a day of practice, the first game, footage of college life, and interviews with family, coaches, fellow players, and friends. What you don't know is what people will say or how the experience will play itself out. It's not until after you shoot and you know that the team had a losing year and your subject is injured that you know your story and can write your script. Even for a project like this, preproduction planning is very important. You can create a list of interview subjects and write lists of questions. You can create a **script outline** that includes different shooting locations and describe the shots you envision, so you can go into production prepared. A script can be written after the production is complete.

VISUALIZING THE SCRIPT

For media projects with a visual component, a storyboard is often created A **storyboard** is a series of frames, much like a comic strip. The frames can be hand drawn, made up of still photos, or computer generated. Each frame represents a shot or part of a shot when camera or subject movement changes the shot composition (Figure 1.7). Storyboards are helpful in allowing others to previsualize the project that is taking form in the maker's head. Storyboards are not used for talk shows or situation comedies, where the framing and camera angles are usually routine. Nor are they used in documentaries, where shooting is done in uncontrolled situations. For dramas, TV commercials, and music videos, however, storyboards can be very helpful. In feature films, a storyboard organizes the director's thoughts and helps her communicate her vision clearly to the cameraperson or director of photography and, later, the editor. In TV commercials, a storyboard and script are combined to help sell the client on the idea for the ad.

Announce, Narrative, Dialogue

Announcer:
Economic Revitalization. From Recession to Recovery, with Dr. Christopher Outwin
Host: (Dr. O.)

Narrative: (Chris Outwin)
In contemplating the financial reversals that many investors and businesses are experiencing today, it is both instructive and comforting to consult history. In the early twentieth century, philosopher, George Santayana, observed that, "Those who do not learn from history are condemned to repeat it." We have faced these economic circumstances before, and apparently, not learned enough to avoid them. To illustrate, here is a brief scene from Archibald Macleish's Great Depression era drama, PANIC, produced by NBC in 1935 for the radio series, *March of Time*. The action opens in the office of an anxious banker, McGafferty, as he receives a situation update from an assistant.

Secretarial Voice: (over an intercom)
Mr. Immelman. Mr. Immelman. Report to Mr. McGafferty's office.

Engineering, Music, Sound Effects

Music Bed: 5-second segments of **Money performed by Pink Floyd,** (5 seconds and cross fade) **Money performed by the Beatles,** (5 seconds and crossfade) **Money performed by Ray Charles**
Music under: Music Out:

Bring the following sound effects up under the last sentence of the narrative.

Sound Effects: Typing machines, printing machines, copying machines, chairs being pushed back, the hubbub of a frantic bank office.

Sound Effect: The secretarial announcement is equalized to accentuate high frequencies as if on a public address system.

Figure 1.5   An example of a two-column radio script with voice and sound effects. (Courtesy of writer Christopher Outwin.)

One Plus One

VIDEO	AUDIO
VT OPEN (:15)	THEME up and under
	ANNOUNCER: Yes it's the show that that proves to you why math counts— *One Plus One*.
DISSOLVE to CU Jack's hand rolling dice	JACK: Hi kids. Do you know what I'm doing? Playing a game? That's a good guess. But actually I'm doing an experiment in probability.
LS Jack sitting at table	
KEY GRAPHIC (Probability)	*Probability* is the likelihood that a certain event will happen.
(Jack gets up and walks over to the bookcase where he picks up a piggy bank and shakes out a coin.)	When I flip this coin, how likely is it that it will land heads? How likely is tails? To help explain probability we have with us Dr. Joan Gonzalez from Columbus University Department of Mathematics.
PAN with Jack to bookcase	
(Jack flips the coin.) (Jack walks back to table as Joan enters.)	
2-SHOT Jack and Joan	JACK: Hi Joan. Thanks for stopping by. So tell us, how likely is it that the coin will land heads up?
MCU Joan INTERCUT with MCU Jack	Ad-lib response and follow up questions (2:15)
2-SHOT Jack and Joan	JACK: Thanks Joan for coming to talk to us today. Next, I want to show you what happened when I went to the county fair and tried the games of chance.
CU Jack (to camera)	
VT SEGMENT (1:30)	

Figure 1.6 A two-column script often has video on the left and audio on the right. This is a script from a semiscripted children's show in which some of the dialogue and shots are prescripted and some portions of the script are outlined. Because interviews cannot be prescripted, a time limit is given, and the director can choose shots from a list as the interview progresses.

natural sound
(Man opening door)

natural sound
(Man climbing stairs)

Ed: I thought I'd
find you here.

Lana: I almost left.

Ed: But you didn't.

Figure 1.7 A storyboard visualizes each shot, allowing others to see the maker's vision. A downloadable PDF of this storyboard form is available on the book's companion website books.elsevier.com/companions/97802408076 in the *Storyboard and Releases* activity.

BRANCHING STRUCTURES

Nonlinear, interactive media projects require a different type of scripting. Although components of some interactive media may be scripted or storyboarded, the branching structure requires a **flowchart** to visualize the user's different choices and how the material links together. The home page of a website about coral reefs might feature a short linear movie with narration that describes how coral reefs are formed. Before footage is shot and animations are created, storyboards would be drawn. From that home page, however, the user might be able to navigate to four different sections of the site, dealing with types of coral reefs, animal life on or near the reefs, locations throughout the world, and the threats to reefs from pollution and overuse. From any of those pages, there might be a variety of options to continue to other pages, with the opportunity to return at any time to the main menu or to travel sideways to another information flow. With a large interactive piece, it can get quite complicated, and the flowchart is important in terms of keeping track of content and gauging usability (Figure 1.8).

ALTERNATIVES

Not every media project lends itself to a script or flowchart. A non-narrative film in which many images are edited together to evoke an emotional response would be difficult to script. If you were seeking a grant to make such a video, you might write about the emotion that you were seeking to evoke and list the types of shots you were

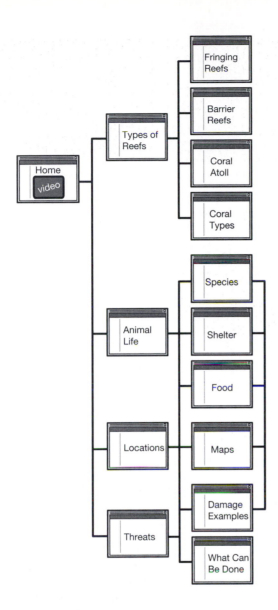

Figure 1.8 A flowchart visualizes the branching structure of interactive nonlinear projects, such as a website or DVD.

planning to shoot. The order of the shots might not be known until different options were tried in postproduction. A gallery installation might need a diagram and written explanation to make your intention clear. A changing media landscape demands flexibility in process expectations as well.

ETHICAL AND LEGAL RESPONSIBILITIES
ETHICAL RESPONSIBILITIES

You are undoubtedly aware of the power and pervasiveness of the media—be it TV, Internet, movies, or radio. It is indeed that pervasiveness, and the subsequent ability to have our message seen and heard, that draws

Go to the Source—
Fair Use and the Center for Social Media

In 2005, The Center for Social Media released *Documentary Filmmakers' Statement of Best Practices in Fair Use*, a landmark publication defining and explaining the concept of fair use. Fair use aims to be just that—fair. It balances the intellectual and economic rights of the copyright holder with the rights of all makers to create and comment on the ideas of others. The *Statement of Best Practices* describes four situations in which fair use can be legitimately claimed:

"1. Employing copyrighted material as the object of social, political, or cultural critique.

2. Quoting copyrighted works of popular culture to illustrate an argument or point.

3. Capturing copyrighted media content in the process of filming something else.

4. Using copyrighted material in a historical sequence."

The relative amount of material used is a consideration. Also, fair use requires that the copyrighted material be used in a new way and for a different purpose than the original. Ultimately the decision as to whether fair use was employed is that of the courts, but the work of the Center for Social Media has helped to demystify this issue for media makers and encourage distributors, broadcasters, etc. to show the work of makers who employ fair use, with less concern about litigation. See www.centerforsocialmedia.org for more information.

many to the field. With power goes responsibility. We hear much about the news media's responsibility to be unbiased and balanced but less about the responsibilities of those who make art and entertainment. Yet these are the people who define our cultural landscape. The media show us our middle ground and our extremes. Where you decide to focus your media-making attention and what you choose to say or not say about it becomes part of the definition. The attempt here is not to prescribe the ethical stance you take—far from it—but instead to ask that you consider it always. Consciously or not, you are making statements about yourself, your values, and the kind of world you want to make. As makers of media, we are in a privileged position. Let's try to be worthy of it.

LEGAL ISSUES

Similar to the ethical decisions you make, but not the same, are many legal issues that face us as media makers. You should refrain from defaming anyone's character. You should obtain permission to use anyone's voice, image, or creative work as part of your media production. That is the ethical thing to do. It is also the law.

Copyright

Any work that you use that was created by someone else (e.g., music, image, text) can only be reproduced or excerpted with permission. Official copyright registration with the U.S. government generally protects the work for 70 years after the creator's death. After that, the work falls into the **public domain** and may be used by others without permission. Short excerpts of copyright-protected material can sometimes be used under a legal concept called fair use. **Fair use** can be claimed when you are critiquing the media or quoting a work to make an argument. Historically, distributors or exhibitors of media programming have been unwilling to take the chance of a lawsuit by relying on this largely untested concept, but recently filmmakers and other activists have been working to more clearly define the concept and increase its acceptance with broadcasters, cablecasters, film festivals, etc. (Go to the Source: Fair Use and the Center for Social Media). Often students think that it is all right to use a piece of copyright-protected music in a class assignment, but this greatly restricts what you can do with a finished piece. Showing it in your classroom would be okay, but submitting it to a film or video festival or mounting it on your website would not be all right. To have the legal right to use someone else's work, you need to request permission from them or their representative. Sometimes the permission can be obtained without charge for a noncommercial project; sometimes it can be very expensive.

Permission to use quotes from books or published photographs or artwork can be requested from the publisher. The use of a piece of music requires the permission of the composer. Many composers and music publishers are represented by the American Society of Composers, Authors and Publishers (ASCAP), Broadcast Music Inc. (BMI), and an organization that was originally called the Society of European Stage Authors and Composers and now goes only by the acronym of SESAC. These three organizations collect royalties for composers (Go to the Source—ASCAP,

BMI, and SESAC). Large organizations such as TV, cable, and radio stations pay for blanket or pay-per-program licenses. This gives them the right to perform music represented by the license granter.

If you are going to record copyrighted music as part of a media production, a different process is followed. If visuals are involved, you need to obtain **synchronization rights**. If the production is audio only, **mechanical rights** are needed. If you are going to have the music performed yourself, you need to obtain permission for the composition from the music publisher. If you want to reproduce an existing recording, such as a track from a CD, permission must also be secured from the copyright holder, usually the record label. This can be a time-consuming and costly process. Many producers working on a budget opt instead for originally composed music, performed by amateur or emerging musicians, or they use a cut from a *music library*. Music libraries are collections of songs written for the purpose of supplying background or title music. The music is written in many styles and tempos. You get rights to the music by purchasing a music library CD or piece of music downloaded from the Internet, or by paying a **needle drop fee** (dating back to the days of phonograph record) to a sound studio or postproduction company for one-time use of a selection. Music library compositions sometimes sound quite generic, but it provides a good, low-cost solution to music needs for some productions. Online music services have expanded the range of possibilities, but just because you have paid for a music download or purchased a CD does not give you rights to use it in a media production.

Talent Releases

Unless you are working for a recognized news organization, any person featured in your media production should sign a release. A **talent release** is written permission by an individual (or the parent or legal guardian of anyone under age 18) to reproduce his or her voice and/or image. A simple talent release is shown in Figure 1.9 and included as a PDF on the book's website books.elsevier.com/companions/9780240809076, but any form that clearly states that the talent is agreeing to appear in your production and includes the names and addresses of both the producer and subject or talent is adequate. Some producers record their releases on film or tape, which works as well, though it is not always as easy to archive and retrieve. In a public space, people appearing incidentally in the background do not need to sign releases. The guideline seems to be this: If people are in public where they should have no expectation of privacy, then no release is needed. If you speak to them or feature them in your production, though, you should have them sign a release, even when on public property. On private property, such as a nightclub or building lobby, often a sign is posted or announcement is made, which states that a production is being made and a person's presence within the space is interpreted as willingness to appear in the production.

A release also provides a certain level of legal protection for you, the producer, but a signed release does not prevent someone from suing you for falsely representing the production's purpose or subject matter or for presenting a subject in such a way as to damage his or her reputation or livelihood. (*Libel* is the written form of character defamation;

Go to the Source—
ASCAP, BMI, and SESAC

ASCAP was created in 1914 to represent the rights of composers, songwriters, and music publishers. ASCAP collects license fees from users of music—radio, TV, cable stations, and nightclubs—and distributes royalties to members.

BMI was founded in 1940 by the broadcasting industry as a competitor to ASCAP, which they considered to be an unfair monopoly and too expensive. The two organizations now coexist and even collaborate, such as on a 2001 policy statement about Internet music use.

SESAC (which was originally the Society of European Stage Authors and Composers, an acronym that is now outdated) was founded in 1930 to represent European artists in the United States. Though smaller than its two competitors, SESAC now represents all types of music.

Talent Release Form

Name of Producer _____

Address   _____

                 _____

Phone   _____

I irrevocably consent to and authorize any sound or image taken today, for any purpose, without further compensation. The resulting media project remains the sole property of the producer.

Name of Talent   _____

Address   _____

                  _____

Phone   _____

Signature _____ Date_____

Witnessed by
Name   _____

Address   _____

                  _____

Phone   _____

Signature _____ Date_____

Figure 1.9 Here is a simple talent release. A downloadable PDF of this release is available on the book's companion website books.elsevier.com/companions/9780240809076 in the *Storyboard and Releases* activity.

slander is the spoken form.) A signed release, however, is a good starting point and a sound professional practice.

Having participants in your production sign releases is not only a legal protection, it is ethically appropriate. People have a right to decide if they want to be part of your production and to be informed of its content and purpose. A talent release may not be enough. For "real" people involved in your productions (as opposed to actors) a talent release does not guarantee that the person is giving "informed consent." Is the person (because of age or mental capacity) unable to understand the implications of their involvement? A woman with diminished mental capacity talking about her drug use in a documentary interview may not understand that she is risking legal action or damage to her reputation if the interview is broadcast. It is the media maker's ethical responsibility to inform their subjects of potential risks and benefits of participation and of their right to end their involvement at any time. A more detailed consent form is good ethical practice for nonfiction projects and may be required by your school or funding institution.

Location Releases

It is also important to obtain permission to use locations. When on public property, different towns and cities have different regulations about the need for permits. Often, if the production is a small one and you are not blocking vehicular or pedestrian traffic, no permit is needed. Larger productions, however, require permits in advance and may require the presence of police. Major cities have film offices to help you determine the requirements. In a smaller city or town, contact the police department or city hall.

On private property, permission is needed, and the owner or manager of the property should sign a location release or put the permission in writing (Figure 1.10). Do not just go with someone's verbal okay. They might not be there the day you go to shoot or record and someone else might be unwilling or unable to approve your use. If a piece of private property appears in a shot taken from public property (e.g., the outside of a house seen from a public sidewalk), generally no release is required.

CONCLUSION

Media making is about telling your stories through sounds and images. There are an infinite number of stories to be told and many ways to tell them. Defining your message and deciding on the most appropriate medium are the first big challenges. Many other tasks need to be accomplished before you ever touch a camera or a microphone, though. Thorough preproduction is an absolute requirement for success. Conceptualizing; determining your audience; completing a distribution plan and budget; hiring your cast and crew; creating a plan (e.g., a script, flowchart, or outline); scouting locations; arranging for equipment, transportation, catering, props, hair, and makeup; and resolving legal issues are just some of the responsibilities of media making. Whether it is a personal medium artwork or a large commercial production, whether for an audience of a few or millions, you are responsible for your stories. You are responsible for the joy and knowledge they

Location Release Form

Name of Producer _____

Address   _____

                _____

Phone   _____

As the owner, or authorized agent of the owner, of the property described below, I grant the producer permission to record and/or film sound and/or images of

Name of Property or Description _____

located at

Address   _____

                _____

on

Date _____

between the hours of _____ AM PM (circle one) and _____ AM PM

Name   _____

Address   _____

                _____

Phone   _____

Signature _____ Date_____

Figure 1.10 A location release gives you permission to shoot or record on private property. A downloadable PDF of this release is available on the book's companion website books.elsevier.com/companions/9780240809076 in the *Storyboard and Releases* activity.

bring to people, for the effects that they may have on the participants or audience, and for the vision of the world that you put forth.

PUTTING IT INTO PRACTICE
OBSERVING

Observe three examples of media programming from the following list: a fiction narrative film or video, an interactive documentary or informational program on DVD or the Internet, a radio talk show, a video or multimedia installation in a museum or gallery, a music video. For each one, define the story and then describe how that story could have been told using the other two programming types. For each example, note when and what type of script or preproduction planning technique would have been most useful.

WRITING AND DOING

Start a notebook for the following exercises. Keep it for exercises in subsequent chapters. Follow each direction before reading the next.

1. List 10 people you would like to interview.
2. List 10 locations that would be visually interesting to shoot.
3. List 10 things you feel passionate about.
4. Take choices 3 and 7 from the first list and put them in choice 4 from the second list and have them talk about choice 1 from the third list. Write a one-page script of the conversation.

Think about being six years old. Write down your memories in the order they occur to you. Now storyboard your list or memories. Is it a linear narrative with cause-and-effect chronology or is it a nonlinear narrative based on association?

KEY CONCEPTS

budget	nonnarrative
convergence	postproduction
documentary	preproduction
exposition	producer
fair use	production
fiction	proposal
flowchart	public domain
foreshadowed	run-down sheet
fully scripted	screenplay
installation	script outline
linear	shooting script
mechanical rights	storyboard
narrative	subject
needle drop fee	synchronization rights
nonfiction	talent release
nonlinear	

CHAPTER 2

The Frame

SEEING THE WORLD THROUGH A FRAME

The frame defines what we see and hear. It also defines what is implied beyond what we see and hear. By putting a frame around something, by including it within a frame, we call it art. We carve out a rectangle of reality (or fantasy) and claim it for ourselves as media makers. The word **frame** can have many meanings—from the slats of wood we place around the edges of a painting to the single exposure on a strip of photographic film to falsifying the evidence that unjustly sends someone to jail. All of these meanings, however, include the idea of defining or shaping a certain reality. It is the crux of what we do as media makers. Understanding the power of the frame and the aesthetic principles at work within the frame are key to effective visual and aural storytelling.

Some media makers resist the idea of analyzing or intellectualizing the creative process. Such a film director or web designer "just knows" that something works. The truth is that—whether you consciously acknowledge it or not—every time you set up a camera and frame a shot, every time you arrange text and images within a computer screen, and every time you place one sound source in the foreground and another in the background, you are making aesthetic decisions. Those decisions have implications in terms of how your product will be received by an audience. The results of those decisions either conform to accepted conventions of media making or break those conventions. If you learn to externalize and understand those decisions, you will have more control over the power and meaning of your message.

THE STILL IMAGE

Photography has been around since the 1800s when large-view cameras and wet-plate developing required a strong back and a chemist's knowledge to create black-and-white portraits, landscapes, and documents of major events (Go to the Source—Daguerreotypes). A photograph possesses the power to freeze a moment in time. It creates a representation of reality but also a new entity—an art object. Once you separate the photographed subject from its context and translate the light reflected from an object into grains of silver on a sheet of paper, it is both the same and different from the original. You have mediated the experience. You have made media.

Go to the Source—
Daguerreotypes

Daguerreotypes, invented in 1839, were the first of the early photographic process to become commercially available. The one of a kind image was created through a complex process where copper plates with a silver surface were washed with an acidic solution and coated with iodine. This plate exposed to an image reflected through a lens for several minutes. The image was "developed" or made visible by heated mercury fumes and "fixed" or made permanent with salt water. The result was a unique, metallic looking image. This process was soon replaced by paper prints, which allowed for more than im-age to be produced. (Daguerreotype by E.T. Whitney, Portrait of Mary Eloise and Emma Walbridge, c1852. By permission of George Eastman House.)

Even though advanced technology has made the process of creating a still photograph as simple as "point and shoot," the potential power of the image has not been diminished. We are still awed by a fast-moving object frozen poetically in time, or a heartbreaking expression or gesture plucked from the chaos of a tragedy. Although it is the most obvious, it is not merely the subject matter of a photograph that grabs us. It is the placement of objects within the frame. It is the play of light, dark, and color. It is the movement implied by frozen action. Those are the aesthetic principles that enhance the content for the viewer and become the media maker's tools for making a slice of reality their own expression.

CONTROLLING THE FRAME
THE SHAPE OF THE FRAME

When we put a frame around media, theoretically, it can be any shape we like. Paintings are most commonly in rectangular frames—sometimes horizontal and sometimes vertical. But a frame can also be round, oval, or triangular. Convention (and the relative ease of stretching a canvas to a rectangular shape as opposed to a round one) dictates our expectations. The technology involved in making mediated visual images (e.g., photographs, motion pictures, video, or computer images) demands even more conformity. In order for multiple rolls of film to be able to run through a camera, they need to be the same size and shape. An exposed frame of film used for still photography can be square, horizontal, or vertical and, when printed, can be cropped to any proportion. It is different with media where the means of exhibition (e.g., the TV set, computer screen, or movie projector) are mass produced. The shape and proportion of a mass-produced frame must remain constant. A horizontal rectangle is the rule. (Remember, though, every rule can be broken! A TV or film image can be masked to create even a round shape, but that is very rare.)

However, the proportions of the rectangle (its relative width and height) vary from medium to medium. This is called **aspect ratio**. A frame of 35mm film used for still photography has an aspect ratio of 3:2. That means a frame of film that is 35mm wide is 23.3mm high and 34.9mm wide. A typical snapshot printed full frame from 35mm film measures 3.5 × 5 inches or 6 × 4 inches. Standard television and computer screens have an aspect ratio of 4:3 (sometimes described as 1.33:1). New digital, high-definition television (HDTV) systems and wide-screen computer monitors, however, have a 16:9 aspect ratio. A 16:9 image is proportionally wider and more panoramic than one that is 4:3.

Film used for motion pictures has a range of aspect ratios. The specifics are discussed later in the chapter, but 35mm motion picture film is generally projected in the United States at a dimension of 1.85:1, similar to the 1.78:1 or 16:9 aspect ratio of high definition television (HDTV) (Figure 2.1).

Differences in aspect ratio become an issue when one medium is transferred to another medium with a different dimension. When a film is transferred to video for home video distribution or broadcast on National Television Systems Committee (NTSC), or traditional

Figure 2.1 Common media aspect ratios are compared. The common photographic snapshot ratio is 3:2. The shape of a traditional television screen is 4:3. The aspect ratio of an HDTV screen is 16:9, very close to the 1.85:1 dimension of most movie projections in U.S. theaters.

3×2

4×3

16×9

television, the difference in aspect ratio needs to be adjusted. This is also true for HDTV images shown on 4:3 televisions. The movie is either cropped along the sides or the entire frame is shown on the television screen, leaving a band of black along the top and bottom, a technique known as **letterboxing** (Figure 2.2). With the first option, indiscriminately cropping both sides of the frame equally can cause loss of pertinent information for the viewer. Therefore, a technique called **pan and scan** is used, in which the cropping shifts from side to side according to the content of the frame (Figure 2.3). Film directors often prefer the letterboxing technique because they have carefully composed shots for the shape of the film frame and don't like to see their original vision compromised by any type of cropping. Some viewers, however, do not like how letterboxing essentially reduces the size of the image.

When programming produced in standard television format (4:3) is shown on wide-screen TV (16:9), the black bars appear on the sides of the screen (Figure 2.4). This is referred to as **pillarboxing**. When showing programming with one aspect ratio on a monitor with a different ratio, you have three choices, all of which have their own disadvantage. The first is "**windowboxing**"—a term that includes both letterboxing and pillarboxing—which results in black bars and unused screenspace. The second is cropping, which results in lost picture information. The third is manipulating the image—either stretching a 4:3 image into a 16:9 frame (Figure 2.5A) or squeezing the 16:9 image into a 4:3 frame (Figure 2.5B). This obviously creates distortion of the image that is not generally desired.

The development of new digital television standards, with an aspect ratio compatible with widescreen motion pictures, is solving the problem created by conflicting aspect ratios. This change is not without implications, however. The "boxier" aspect ratio of original TV is the ideal shape for a head and shoulders shot—the staple shot of many

Figure 2.2 Letterboxing allows the full 16:9 image to be seen on the 4:3 TV screen. It does, however, essentially reduce the image size by not utilizing all of the screen space.

Figure 2.3 Pan and scan uses the full 4:3 screen but results in some loss of information. Essential information is retained by adjusting the transfer according to what is on the screen.

Figure 2.4 Pillarboxing allows for an undistorted 4:3 image to be displayed on a 16:9 monitor.

A

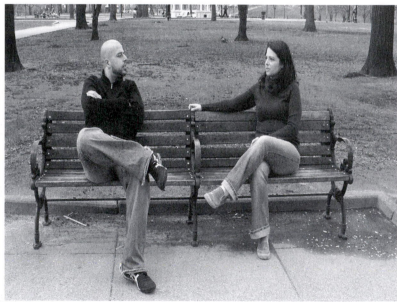

Figure 2.5 The transition from 4:3 to 16:9 televisions results in distortion when **A**. 4:3 images are stretched to 16:9 or **B**. 16:9 images are squeezed to 4:3. Windowboxing and cropping are preferred alternatives.

B

forms of television. Television, sometimes called a *close-up medium*, invites intimacy between the viewer and the on-screen character or personality (Figure 2.6). Close-ups were necessary when television screens were small, but are not necessary with today's large-screen monitors. The wider rectangles of motion pictures and HDTV encourage a more panoramic vision, ideal for landscapes and shots with at least two people (Figure 2.7). This is appropriate for the larger screens of movie theaters and big TVs. The use of the 16:9 aspect ratio is changing the way television directors frame their shots and bringing a more "cinematic" look to television programming. Interestingly, at the same time that directors are getting used to creating content that works on large wide-screen TV monitors, an increasing amount of programming is

Figure 2.6   The proportion and small size of early television screens contributed to its reputation as a close-up medium. Its location within the living rooms of viewers also adds to the sense of intimacy that movies in a theater do not have.

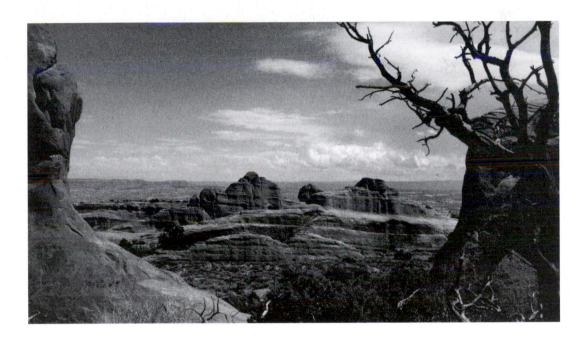

being distributed for the very small screens of cell phones, MP3 players, and iPods. While a detailed panorama might look great on a 60-inch high-definition monitor, the close-up, favored by 1950s low-definition television, might be best on the tiny screen of your cell phone.

Figure 2.7   Aspect ratios of 16:9 and wider lend themselves to panoramic scenes and action.

WHAT'S IN THE FRAME AND WHAT ISN'T: SHOT SIZES

As we capture an image within the frame, we make decisions about size of the subject within the frame and how much of the subject we will show. These are called **shot sizes**. Shot sizes apply to the human figure, but they can be used to describe objects as well (Figure 2.8):

A

Figure 2.8 Shot sizes: ECU, CU, MCU, MS, MLS, LS, WS.

ECU—extreme close-up—crops the top of the head and the bottom of the subject's chin
CU—close-up—shows head of subject with just a bit of the shoulder line
MCU—medium close-up—shows head and shoulders of subject
MS—medium shot—shows subject from just above or below the waist
MLS—medium long shot—shows subject from just above or below the knees
LS—long shot—just wide enough to show subject's full body
WS—wide shot—shows subject and surrounding environment.

Note that in the above definitions, the crop points on the human body avoid the natural cutoff points, like the neck, waist, and knees. This is because of a phenomenon called **closure**, short for *psychological closure*. Closure results from a human psychological desire for wholeness and our need to make sense out of chaos. When we look at a framed image, we try to perceive it as a completed pattern. When visual elements create simple geometric shapes, closure within the frame can create a strong graphic composition (Figure 2.9). Often though, the frame shows just part of a figure or object. If framed with the appropriate visual clues that suggest that the figure continues beyond the frame line, the viewer is

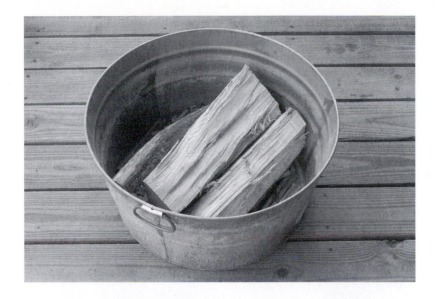

Figure 2.9 Closure within the frame can create a strong graphic composition.

Figure 2.10 When given the appropriate visual clues, the viewer's mind creates closure beyond the frame.

comfortable with a sense of closure beyond the frame (Figure 2.10). If, however, the frame line intersects with a point on the body that separates discrete body parts (i.e., the neck, waist, elbow, knee, or ankle), we accept the body part as the complete image, even if intellectually we know that the body continues beyond the edge of the frame. This makes the image disturbing. If cut off exactly at the knee joint, the subject appears to have no lower legs. If cut off right at the neck, he or she appears to be a disembodied head (Figure 2.11). If, however, a subject is cropped just above or below the knee for a medium long shot or if the frame shows just a suggestion of the shoulder line for a close-up, our minds see the continuation of the subject beyond the frame line. We mentally complete the figure beyond the edge of the frame (Figure 2.12).

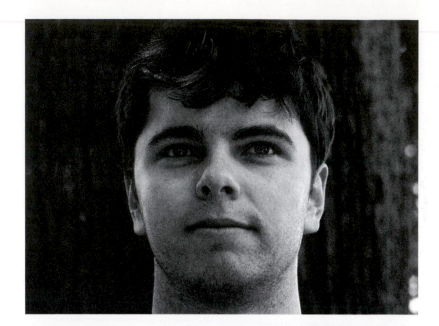

Figure 2.11 Closure causes us to see this shape as complete. Even though we logically know better, it seems that this is a disembodied head, not an image of just part of a person.

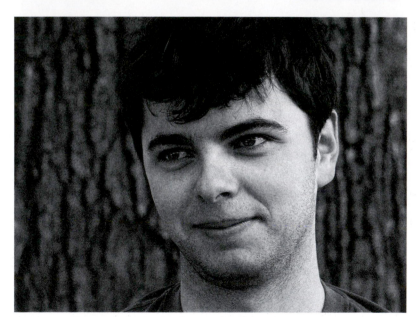

Figure 2.12 Here, a glimpse of the continuation of the body is given by showing the shoulder line. We see the head as part of a body that extends beyond the frame. We also mentally complete the top of the head beyond the frame.

THE WEIGHT AND MAGNETISM OF THE FRAME

Subjects within the frame have psychological weight. Too much mass on one side of the frame makes the viewer feel like the frame is about to tip over. Even if a viewer is not conscious of it, the lack of balance conveys a feeling of uneasiness (Figure 2.13). During a suspenseful moment in a film or in a photograph of a danger-ous situation, nervousness may be just the message you want to

Figure 2.13 An unbalanced composition creates a feeling of uneasiness (often unconscious) in the viewer.

convey. Generally, we try to reinforce the content of the shot with our formal choices. If you want the viewer to feel a sense of control and well-being about what is happening on screen, a balanced composition is most appropriate. There are many ways to accomplish a sense of balance. You can center the subject within the frame. Our eyes are drawn to the center of the frame; we expect to find the subject or object of most importance there. This **symmetrical balance** conveys a scene that is stable or static (Figure 2.14). The news

Figure 2.14 Symmetrical balance gives the sense of stability and calm. There is usually a lack of dynamic energy.

Go to the Source—
The Golden Mean

The Golden Mean or Golden Section is a concept that applies to many academic areas ranging from Aristotelian ethics and philosophy to mathematics to visual composition in art and architecture. Simply, the Golden Mean is a proportion of 1:1.618. That proportion creates a frame somewhere between the aspect ratio of standard television (1:1.33) and that of HDTV or projected 35mm film (1:1.85). The Golden Mean also defines the division of the frame (see Figure 2.14). The relationship of B to A is the same as A to A + B. Placement of subjects or objects according to the Golden Mean creates aesthetically pleasing images because of their mathematical relationships.

anchor, for example, framed in the center of the screen, holds our attention, and does not seem likely to mislead us.

The primary subject does not have to be centered, however. Often, more effective composition is achieved by placing your subject off-center. There is a fine arts concept, dating back to the ancient Greeks, called the **rule of thirds**. The rule of thirds is derived from an ancient principle called the Golden Mean (Go to the Source—The Golden Mean) (Figure 2.15). It describes an approach to strong visual composition where a rectangular frame is divided into thirds both vertically and horizontally. The intersection of these lines defines placement in the frame that can be both pleasing and dynamic.

A subject placed on one of the lines of thirds can be balanced symmetrically or asymmetrically. A subject of similar size and mass could be placed on the opposite line of thirds. This creates a balanced but static feeling (Figure 2.16). **Asymmetrical balance** can also be achieved with a smaller, distant object or a shadow (Figure 2.17). Balance does not even have to involve a visible object. A subject's gaze, a pointing gesture, and sense of direction portrayed by movement all carry psychological weight. That is the reason that we use lookspace and leadroom. **Lookspace** is extra space allowed in the frame to balance a subject's gaze in the direction the eyes are looking. The more profiled the subject, the more lookspace needed (Figure 2.18). Without it, even a subject placed directly in the center of the frame can appear unbalanced (Figure 2.19). (See the *Visual Aesthetics: Lookspace* activity on the book's companion website books.elsevier.com/companions/9780240809076 where you can experiment with changes in lookspace.)

Leadroom is the extra space that balances the momentum of movement or implied direction. A subject walking toward the right edge of the frame should be placed to the left of the centerline (Figure 2.20).

Parts of the frame have a psychological magnetism. The center of the frame draws our greatest attention. The most important object or subject should be placed near the center. The edges and corners of the frame have magnetism. The closer to the edge of the frame an object is, the more it seems to be pulled off the frame, creating an unbalanced frame (Figure 2.21). For that reason, we leave a little space above the person's head when we frame them. This is called **headroom**. The wider the shot, the more headroom needed. Therefore,

Figure 2.15 The Golden Mean defines ideal proportions of the frame itself and of division of the frame. This rectangle has a 1:1.618 aspect ratio. Within the frame the ratio of the length of B to A is 1:1.618. The ratio of A to A + B is also 1:1.618.

Figure 2.16 Symmetrical balance can be achieved by placing similar objects along opposite lines of thirds.

Figure 2.17 Asymmetrical balance can be achieved by balancing a primary subject with a background object.

a close-up requires less headroom than a long shot. A good rule of thumb is that the eye line of the talent is placed one-third of the way down the frame. This automatically increases the headroom with a wider shot and avoids leaving too much space (Figure 2.22). Once again, this rule is for standard, accepted framing. Break the rules if you want to create a sense of uneasiness. (See the *Visual Aesthetics: Headroom* activity, where you can experiment with changes in

Figure 2.18 Lookspace compensates for the implied weight of a person's gaze. The more profiled the shot, the more lookspace needed.

Figure 2.19 Lack of lookspace results in an unbalanced composition, even if the subject is centered in the frame. The right side of the subject's face seems crowded by the right side of the frame.

Go to the Source—
Gestalt Theory

Gestalt theory was developed in Germany and Austria in the late 20th century. Gestalt experiments in perception have influenced thinking in both psychology and visual aesthetics and are the foundation for an approach to therapy. Simply put, Gestalt thinking states that the whole is more than a sum of the parts and that perception is not a passive activity. The brain searches for and completes patterns out of the stimuli presented to it. The phi phenomenon, which is discussed in Chapter 3, was discovered by Gestalt theorists.

headroom, on the book's companion website books.elsevier.com/ companions/9780240809076.) There is also magnetism between objects in the frame, This is called the *law of proximity* (Figure 2.23). Two objects placed close together in the frame seem to attract each other and belong together. Gestalt theorists in the early 1900s identified the concept of proximity, which affects the process of closure. Objects that are close to each other create closure more readily than those farther apart (Go to the Source—Gestalt Theory).

Figure 2.20 Leadroom compensates for the momentum of movement within the frame.

Figure 2.21 An object or subject too close to the edge of the frame will seem to pull out of the frame, creating an unbalanced composition.

Balance is also affected by the positioning of horizontal and vertical lines. A tilted horizon line or vertical element can create a lack of balance and viewer discomfort and, like other unbalanced compositions, can be used to create the desired emotional response (Figure 2.24).

Figure 2.22 Proper headroom increases as the shot size increases. If you keep the subject's eye line one-third of the way down the frame, proper headroom is achieved.

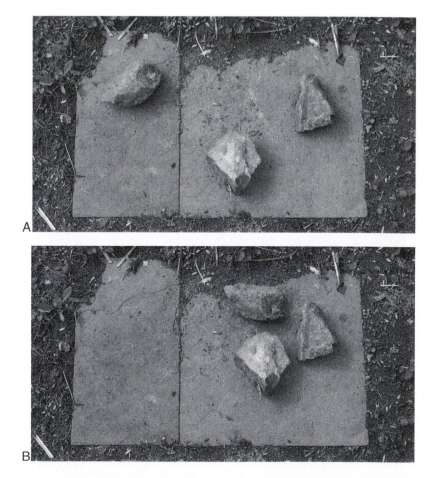

Figure 2.23 The law of proximity causes objects placed closely together to seem to form a cohesive group. **A**, Separate objects don't seem related. **B**, When the images from part A are placed closer together, they seem to be part of a group.

Figure 2.24 A tilted horizon line can give a feeling of danger or chaos.

REPRODUCING THE FRAME

Cameras are used to create our visual frames. Cameras (still or motion picture, film or digital) are made up of a lens, through which light travels, and a camera body. Within the camera body is the **image plane**, the surface onto which the image is reflected. Understanding lens theory—the type of lens used and its characteristics—is central to all forms of image making. Understanding the different types of materials that can reproduce images gives you an idea of the many choices available.

LENS

When you look at something, a series of reactions takes place. Light waves bounce off the object. A light-colored object will reflect most of the light waves that strike it, absorbing only a small amount of light. A dark object will reflect fewer waves and absorb more of them. The reflected light waves enter the cornea of your eye, and the lens focuses an upside-down reflection of the original object onto the retina at the back of your eyeball. The retina converts the light energy into electrical impulses that are read by your brain as a right-side-up, reproduced image. Mediated images work much the same way. Light waves enter a camera lens. Lenses are made up of a series of curved glass elements that bend the light and focus an upside-down reflection onto a light sensitive surface or *image plane* (Figure 2.25). The image plane might be a strip of film in a still or motion picture camera or a **charge-coupled device** (**CCD**) in a digital still or video camera. A CCD creates electronic signals in response to the presence of light striking it. The silver halide particles in film chemically respond to the presence of light.

Focal Length

The number, size, position, and shape of the glass disks in a lens determine how much of the scene in front of the lens is included in the frame. This is the lens's **field of view**. The mathematical angle of a lens's field of view (**angle of view**) can be normal, wide, or narrow. A normal lens approximates the human angle of vision; that is, what

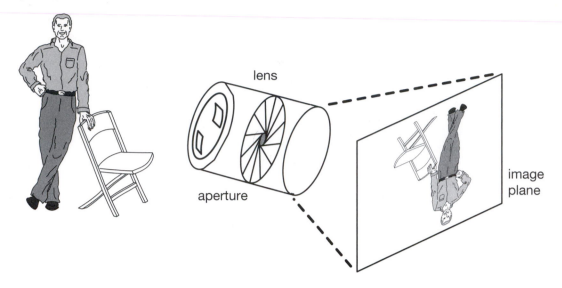

Figure 2.25 Light reflects off the subject, travels through the lens and is reproduced (upside down) on the image plane of the camera.

your peripheral vision allows you to see. The view of a wide-angle lens takes in more of a scene, making objects in that scene appear farther away than they would to the eye. The narrow angle of view of a telephoto lens chooses a small segment of what is in front of the lens and makes it seem closer and larger than it would to the eye. The angle of view is closely related to another measurement within the lens, called its focal length. The **focal length** is the distance from the center of the glass elements making up the lens to the image plane. This measurement is made when the lens is focused to infinity or the furthest possible point visible because the positions of the glass elements shift slightly when you focus the lens (Figure 2.26).

Lenses are categorized by their focal length. Lenses with a short focal length allow a wide field of view and are called **wide angle**. A short focal length lens produces a relatively smaller image, so the entire field of view will fit in the film frame or CCD. Lenses with a long focal length are called **telephoto**. Long lenses produce a larger image so only a portion of the image is reproduced, seeming to magnify the image. Lenses that have only one single focal length in one lens casing are called *prime*. Lenses can also have a *variable focal length*. Another name for a variable focal length lens is a *zoom* lens, which allows for a full range of focal lengths within one lens housing. You can zoom in on a subject, creating a long focal length or telephoto view, or you can zoom out, shortening your focal length and creating a wide-angle field of view. The normal field of view falls somewhere in between. Prime lenses result in a sharper image, but the convenience and improved quality of the zoom lens has made it the most common choice on all types of cameras.

The concept of focal length is complicated by the fact that there are different sizes or formats of cameras, so the focal length of a wide-angle lens for 35mm film is different from the focal length of a wide-angle lens for 16mm film. For example, for 35mm film (either still or motion picture), a normal lens has a focal length of 50mm, a typical

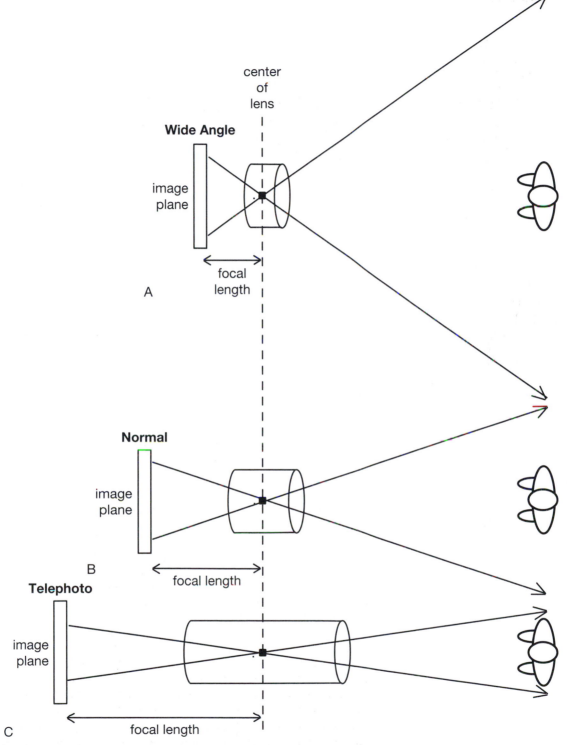

center
of
lens

Wide Angle

image
plane

focal
length

A

Normal

image
plane

focal length

B

Telephoto

image
plane

focal length

C

Figure 2.26 A lens's field of view determines its focal length. **A**, A wide field of view results in a short focal length or wide-angle lens. **B**, A field of view comparable to that of human vision results in what we call a normal lens. **C**, A narrow field of view results in a long focal length or telephoto lens.

wide-angle lens 24mm, and a telephoto lens 100mm. To reproduce the same field of view on the smaller image plane of 16mm film or video, a normal lens is 25mm, a wide-angle lens is 12mm, and a telephoto lens is 50mm. The relative nature of the relationship remains the same.

LENS CHARACTERISTICS

In addition to having a wide field of view, a wide-angle lens has other visual characteristics. In extending its angle of view beyond normal vision, some distortion occurs. Objects at the extreme edges of the frame start to curve toward the center of the frame. This is called *barrel distortion* (Figure 2.27). The more wide angle the lens is, the more extreme the distortion. You can get the idea of wide-angle distortion by looking at your reflection in the back of a metal spoon. You'll see that it is not a very flattering lens for the human face. Wide-angle lenses also exaggerate the appearance of depth between objects in the foreground and background. This can be beneficial if you are trying to create a sense of isolation or emphasize distance between subjects (Figure 2.28). A wide-angle lens also minimizes the appearance of camera shake, which is helpful when hand-holding a camera.

Figure 2.27 Wide-angle lenses have the characteristic of barrel distortion. It is most noticeable when the image has a strong horizontal line as with the steps and horizontal lines of this building, or in its unflattering effect on the human face.

Figure 2.28 Wide-angle lenses exaggerate the sense of distance between foreground and background subjects. **A**, A scene taken with a wide-angle lens. **B**, The subjects have not moved, but a normal lens has been used. **C**, A telephoto lens was used, compressing the sense of distance between the subjects.

As you might expect, the characteristics of a telephoto lens tend to be the opposite of a wide-angle lens. Telephoto lenses seem to compress depth, making subjects in the foreground and background appear closer together than with a normal lens. When trying to emphasize the crowding of a city street, this distortion could be used to reinforce the emotional impact of an image. Telephoto lenses also flatten and soften facial features. Generally, a slightly longer lens gives a flattering portrait or close-up. Because they are magnifying a small portion of the frame, telephoto lenses exaggerate camera shake and should be avoided when using a hand-held camera.

Aperture

Within the lens housing is an opening made of movable blades that can be opened and closed to determine the quantity of light that strikes the image plane. This opening is called the **iris** of the lens. It is analogous to the pupil of the human eye, which adjusts according to the lighting conditions and provides the retina with a comfortable amount of light. The diameter of the lens opening is called the **aperture**. The aperture is one component that helps you determine the proper *exposure,* or amount of light that a given medium requires for image reproduction.

Aperture is measured in **f-stops**—incremental settings on the lens that indicate how large the opening is. A lower number f-stop setting indicates a larger opening. A typical range of f-stops would be F2, F2.8, F4, F5.6, F8, F11, and F16 (Figure 2.29). F2 would indicate a wide open lens. F16 would indicate the smallest possible opening. Some lenses have more extensive ranges. One stop beyond F2 is F1.8; the next stop beyond F16 is F22. Many lenses allow for half-stop or continuous adjustments in aperture. Each change in standard f-stop setting (opening the lens to a smaller f-stop number) doubles the light allowed through the lens.

Shutter Speed

Another determinant of exposure is **shutter speed**. Whereas aperture refers to the size of the opening that allows light in, shutter speed refers to the length of time that each frame of media receives light through that opening. A **shutter** is the mechanical or electronic mechanism that allows light to enter the lens and expose the light-sensitive material on the image plane for a given period of time. The shutter then closes to allow the camera to reposition for the exposure of the next frame. (The different types of shutters are discussed later in this chapter.) When capturing a moving image, the length of time a frame is exposed will determine how much range of movement is reproduced. It might be 1/1000 of a second in an action-freezing sports photograph (Figure 2.30A), or it could be 1/8 of a second in a blurred dance image (Figure 2.30B). Aperture and shutter speed work together to determine exposure. Opening up the aperture (making the opening larger and letting more light into the lens) while shortening the shutter speed (making it faster, thus decreasing the amount of light reaching the frame) can result in the same total amount of light exposing the frame (more light for less time), while the converse—closing the lens somewhat while lengthening the shutter speed (making it slower)—could do the same.

Figure 2.29 Small f-stop numbers indicate a more open lens aperture, higher numbers more closed down. With the standard f-stop increments shown here, each change in stop indicates a doubling (or halving) of the amount of light. An f-stop setting of F5.6 lets twice as much light into the camera as a setting of F8. Some cameras have incremental f-stop settings.

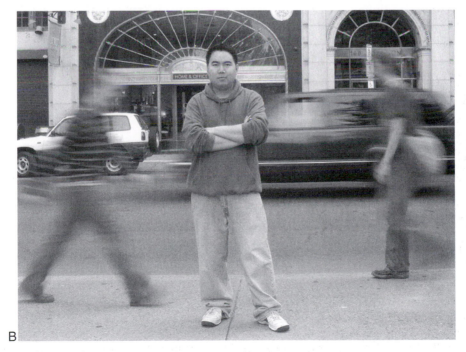

Figure 2.30 **A**, A fast shutter speed will seem to freeze action. **B**, With a slow shutter speed, movement will result in a blurred image.

Sensitivity

The third determinant of exposure is the **sensitivity** of your medium. Some types of film (film stocks) require less light to create a properly exposed image than do other types. Newer digital cameras are more light sensitive than older models, requiring less light to create a high-quality image.

FOCUS

Focus is important when framing an image through a lens. Focus is achieved when the lens elements are adjusted to the position that allows the reflected light waves to converge, creating a sharply defined image. Ideally the light rays reflected off a specific point on the subject will converge to create a point of light on the image plane. The convergence does not always take place on the image plane, however. Some light rays converge in front of or behind the image plane, forming not a point but a blur or a **circle of confusion**. A circle of confusion that is not very large still appears to be sharp. (Figure 2.31)

Focus is relative to the distance from the subject to the image plane. You can shift the focal plane by rotating the focus ring on the camera's lens, which adjusts the different glass elements in the lens. This allows

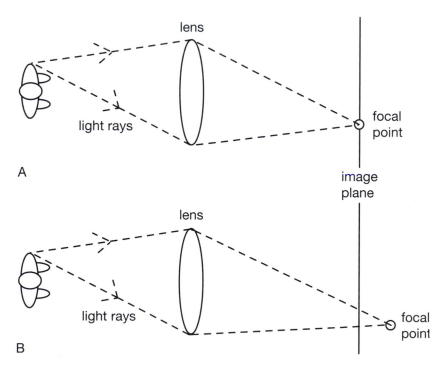

Figure 2.31 Focus is created by the convergence of light rays on the image plane. A point of light that does not converge on the image plane creates a circle of confusion. A small circle of confusion might still appear relatively sharp. A large circle of confusion appears blurry. **A**, Light reflected off the shoulder of the subject travels through the lens and converges on the image plane, creating a focused image. **B**, A point of light does not converge on the image plane, creating a circle of confusion.

you to choose the specific distance from the lens that will be in focus. You generally focus on the most important subject or object in the frame because our eyes are naturally drawn to what is in focus. Only one plane in space, parallel to the image plane, can be in true focus. If the subject or the camera moves forward or back, the lens is still focused at the original camera/subject distance, and the subject may fall out of focus or become blurry. Even though there is only one plane at one specific distance from the camera that is really in focus, a certain range of distance in front and behind the subject appears to be in focus, or is in *acceptable focus*. This is because the circles of confusion within this range are relatively small. This range of acceptable focus is called **depth of field** (Figure 2.32).

If objects that are several feet in front of and behind the subject on which you are focused appear to be sharp, this is called *deep focus* (Figure 2.33). *Shallow focus* occurs when objects that are only a few inches (or less) in front of or behind the subject are unfocused or blurry (Figure 2.34). Deep focus allows the viewer to choose what part of the frame to look at. Shallow focus directs the attention of the viewer to what is sharp.

Figure 2.32 There is only one distance from a lens that will be in true focus, but depending on the situation, a distance in front of and behind the focal plane will hold acceptable focus. This is called the *depth of field*. One-third of the depth of field will be in front of the focal plane, two-thirds behind it.

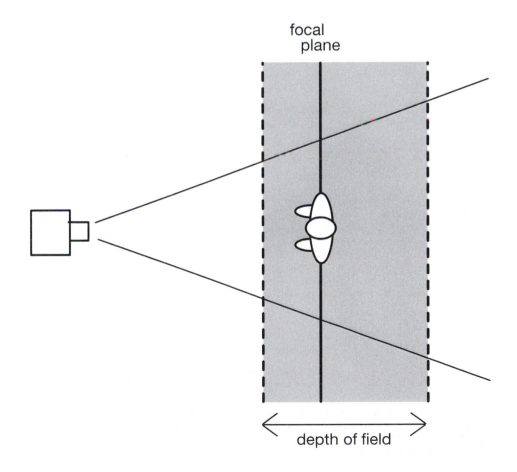

focal
plane

depth of field

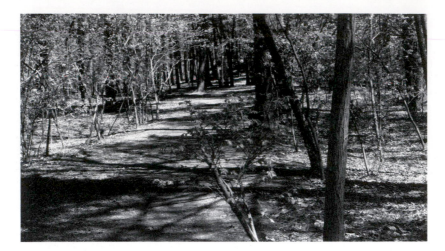

Figure 2.33 An image with a great depth of field is said to have deep focus. Foreground, middle ground, and background all hold acceptable focus.

Figure 2.34 An image with a small depth of field is said to have shallow focus. Shallow focus is good way to direct the viewer's attention. We look at what is in focus.

In practice, depth of field can be controlled by manipulating three variables:

1. aperture,
2. camera/subject distance, and
3. focal length.

As aperture decreases, the depth of field increases (Figure 2.35). This is why that is so: Light rays reflect off a subject. Aperture, as we know, is the size of the lens opening allowing light to enter. A small aperture opening allows fewer rays, which are closer to parallel, to enter the lens. This causes the reflected rays to create smaller circles of confusion on the image plane. Therefore, more of the image seems sharp.

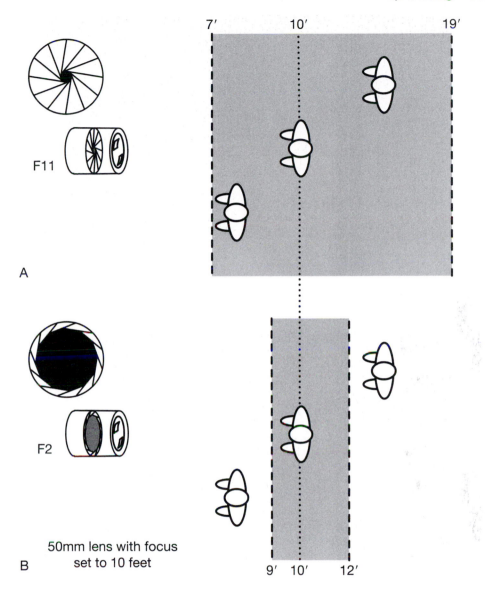

7' 10' 19'

F11

A

F2

50mm lens with focus
B set to 10 feet

9' 10' 12'

Figure 2.35 A, A small aperture opening (high f-stop number) contributes to greater depth of field. **B**, A larger aperture opening (low f-stop number) contributes to less depth of field.

The camera/subject distance and the focal length of the lens used both affect the magnification of the image. The more the image is magnified, the less the apparent depth of field. This is not because the focus really changes but because we can more readily see the circles of confusion and realize that objects in front of and behind the image plane are not really in focus. Therefore, the greater the distance between the subject and the camera, the greater the depth of field. Conversely, the closer the camera is to the subject, the shallower the depth of field.

Zooming in on a subject also magnifies the image and decreases the apparent depth of field. The shorter the focal length of the lens used (the more wide angle it is), the greater the appearance of depth of field.

Determinants of Depth of Field

	Aperture	Focal Length	Camera/Subject Distance
Minimum Depth of Field	open (large)	telephoto	close
Maximum Depth of Field	closed (small)	wide angle	far

Figure 2.36 This chart shows the three determinants of depth of field.

To have the absolutely deepest focus possible, you would need a very brightly lit scene (resulting in a small aperture opening), a long distance between subject and camera, and a wide-angle or "zoomed out" lens. If you visualize these conditions, you will see that this would result in only wide shots. However, you don't have to maximize all three variables to achieve deep focus (Figure 2.36). An f-stop setting of F11 or even F8 would result in reasonably deep focus even with a normal lens and enough camera-to-subject distance to create a medium shot. If you can't get enough light to warrant a small aperture setting (i.e., F11), you could also achieve a small aperture opening by slowing the shutter speed or increasing the sensitivity of your image-making material. To create shallow focus, you can use a larger aperture opening (created by low light, a fast shutter speed, or decreasing the sensitivity of your image making material), use a telephoto lens, and decrease your camera-to-subject distance.

RESOLUTION

The clarity of the reproduced image is called the **resolution**. For still and moving images produced by both analog and digital methods, the quality of the lens affects the resolution of the reproduced image. High-quality materials and workmanship (resulting in higher cost and larger size and weight) make a big difference. Generally speaking, the larger, more expensive cameras, which are designed for professionals, have better lenses and produce sharper, clearer images. Other determinants of resolution are particular to the medium and are discussed in the next section.

THE FRAME APPLIED TO DIFFERENT MEDIA

We have been speaking mostly about concepts shared by visual media. There are, however, medium-specific aspects that are important to understand. This discussion includes the following four media:

1. film still photography,
2. digital still photography,
3. motion picture film, and
4. video motion pictures, both analog and digital.

Later we will consider audio as both a stand-alone medium and combined with visuals.

ANALOG VS. DIGITAL REPRODUCTION

Methods of image and sound reproduction can be characterized as analog or digital. Both sound and image reproduction involve changing one form of energy into another (transduction). Light, sound, and electrical energy travel in waves. When one form of energy is transduced into another using analog technology, the full wave of original energy is reproduced. This includes both wanted and unwanted information, or *noise*. The result is a full translation of the original image or sound (a *continuous wave*). When analog media is copied or *dubbed*, it produces an amplification of the noise. This degradation of the original quality is called **generational loss**, and it is a disadvantage of analog methods of media making. Digital reproduction does not reproduce the entire wave. Instead, it samples the original signal, reading the signal's information at very small intervals. Then the information is encoded as digital data, a series of on and off pulses (ones and zeros). Encoded into the digital signal is the information needed to reproduce the information from the original source. The process of **sampling** allows reproduction of the signal's wanted information without its noise (Figure 2.37). Thus an audio CD does not have the hiss (noise) of a phonograph record or analog audiocassette. When digital media are compressed and uncompressed some generational loss can occur, but not to the extent that it does with analog media. (Compression will be covered later in this chapter and in Chapter 9.) Some feel that there is a loss of richness and authenticity with digital sampling—that it sounds or looks too clean to be real.

Figure 2.37 **A,** An analog process reproduces the entire signal (continuous wave) and is susceptible to noise. **B,** A digital process samples the signal, converting the measurements into a mathematical value. Noise can be avoided.

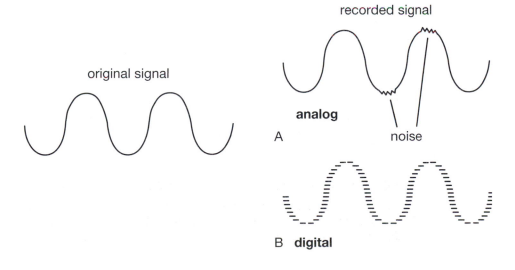

original signal

recorded signal

analog

A   noise

B **digital**

STILL IMAGE MAKING

Still images are now captured using either the traditional method of exposing silver-based film or through digital means.

Film

When exposing a frame of film, light waves reflecting off the subject are focused by the lens onto the surface of the image plane. In this case, the image plane is a strip of plastic coated with a light-sensitive emulsion. An analog still camera is a largely mechanical device that relies on a chemical process to produce an image. The strip of film is pulled through the camera by a manual or motorized gear system. A mechanical shutter blocks the light from striking the image plane until you are ready to expose the film. When you press the shutter release button, the shutter opens for a fraction of a second, exposes one frame of film, then closes again. The strip of film is then advanced so another picture can be taken.

The emulsion or coating on the film contains particles of silver halide that have a chemical reaction to the presence of light. The particles are called the *grain* of the film. More grains of silver halide coating the frame of film means that each grain is smaller, so the film can respond more accurately to the differences in exposure throughout the image reflected by the lens. The finer the grain, the sharper the image or the higher its *resolution*. More grains also means that more light is needed to properly expose the film.

The amount of light needed by a particular film stock to produce optimum image quality is called its *sensitivity*. The sensitivity of film can be measured in different ways. ASA, a rating system developed by the American Standards Association, and DIN, a standard developed in Germany, are both reflected in an International Organization for Standardization (ISO) designation. Film with an ISO of 100/21 has an ASA of 100 and a DIN of 21. This indicates a film that has a medium range of sensitivity. These numbers measure a film's *exposure index* (EI). The higher the number, the less light needed to expose the film (meaning increased sensitivity). But as film becomes more sensitive to light, an increase in grain size and a subsequent reduction in resolution result.

There are two types of film—negative and reversal. **Negative film** for still cameras is used to create printed photographs. When negative film is treated with developing chemicals, the bright parts of the subject cause the corresponding parts on the film to turn dark. The dark parts of the subject cause little to no reaction. This creates a negative image. The light is focused through this negative image and strikes a sheet of light-sensitive paper, once again reversing the bright and dark relationships. Through this printing process, the reproduced image now has the same relationship between light and dark areas as the original subject (Figure 2.38). The printing process also allows for cropping of the images and manipulation of brightness and contrast in black-and-white reproduction. (We will discuss color in the Chapter 4.)

Reversal film for still cameras is used to create slides, or *transparencies*. With reversal film, a single strip of film is chemically treated to

A

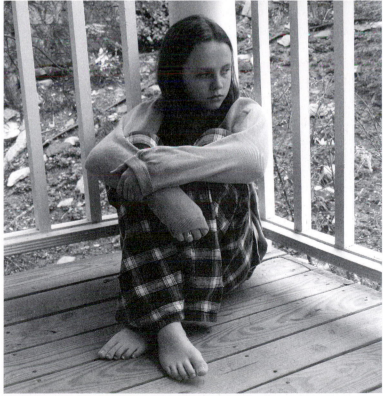

B

Figure 2.38 Light is focused through
(**A**) a negative onto photographic paper to
create (**B**) a positive image.

first become a negative image. Then, when reexposed and treated with more chemicals, a positive image is formed. The final image exists on a strip of film that is usually cut into individual frames and mounted in plastic or cardboard mounts. Transparencies require transmitted light from a slide projector or light table to be viewed.

Formats or sizes of still film vary but, by far, the most common is 35mm. In addition to 35mm, professional photographers use 120mm film, often producing a square image or even using single sheets of film that are 4×5 or 8×10.

Digital

In a digital camera, the light is focused through the lens and strikes a CCD that is covered with light-sensitive dots or **pixels** (short for *picture elements*).The pixels create an electronic charge relative to the amount of light hitting them. A brightly lit object will reflect a lot of light onto the CCD, creating a strong signal. A dark object will result in a weaker charge. This electronic signal is converted into a series of off and on pulses that form a digital representation of the object being captured. Digital cameras have shutter systems, too, but they are electronic, not mechanical, and work a bit differently. Instead of a shutter opening to let light strike the image plane for a specific amount of time, a digital camera's shutter controls how long the CCD holds the reflected image before releasing the encoded digital information. The result is the same, as a shortened shutter speed would cause less light to strike the image plane. Less light would mean a darker image, unless compensated for by opening the aperture. A shorter time of exposure results in a less blurred moving image or frozen motion.

Resolution Resolution is an issue in digital imaging as well as analog. Simply, the number of pixels on the CCD determines the resolution or amount of detail in the image it can produce. The more pixels, the sharper the picture and the higher the resolution (Figure 2.39). In this way, the pixels of a CCD are analogous to the grains of a film stock. The *pixel count* is the maximum number of pixels that can be recorded by a single image. Pixel count is expressed in *megapixels* or millions of pixels. The camera used to take the photographs in this book records 5 megapixels or 5 million pixels per image. The more pixels, the better the image; but, also, the more pixels, the greater the file size or amount of digital information encoded.

Most digital cameras allow you to choose from a range of resolutions. The 2650 × 1920 resolution setting on my camera takes advantage of virtually all of the 5 million pixels available. The numbers describe an image 2650 pixels across and 1920 pixels high. You get the total number of pixels by multiplying the two. A 1280 × 960 setting would mean fewer overall pixels and therefore a smaller file size, allowing for more pictures to fit on the camera's storage medium, but less detail when compared to the image with higher resolution.

Less simple is the issue of resolution when it comes to displaying the image on a computer screen or printing it onto paper. It is important to remember that pixel count doesn't necessarily define the *size* of your image—just how many pixels it is made up of. The image size

A

B

Figure 2.39 The same image is reproduced in (**A**) high resolution and (**B**) low resolution.

is determined by how close together those pixels are displayed, or the *pixel density*. The same image can be displayed at a high density, resulting in more detail and a smaller size than the same image displayed at a lesser density. Pixel density is expressed in pixels per inch (ppi).

With digital prints, resolution is ultimately determined by the size of the image you print and the dots per inch (dpi) of the printer itself. A 5-megapixel image reproduced at 4 × 6 inches has a higher ppi value (higher density of pixels) than that same image enlarged to 16 × 20 inches. With the larger print, you've taken that same number of megapixels and stretched them out over a larger area. It's the same as printing a film image. The larger the print, the less detail it will appear to have. It's a matter of matching the appropriate resolution with the needed print size. A minimum of 300 ppi is generally desired for printed images.

Computer printers reproduce images as tiny dots of black or color. The more dots per inch a printer can print, the smaller the dots are and the clearer the image. A printer has a fixed number of dpi that it is capable of printing. If the dpi is less than the ppi of the digital image being printed, you'll lose resolution in the print.

Computer and video monitors have a much lower number of pixels per inch than most printed images. Video monitors have a set number of pixels displayed. On computer monitors you can choose from a range of resolutions. When reproducing an image on a computer or video monitor, an image pixel will line up with a monitor pixel. So an image that has a pixel dimension of 2650 × 1920 would more than fill a computer monitor set to a resolution of 1024 × 640. To make your image fit on the screen, you can rescale the image, making it smaller. The resolution, though, can only be as good as the monitor on which the image is displayed. Generally, a monitor has a maximum resolution density of 72 ppi. If you know your images are going to be used on the web, there's no reason to shoot them at maximum resolution as you would for an image that is to be printed. It just wastes room on your camera memory card and causes the image to take longer to load in a web page.

Compression   It takes a good amount of digital information to reproduce a high-quality image, much more than it takes to store a text document. For that reason digital images are often compressed. **Compression** mathematically reduces file size by either discarding redundant information or reorganizing the digital files more efficiently. Digital cameras generally allow you to choose whether to compress your images and, if so, what type and amount of compression to use. Compression allows you to fit more images on the digital storage medium, such as a flash drive or CD, and it facilitates faster transmission of information if the image is distributed through the Internet, where digital information has to flow through a phone line, cable connection, or wireless channel. Common types of compression for digital images are TIFF, a type that compresses an image only a little but loses no information, and JPEG, which allows more compression but at high levels can result in a visibly degraded image. Generally, compression negatively affects image quality. The higher the compression, the lower the image quality. Compression does not affect resolution, though. Compression and resolution are both aspects of image reproduction that affect file size and image quality, but in different ways. A highly compressed high-resolution image and an uncompressed low-resolution image could both lack the image quality you're looking for. Compression is discussed more fully in Chapter 9.

Digital images can be viewed on a computer screen, burned to a DVD, transmitted to a cell phone, or printed on paper. Digital images can be imported into many software applications, such as Adobe's Photoshop, that allow manipulation of the original image, from simple cropping or increasing contrast to sophisticated digital effects. Knowing how an image will be used affects decisions about what resolution and how much compression to use. An image for a web page requires less resolution and can withstand more compression than an image that is to be reproduced in a magazine.

The aspect ratio of a still image can be whatever dimension it is cropped to be. It can be horizontal or vertical. Standard snapshots follow the 3:2 ratio of 35mm still film. If a still image is used to fill a computer, television, or movie screen, it needs to adopt the aspect ratio of the medium in which it is being used.

MOTION PICTURE FILM

Just like still film, motion picture film can be negative or reversal. Most filmmakers prefer negative film because it allows multiple prints to be made from the original camera negative. This protects the footage and allows darkroom manipulation of brightness, contrast, and color. With negative motion picture film, the printing is done onto another strip of film that must be projected with light to be seen.

Formats or gauges of motion picture film range from 8mm to 70mm. This measurement relates to the width of the strip of film. Use of 8mm has been effectively replaced by video. Student and independent filmmakers commonly use 16mm, and major motion pictures, high-budget commercials, and television series use the more expensive but higher-quality 35mm. Films that are to be projected on a very large screen sometimes use 65mm and 70mm formats. The less the filmed image is enlarged when projected, the sharper the image seems.

As discussed earlier in the chapter, film aspect ratio varies, based on the specific film size or gauge, the camera used, and how it will be projected. For example, 16mm film has an aspect ratio of 1.37:1, close to the 1.33:1 (4:3) aspect ratio of traditional television, and is generally projected at that dimension. Super 16 uses the same size film but shoots a wider frame (1.66:1) that is more compatible with commercial film projection or widescreen TV. For that reason Super 16 is more commonly used now than standard 16mm.

The standard for commercial motion picture production is 35mm film, which is also still used for some television production and commercials. Digital production is making inroads into the use of all film, but both film and digital image acquisition are prevalent in the industry. Aspect ratios for projecting 35mm vary, but 1.85:1 is the most common in the United States, whereas 1.66:1 is the most common ratio in Europe (Figure 2.40).

Extreme widescreen exceeds a 2:1 ratio. This is accomplished in two ways. The first is by means of *anamorphic* lenses used on the film cameras and projectors. These lenses squeeze the image horizontally, into a more extreme oblong, creating a distortion that is corrected by a special projector during exhibition. This method was introduced in the 1950s, and though the

Figure 2.40 The ratio 1.85:1 is the U.S. norm for widescreen 35mm projection. Though the film is the same, 1.66:1 is the European standard.

specific technology has changed, anamorphic widescreen is still used today. Originally the aspect ratio of anamorphic was 2.35:1, and it is often still referred to as that, though the ratio is really 2.39:1. The other method involves shooting on 65mm film (2.29:1) and releasing the finished product on 70mm film (2.20:1). This extremely wide image is often used for epic films with panoramic vistas, big battle scenes, and thousands of extras (Figure 2.41).

Another use of the very large format 70mm film has been developed by IMAX. This technology exposes the frame horizontally, rather than vertically, between the sprocket holes, allowing a much larger image, with resolution that will hold up to extremely large projection sizes, up to eight stories high. The aspect ratio of this format is 1.43:1, very similar to the 3:2 of 35mm still photography (Figure 2.42).

2.20

Figure 2.41 Extreme widescreen can have an aspect ratio of 2.20:1.

Figure 2.42 A frame from an IMAX movie. The image is exposed horizontally on the film to maximize the resolution. (Courtesy of IMAX Corp.)

VIDEO MOTION PICTURES

Video technology has changed radically in the past several years. The terminology surrounding the acquisition, distribution, and exhibition of video or television can get a bit confusing, because multiple and overlapping changes are at work. For one thing, the technology of the video that is shot is often different from the technology of the signal that is distributed by broadcast, cable, or satellite, which can be different yet from the technology of the TV set you are watching. The transition from analog to digital has already taken place in terms of acquisition. Virtually all video cameras are now creating a digitally encoded signal. At this writing, the transition to digital broadcasting and reception is currently in process (Go to the Source: Transition to DTV). However, digital television (DTV) is not necessarily high definition. Nor is digital necessarily 16:9. A higher resolution and a wider aspect ratio are possible features of digital TV.

Analog Video

In the past several years, video has transformed from an analog to a digital medium. The decreased generational loss, increased image resolution, lower price, and portability of digital video equipment have fueled this transition. Analog cameras have all but ceased to exist, but analog VCRs and television sets are still quite plentiful. The way analog video is created is still of interest historically and provides a model of creating a television signal that may be easier to visualize than its digital counterpoint. With analog video, the image is focused onto the light-sensitive surface of a cathode-ray tube (CRT), an electronic vacuum tube that is capable of receiving, amplifying, and exporting electronic signals. The front of the tube (called a *faceplate*) is coated with a light-sensitive compound, containing an element such as selenium or cesium. These elements, or pixels, convert the light waves into electronic energy when struck with light energy. Something that converts one form of energy into another is called a **transducer**.

The strength of the electronic signal that is produced is relative to the brightness of the light that produced it. The brightness information is read by an electron beam through a process called **scanning**. The beam reads the faceplate from top to bottom, moving horizontally across the tube, from left to right (Figure 2.43). The number of times the beam scans left to right for each frame of video is called the *vertical lines of resolution*. More lines result in higher image resolution. Original television standards in the United States required 525 lines of vertical resolution.

In analog video, the frame is scanned in two parts. First the odd-numbered lines are scanned and then the even-numbered lines. Each half-frame is called a *field*. NTSC video with a frame rate of 30 frames per second (fps) has 60 fields per second; PAL with 25 fps has 50 fields. (Go to the Source—Analog Broadcast Standards). The number of horizontal lines of resolution is the number of pixels that make up one scanning line. This number, too, is a determinant of image resolution.

Once amplified, the electronic signal produced by scanning travels through a cable to be recorded onto a magnetically coated videotape or

Go to the Source—
Transition to DTV

In the United States, the Federal Communications Commission (FCC) is the federal agency responsible for the regulation of telecommunications. The FCC set a 2009 deadline for all broadcasters to complete their transition from analog to digital broadcast signals. Cable and direct broadcast satellite services are also making the change. Digital service allows a clearer picture, better sound, and more TV channels within the same amount of bandwidth. It also allows for other services such as captioning and viewing on demand. Digital service also requires that the television be capable of receiving digital signals. This can be done with a digital to analog set-top box that converts the digital signal back into analog or by having a set that has a built-in digital tuner. The FCC also set a 2007 deadline for all television sets, 13 inches or bigger, sold in the United States to have digital tuners.

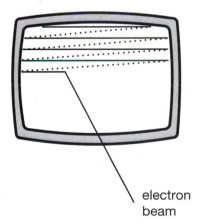

Figure 2.43 Video information is read and reproduced by means of scanning. An electron beam reads left to right, from the top of the screen to the bottom. How many times the beam reads across each frame of video determines its lines of resolution.

Go to the Source—
Analog Broadcast Standards

When television was first introduced, there needed to be agreement on exactly what technical standards would be used. In the United States, a group called the National Television System Committee adopted standards in 1941 that are called NTSC standards. These standards, some of which are discussed further in upcoming chapters, include the following:

- *Composite signal.*
- *4:3 aspect ratio.*
- *525 lines of vertical resolution* (480 of which are visible in the broadcast image).
- *30 frames per second of interlaced video* (resulting in 60 fields per second). This was for black-and-white television. When color was added, the additional information that needed to be transmitted required a reduction in the frame rate to 29.97. Interlaced scanning came about because the pixels used in early television could not hold their brightness for a full 1/30 of a second to allow the electron beam to read it. Shortening the scanning process to 1/60 of a second allowed the signal to be adequately scanned.
- *60 Hz electrical cycle.*
- *The use of frequency modulation (FM) to transmit the audio portion of the signal.*

Different standards were adopted in different parts of the world. In Germany in the 1960s a system called PAL was developed and replaced earlier TV systems in most of Western Europe, Asia, and parts of Africa and South America. Ways in which PAL differs from NTSC include these:

- *625 lines of vertical resolution* (576 visible),
- *25 frames (50 fields) per second,* and
- *a 50-Hz cycle.*

SECAM is similar to PAL in terms of standards, but tapes recorded in SECAM cannot be edited, so tapes are often converted to PAL for postproduction. SECAM is used in France, Eastern Europe, the Mideast, and parts of Africa, though some countries in Eastern Europe have switched to PAL.

converted once again into radio-frequency waves for broadcast. A CRT at the other end, such as the picture tube inside a television, reverses the process. An electron beam scans the phosphors or light-sensitive dots on the TV screen, converting the electronic signal back into an image.

Analog video has many formats and they are often characterized as consumer, industrial, or broadcast in terms of their image quality. VHS (which uses a 1/2-inch videotape) and Hi-8 (8mm) are consumer formats; 3/4-inch or U-matic is a basically obsolete industrial format. Beta (a 1/2-inch tape) is the most common analog broadcast format, but 1-inch type C videotape (on a reel, not a cassette) is still in use. It can be a bit confusing because not only are there many different formats, but there are digital versions of some, such as Beta and Hi-8, as well. When you copy an analog tape to another analog tape of the same or different format or make dubs of digital formats using an analog connection, you will experience significant generational loss, especially with the consumer and industrial formats.

Digital Video

Digital video is said to be have less noise than analog, meaning less signal interference. This is due to the fact that digital video is sampled as opposed to reproducing the entire signal. In sampling, unwanted information can be avoided. This results in cleaner reproduction, particularly in the dark areas of the image. Digital video is subject to other types of image distortion, however, which are often the result of compression.

Digital video cameras have replaced CRTs with light-sensitive CCDs, as with the digital still camera. Images are focused onto the CCD, encoded into digital information, and released as a digital signal to be recorded on videotape or increasingly saved in its original digital form on a hard drive or storage device. The resolution of the digital image is determined by the number of pixels on the CCD. As with analog video, the number of pixels in each row of pixels defines the horizontal resolution. Vertical resolution is determined by how many rows or lines of pixels make up each frame. Grains in film and pixels in video determine resolution. The more there are per frame, the greater the image quality (Figure 2.44). With video, though, we tend to talk more about lines of resolution (rows of pixels) than we do about overall numbers of pixels.

Digital video can be standard definition (SD) or high definition (HD). SD digital video adopts the standards of its analog counterpart. NTSC SD has a 4:3 aspect ratio, 525 lines of resolution, and a frame rate of 29.97 fps. PAL SD, on the other hand, has 625 lines and a frame rate of 25 fps.

With digital video, the term *scanning* is still used to describe the way in which the electronic signal is encoded, though the process is different from the moving electron beam of analog video. A CCD receives the image and converts to the light energy to an electronic signal. The signal generated by the pixels is then shifted row by row, first vertically down the frame, then horizontally to a storage area where the information is quantized, or converted to ones and zeros. Scanning can be either interlaced or progressive. In **interlaced scanning** (as with analog video), each frame of video is separated into two fields

horizontal resolution

vertical resolution

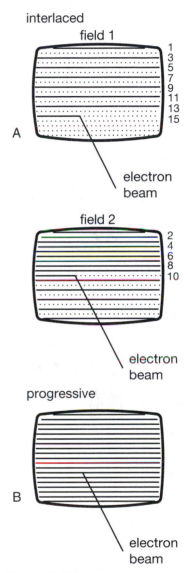

Figure 2.44 Vertical lines of resolution are the number of lines scanned down the frame. Horizontal resolution is determined by how many pixels make up each scanning line.

interlaced

field 1

1
3
5
7
9
11
13
15

A

electron beam

field 2

2
4
6
8
10

electron beam

progressive

B

electron beam

Figure 2.45 A, Interlaced scanning first reads the odd-numbered lines, creating one field, then the even-numbered lines, creating a second field. The two fields are combined to create a single frame. **B**, Progressive scanning reads sequentially down the frame, creating 60 full frames per second.

(Figure 2.45A). First, the odd-numbered lines are scanned, then the even. The letter *i* is used after the resolution or the frame rate to indicate interlaced scanning , such as 1080i or 60i. High-definition digital video offers a variety of scanning methods, resolutions, and frame rates, often within the same camera. With **progressive scanning** each line in the frame is scanned in order, from top to bottom (Figure 2.45B). To provide enough images per second for perception of smooth motion without flickering, the scanning rate is increased to 60 frames per second (as opposed to 30 in interlaced systems). The letter *p* is used to indicate progressive scanning, and 480p and 720p systems are currently dominant. The quality of the progressive systems rivals 1080i because of the increased scanning rate. Progressive scanning also avoids the flicker that can occur when interlaced fields fail to align precisely.

Standard Definition and High Definition

There is a difference between digital video or television and HDTV. Digital refers to the way the signal is recorded—digital sampling as opposed to the continuous wave of analog. Digital video can be standard definition or high definition (Go to the Source—SD and HD Formats). The nature of digital processing means that a single camera can process signals in a variety of ways. Cameras are able to produce signals that are either interlaced or progressive, shoot at a variety of frame rates, and offer an image that has either a 4:3 or 16:9 ratio.

High definition refers to the vertical resolution of the image. Though some claim that an image has to have at least 1000 lines of resolution to be considered HD, 720p is generally accepted as high definition. HDTV is often thought of as a digital-only standard, but early forms of high definition, such as the NHK system developed in Japan in the 1980s, were analog. In the United States, broadcast standards have been agreed on (Go to the Source—HDTV Standards) and include a 16:9 aspect ratio and Dolby audio.

Go to the Source—
SD and HD Formats

Standard Definition

Video that has traditional resolution is standard definition (SD). This includes analog video, as well as digital SD. A variety of digital SD formats are in use in consumer camcorders and professional applications. This includes the common format of DV (originally DVC) as well as Sony's DVCAM format and DVCPRO, developed by Panasonic. All three record onto tape that is 1/4 inch or 6.35mm wide and come in both small cassettes for camcorder use and larger, longer cassettes for studio decks. There is limited compatibility between the formats. DV tapes, because the DV format is marketed to consumers, can be recorded either in standard play (SP) or long play (LP), which allows for longer record time at lower quality. A 60-minute DV tape recorded in SP can play back on any deck (i.e., DV, DVCAM, or DVCPRO; note, however, that the small DV tapes in a DVCPRO deck require an adapter). DV tapes can be used to record DVCAM format, but a 60-minute tape will only hold approximately 40 minutes of material because the DVCAM format records a wider signal. Most digital SD cameras are inherently 4:3, but most allow shooting a 16:9 image by cropping, using more horizontal lines, or the use of a separate anamorphic lens. There are a few 16:9 SD cameras. Digital betacam (or digi-beta) is one of many broadcast quality digital SD formats. It uses a 1/2-inch tape and produces a very high quality image that had been the professional industry standard until the transition to HDTV.

High Definition

There are several competing formats at both the high end (in terms of quality and cost) and the more affordable end. Sony, Panasonic, and JVC each offer a high-end HD format. (Some call these "real" HD.) Sony has HDCAM, Panasonic has D5-HD, and JVC

DVB (Digital Video Broadcasting) is the set of standards adopted by Europe, Australia, South Africa, and India. Many African, Asian, and South American countries have adopted at least some of the standards as well. Japan developed and is using ISDB (Integrated Services Digital Broadcasting). All are digital, high-definition, and widescreen.

CONCLUSION

The frame is your media canvas. By defining the shape of your frame and the arrangements of subjects and objects within it, you begin to create the visual aesthetic that helps communicate your message. Some decisions about framing, composition, and focus are made consciously, based on learned practices; some are done instinctively. All of the choices impact how your audience perceives the content. Whether still or moving, analog or digital, chemical or electronic, strong composition is an important foundation of effective media. In subsequent chapters, you will see ways to extend that foundation through the control of light, color, depth, and movement.

PUTTING IT INTO PRACTICE
OBSERVING

Watch television with the sound off so you can concentrate on the formal aspects, not the content. Watch for difference in balance, depth of field, and shot sizes. Watch for the use of headroom, lookspace, and leadroom.

Cover your television screen with plastic food wrap. Use a marker to divide the screen into thirds both vertically and horizontally. Watch how often the rule of thirds is used in composing shots.

WRITING

Find six photos in books or magazines that have either static or dynamic compositions (three of each). In your notebook, describe the aspects of their composition that contribute to their sense of stasis or dynamism. Are the images pleasing or disturbing? Does their composition reinforce their message?

DOING

Use a still camera (film or digital) to start viewing your world through a frame. Create the following images:

1. one that shows a symmetrically balanced composition,
2. one that is asymmetrically balanced,
3. one that obeys the rule of closure,
4. one that doesn't obey the rule of closure,
5. a close-up with appropriate headroom,
6. a long shot with appropriate headroom, and
7. a balanced image that obeys the rule of thirds, balancing the subject with the weight of his or her gaze.

Figure 2.46 Panasonic's AJ-HPX2000 records DVC Pro HD directly onto a digital storage device—the P2 card. It can simultaneously record onto DV tape as well.

has D9-HD. These are the formats being used by Hollywood and the television networks. More affordable HD has been created as a high-definition version of DV and DVCPRO. These are called HDV and DVCPRO-HD, and they allow for high-definition quality on DV tapes or tapeless digital storage media (such as Panasonic's P2 card, introduced in 2006) (Figure 2.46). All of the HD formats are 16:9. Almost all HD cameras can record both 720p and 1080i at a variety of frame rates. Some can record 1080p and some can record both HD and SD within the same camcorder.

KEY CONCEPTS

angle of view	lookspace
aperture	negative film
aspect ratio	pan and scan
asymmetrical balance	pillarboxing
charge-coupled device (CCD)	pixel
circle of confusion	progressive scanning
closure	resolution
compression	reversal film
depth of field	rule of thirds
field of view	sampling
focal length	scanning
frame	sensitivity
f-stop	shot size(s)
generational loss	shutter
headroom	shutter speed
image plane	symmetrical balance
interlaced scanning	telephoto
iris	transducer
leadroom	wide angle
letterboxing	windowboxing

Go to the Source—
HDTV Standards

The Advanced Television Systems Committee (ATSC) is a voluntary international consortium, created in 1982, to agree on new standards for digital television. They have agreed on 18 acceptable standards for digital SDTV and HDTV that to date have been adopted by the United States, Canada, South Korea, Argentina, Mexico, and Honduras. The high-definition standards are 720p, 1080i, or 1080p. Each of the three can have frame rates of 24, 30, or 60 fps.

CHAPTER 3

Depth and Movement in the Frame

MEDIA ILLUSIONS

Visual media exist in two dimensions. Whether a theater movie screen, a computer monitor, or TV set, the image has height and width (its aspect ratio), but no depth beyond the measurement of light molecules or pixels. In geometry, we call the width the **x-axis**, the height the **y-axis**, and the depth the **z-axis** (Figure 3.1).

Despite the fact that the images we deal with have only two dimensions, most of what we portray in these images are three-dimensional objects. To view these objects as three-dimensional entities in a two-dimensional medium, the creation of an **illusion of depth** is required. An important factor in creating this illusion of depth is the control of **perspective**. Perspective describes our perception of depth and distance from a particular point of view. Our perspective of a scene and the objects in it changes as we move closer or farther away, as we stand or sit, or as we approach from the side as opposed to from the front. In the 15th century, Western European Renaissance painters discovered the convention of linear perspective as a way to represent three-dimensional space on the two-dimensional canvas. Lines converging at the horizon in the way our eyes perceive objects in space from a single vantage point created the illusion of depth in their paintings (Figure 3.2). Painters also discovered how to make light and placement of objects within the painting suggest depth. These are lessons that visual media artists can learn from as well.

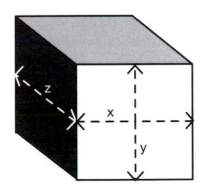

Figure 3.1 The x-axis defines the frame's width, the y-axis its height, and the z-axis its implied depth.

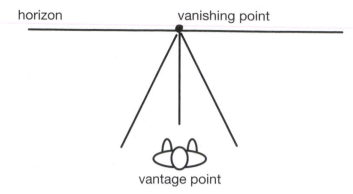

horizon   vanishing point

vantage point

Figure 3.2 In nature, from a single point of view, parallel lines seem to converge at a vanishing point on the horizon line.

As discussed later in this chapter, moving images don't really move. Our brains perceive rapidly projected images as moving, and we fill in missing information to see that movement as smooth and continuous. Through illusions of depth and movement, two-dimensional images can portray a convincing representation of our three-dimensional, moving world. As makers of media, we control how effectively these illusions are carried out.

Although most of the attention to depth and movement within this chapter is paid to visual images, they are concepts that apply to sound as well. Foreground and background sounds lend depth to our listening experience. The sound mixing exercise on the companion website books.elsevier.com/companions/9780240809076 illustrates this. Movement can be achieved in the audio frame and the visual frame.

CREATING VISUAL DEPTH

Different planes along the z-axis can only exist in three-dimensional space (Figure 3.3). By giving visual clues and emphasizing the existence of these z-axis planes, we are proving that our subjects exist in three dimensions but are reproduced in two.

PLACEMENT

The placement, or arrangement, of subjects and objects within the frame is a major way to emphasize the illusion of depth. Placement is determined by several factors. You can physically put portable objects where you want them, you can have talent stand and move in specific places, or you can position the camera so that objects in your frame are positioned just so (Figure 3.4).

Arrangements that emphasize the illusion of depth include placing subjects and objects on different z-axis planes and having them overlap. Placement on different planes is not enough by itself. If size and scale are not obvious, two identical objects placed on different planes but not overlapping may appear to be a large and a small version of the same thing next to each other (Figure 3.5). If the objects overlap (by moving them or moving the camera), it indicates to the viewer that they could not be side by side—one must be in front of the other. Thus

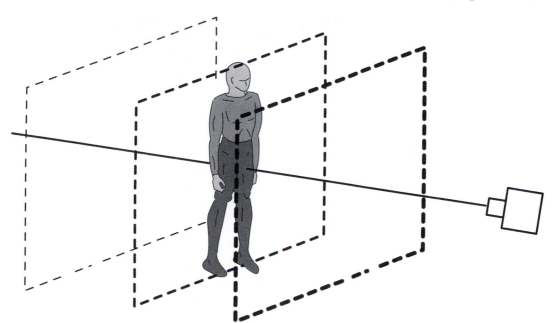

Figure 3.3 The z-axis defines many planes. Techniques that call attention to those multiple planes create the illusion of depth in your two-dimensional image.

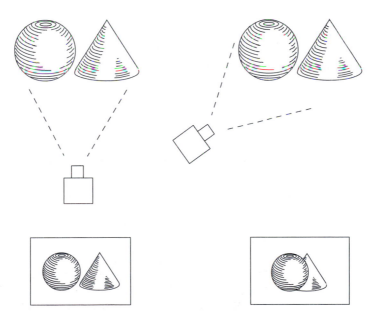

Figure 3.4 Overlapping subjects can be created by changing the camera position.

Figure 3.5 If figures do not overlap, it may be difficult to tell if they are on different planes or if one is just smaller than the other. Overlapping the figures makes it clear to the viewer that there is depth in the frame.

you have multiple z-axis planes and thus, depth. Taking advantage of composition that uses the foreground, middle ground, and background of your scene calls attention to its third dimension.

Positioning objects so that perspective is revealed also adds depth to your frame. From head on, a table can look like a very two-dimensional box. By shifting the camera position up and to the side and revealing the edges of the tabletop converging toward the horizon line, the table now clearly exists in three-dimensional space (Figure 3.6).

LENS CHOICE AND FOCUS

The choice of lens also helps determine the sense of depth in your frame. As discussed in Chapter 2, use of a wide-angle lens exaggerates the perception of distance along the z-axis. The optics of a wide-angle lens reproduces a distorted perspective in which background objects appear smaller than normal, and thus appear further away. The z-axis seems to stretch.

A telephoto lens, on the other hand, "flattens" the image by optically compressing the foreground and background, making background images appear larger and therefore closer than normal. The illusion of depth is less apparent when using a lens with a long focal length.

Camera subject distance also affects depth perception. Two subjects at different distances from the camera will seem closer together the farther they are from the camera. Conversely, the closer you move the camera toward the subjects, the greater the distance between them will seem (Figure 3.7).

Focus, particularly depth of field, affects perception of the third dimension. (See Chapter 2 for a review of the determinants of depth of field.) Deep focus allows the viewer to see clearly from the foreground to the background. Our attention is drawn to objects in focus so that the expanse of the focus emphasizes depth. The combination of deep focus and the exaggeration of depth caused by the use of a wide-angle lens (one determinant of wide depth of field) maximizes the illusion of the third dimension.

Figure 3.6 Changing the vantage point to reveal perspective adds to the illusion of depth.

Shallow depth of field tends to de-emphasize depth because the viewer's attention remains on the plane of action that is in focus. Again,

A

B

Figure 3.7 The same scene taken first with a wide-angle lens and then with a telephoto shows the difference in depth perception. **A**, The wide-angle lens exaggerates the sense of distance along the z-axis. **B**, The combined effect of using the telephoto lens and moving the camera further away from the subjects makes the subjects seem closer together.

Go to the Source—
Rudolf Arnheim

Rudolf Arnheim, born in Germany in 1904, was an influential thinker and writer; his writings attempt to bridge the gap between visual aesthetics and science. A student of philosophy and the then new field of psychology, Arnheim became a professor at the University of Berlin. He conducted research in the area of visual perception, including experiments studying the apparent movement of motion pictures. Being of Jewish heritage, he was persecuted under the Nazis and emigrated to the United States in 1940. Arnheim taught at Harvard University and retired to Ann Arbor, Michigan. His book, *Art and Visual Perception: A Psychology of the Creative Eye*, published in 1954 and revised in 1974, is one of the most influential books written about the perception of art.

the combination of narrow depth of field and the long focal length lens (telephoto), which helps create it, downplays the frame's illusion of depth. An exception to this is the convention of **rack focus**, which is used in motion pictures. In a rack focus, shallow depth of field allows focus and attention on one subject in the frame. Then, on screen, the focal plane is shifted, changing the focus to a different subject on a different plane of action. The viewer's attention is shifted, and he or she is brought forward or backward along the z-axis as the focus shifts (Figure 3.8). This shift of attention emphasizes the foreground and background space of the frame.

Lighting is another important way to create the illusion of depth, as will be discussed in Chapter 4.

MOVEMENT

Movement in the visual media is an illusion, whether it's implied movement within a still frame or the trick our brain plays on us when viewing a film or video.

MOVEMENT WITHIN A STILL FRAME

We tend to think of movement as distinct to motion picture film and video, but movement is a concept that applies to a single still image as well. Rudolf Arnheim wrote that "movement" is an inaccurate term when applied to a still image and that **directed tension** is more descriptive (Go to the Source—Rudolf Arnheim). This refers to the sense of *implied* movement created by either graphics lines, or **vectors**, within the frame or the inherent tension of certain positions within the frame. A vector can suggest movement in many ways; for instance, through a subject pointing or by positioning a subject or object to create a strong diagonal line (Figure 3.9). Chapter 2 described the phenomenon of screen magnetism that seems to pull objects near the edge of the frame and the proximity effect in which objects seem to attract one another. This kind of magnetism creates directed tension as well (Figure 3.10).

Figure 3.8 A rack focus, which shifts shallow focus from one plane in the frame to another, causes the viewer to be aware of the different planes of depth within the frame.

Much research has been done concerning how our eyes move through a still image—what we look at first, for how long, and where our eyes are drawn from there. There are obvious implications for print advertising and website design. In Western culture we tend to "read" images from left to right. The visual dynamic of implied movement is an important part of how we look at an image.

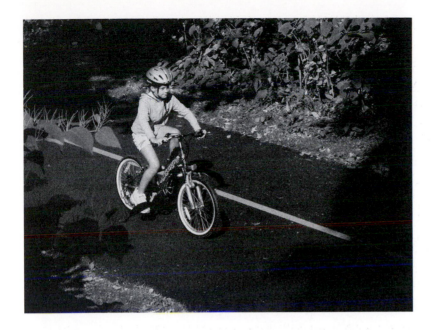

Figure 3.9 The diagonal vector creates a suggestion of movement.

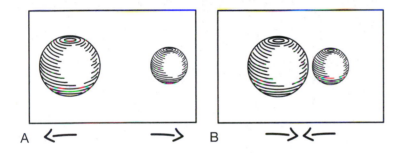

Figure 3.10 **A**, The two objects are pulled to the edges of the frame. **B**, The objects are attracted to each other.

MOVING IMAGES

It wasn't long after the advent of still photography that the idea came along to make the still photographs move (Go to the Source: Early Motion Pictures). Moving images created by film and video cameras do not really move, however. The apparent movement is the result of two optical illusions—**persistence of vision** and the **phi phenomenon**. Motion picture cameras expose a series of still frames to be played back rapidly. The projected images are not showing continuous movement, yet they seem to be. The phi phenomenon occurs when our eyes view two lights, in proximity, flashing in quick succession. Instead of perceiving this occurrence as two separate lights acting independently, we see it as a light moving from the first position to the second. So when a frame of film is projected showing a subject in one position and the next frame of film shows the same subject it a slightly different position, we perceive that the subject has moved. Persistence of vision is a characteristic that enables the retina to hold an image for a brief time beyond reception. When a series of images is projected in

Go to the Source—
Early Motion Pictures

Many inventors participated in the development of motion pictures. Thomas Edison and the Lumière brothers are generally given the most credit. The laboratory of the prolific American inventor Thomas Edison created the kinetoscope and patented it in 1891. It was a camera and peephole viewer in one wooden cabinet that allowed the viewer to look inside the box and see the rapidly moving frames of film, briefly illuminated by a flash of light through a shutter. At the same time, in France, Louis and Auguste Lumière were inventing their cinèmatographe, a combination camera, printer, and projector. It was portable and hand cranked, allowing them to create their famous films of actualities of everyday life, such as a worker leaving a factory or a train pulling into the station.

A frame from the 1909 motion picture, *A Bird in a Gilded Cage*, produced by the Edison Co. Courtesy of the Library of Congress, LC-USZ62-86736.

rapid succession, persistence of vision fills in the gaps. Even though some parts of the action are not shown, there is enough information for our brains to supply the rest. The action seems continuous and smooth. These concepts are illustrated by activities, *Persistence of Vision* and *Phi Phenomenon*, on the companion website books.elsevier.com/companions/9780240809076.

Motion picture film cameras expose 24 frames each second—24 frozen moments, which break an action down into incremental parts. The frame rate for video varies. It gets a little complicated, because not only do different parts of the world use different television standards with different frame rates, but the advent of digital video has resulted in technology that allows for a variety of frame rates. Traditional video technology in the United States, Japan, and much of Central America operates at approximately 30 frames per second, as discussed in Chapter 2. The traditional systems used in other parts of the world operate at 25 frames per second. In order for motion to be perceived as smooth and without flicker, movement needs to be broken down into approximately 50 increments per second. With projected film, this is accomplished by projecting each film frame twice (resulting in 48 projections per second). With traditional video, each frame of video is separated into half-frames or fields, resulting in the scanning of 50 or 60 images per second.

SUBJECT MOVEMENT

Subject movement always has to be considered in relation to the camera. It's a bit like a dance between the talent and the lens. The choreography of this dance is called **blocking the talent**. Blocking is the plan the director makes for when, how, and where actors will move. The actor may say his line as he enters the door, stop at the coat rack to hang his jacket, then walk to his son and greet him. If so, then where is the camera? Perhaps the camera will be positioned so the actor enters through the door on the left edge of the frame, walks screen right to hang his jacket, then steps toward the camera to greet his son (bottom right in the frame) (Figure 3.11). This particular talent blocking and camera position will result in x-axis talent movement as the actor enters, followed by z-axis movement as he approaches the child. X-axis movement gives the viewer a sense of direction and space covered, but it usually isn't as engaging or dramatic as z-axis movement. A subject moving along the x-axis (and looking where she or he is going) will show her or his profile to the camera. Profiles do not involve the viewer as much as frontal views because we pay more attention to someone looking toward us than someone looking away.

Z-axis movement engages the viewer with the frontal view and emphasizes the illusion of depth while the actor moves from the background to the foreground. Z-axis movement also creates more visual variety within the frame by having the actor's shot size change gradually on screen from a wide shot to close-up (Figure 3.12). Movement along the z-axis is demonstrated in the *Depth Through Blocking and Camera Placement* exercise on the companion website books.elsevier.com/companions/9780240809076.

Composing depth by strategically placing the objects and blocking the action only works when subjects in the frame can be directed, such as in a fiction narrative or other scripted program. However, in a documentary,

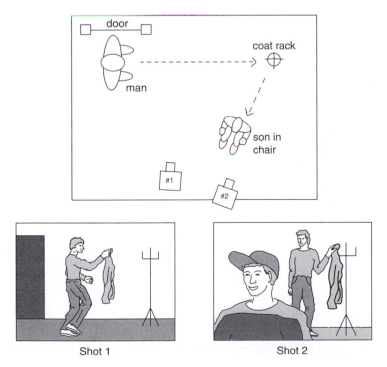

Shot 1   Shot 2

Figure 3.11 The action here is blocked to include both x-axis and z-axis movement. Z-axis movement engages the audience.

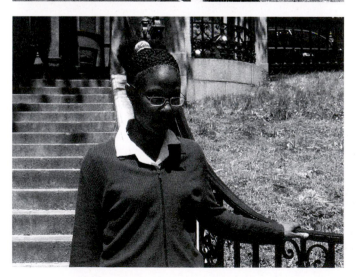

Figure 3.12   Moving the subject along the z-axis provides shot size variety within a single shot.

action is being observed and documented, not controlled. Even in a nonscripted situation, however, the illusion of depth can be obtained by perceptive prediction of action and careful camera placement.

CAMERA MOVEMENT

The viewer experiences a photograph, film, or video through the point of view of the camera's lens. With motion pictures, that point of view can change as the camera moves. A moving camera allows the viewer to explore and move through the mediated space in the same way he or she could experience the real space. The quality and specific movements of a camera depend largely on whether a camera is *mounted* or *handheld.*

Mounting a camera means attaching it to an apparatus that supplies stability and controlled movement. This could be a **tripod** (a three-legged stand with *spreaders*, or supports, that keep the legs steady), a **pedestal** (a heavy wheeled mount used in studio production), or a **dolly** (a tripod on wheels). Dollies can roll on smooth floors or on tracks, which are laid down to accommodate the plan for camera movement. All of these techniques prevent camera shake and, with the camera attached to a mounting head, allow for smooth movement. There is a vast range of tripods and pedestals, ranging from very inexpensive, lightweight tripods for still cameras (where smooth movement is not an issue) or small consumer camcorders to studio dollies with **cranes** that allow sweeping camera movement through space (Figure 3.13).

Hand-holding a camera is a skill that takes practice. It is extremely difficult to hold small consumer cameras, which are designed to be held in front of you with two hands, steady. The very qualities that make them desirable (small size and lack of weight) also defy stability. The result of an unsteady camera on a still image is a blurry picture, especially if the shutter speed is one-sixtieth of a second or slower. For motion pictures, a jittery image can be unpleasant to watch. Built-in image stabilizers, a feature of many camcorders, help a little. A steady hand, a grounded pose, and bracing your forearms against your chest also help. Monopods, or camera mounts with one leg, still require holding the camera but are inexpensive, lightweight compromises to a full-size tripod.

Motion picture film cameras and professional video camcorders are designed to be handheld by setting the camera, which is attached to a *shoulder mount,* on your shoulder. The same rules apply, but with practice, the results can be much smoother. Well-done handheld camera work allows the viewer to enter the scene and feel like a participant in a way a mounted camera can't. It is associated with news gathering and documentaries because it is the only way to get cameras into many situations that do not allow obtrusive dolly tracks or cranes. Handheld camera work that is not done well can elicit motion sickness and is a sign of an amateur.

The Steadicam was developed to enable more control over handheld camera work and make it realistic to hand-hold large, professional film and video cameras. It is a body brace worn by the camera operator that includes springs and gyroscope technology to absorb the shakes and jitters of the handheld camera, and makes it possible to go anywhere the operator can walk or run. However, it requires extensive training to

Figure 3.13 Cameras can be mounted on (**A**) a tripod (portable for field work), (**B**) a pedestal (for moving along smooth studio floor), or (**C**) a crane (for very high shots or large camera movements through space). [Courtesy of (A) Bogen Photo Corp., (B) Vinten Broadcast Limited, and (C) Chapman/Leonard Studio Equipment, Inc.]

master. There is also a Steadicam Jr. model, which is less cumbersome and a bit easier to operate, made for smaller cameras (Figure 3.14).

A stable, mounted camera with smooth, fluid movement is traditionally a sign of professional camera work and high production values. It was the amateur home movie makers and independent film and video-makers, working with very low budgets, who handheld the camera, resulting in that telltale jitter. That held true until the last several years. Now, the handheld look is common in almost every kind of film or video production.

Portable film and video cameras that could be handheld were first developed in the 1960s. Production equipment that was less intrusive, less expensive, and capable of shooting virtually anywhere led to a new stylistic and philosophical approach to film and video that was embraced by makers working out of the mainstream. Many makers of documentaries and experimental films and videos rejected slick Hollywood production values in favor of an immediacy and sense of realism resulting from an "off-the-shoulder" shooting style. As is often the case, techniques developed by avant-garde artists or subcultures for aesthetic or political reasons were appropriated by mainstream media as a fresh style. *Hill Street Blues* (1981), a prime time dramatic series that was created by Stephen Boccho, used handheld camera work to give the show the same look as the 1977 independent observational documentary *Police Tapes*, produced by Alan and Susan Raymond.

The erratically moving camera, sometimes even including reframing and focusing of shots, has become an accomplished stylistic convention of its own, seen everywhere from Hollywood films to music videos to television commercials. There is a big difference, though, between the professional handheld style and an amateur home video. Professional handheld camera work is carefully blocked and rehearsed, resulting in an intentional aesthetic style. Even though it is planned out and artfully executed, it maintains a sense of immediacy and improvisation.

Figure 3.14 The Steadicam allows the best of both worlds—a mobile camera without the jitter. (Courtesy of the Tiffen Company, LLC.)

Types of Camera Movements

Camera movement terminology differs slightly in film and video. Some camera movements are accomplished from a static position, and some require the operator or camera mount to travel through space.

The **pan** and **tilt** are pivoting movements in which the mount or operator stays in one spot. A pan pivots right or left; a tilt pivots up or down. Smooth pans and tilts, along with all camera movements, are dependent on operator technique. Pans and tilts on a camera mount are also dependent on a good-quality mount head with appropriate *friction* or *drag* (resistance to the movement). You're better off with a static shot than a pan that jerks along in increments.

Dolly, truck, arc, pedestal, tracking, and crane shots all travel through space. Exact use of the terminology can vary a bit. Strictly speaking, a dolly shot is one in which the camera moves on wheels toward or away from a subject. You can *dolly in* or *dolly out*. A truck or tracking shot moves through space to the right or left, and you can *truck* or *track right* or *truck* or *track left*. A **truck** is done on a wheeled dolly on a studio floor; a **track** is done on dolly tracks. An *arc* is a truck that follows a curved line as opposed to a straight path (Figure 3.15).

Pedestal and crane shots rely on particular equipment. A pedestal shot moves the camera up or down through space with the use of the hydraulic column, called a *pedestal*, which is part of the professional studio tripod. A crane shot can move the camera up, down, right, left, in an arc, or diagonal as the camera and operator move through space.

While not generally considered a camera movement, a **zoom** is an optical adjustment that changes the viewer's vantage point. By changing the focal length of the lens, we change the frame's field of view. Zooming in transitions from a wider shot to a closer shot and takes the viewer visually, but not actually, closer to the subject. Zooming out does the opposite. The difference between a zoom and a dolly, in which the camera actually moves, can be subtle but important. Zooms are quicker, easier to accomplish, and might seem like a good alternative, but in executing a zoom, the change in focal length brings more changes than just shot size. Wide-angle shots exaggerate depth between planes along the z-axis and give the appearance of greater depth of field; telephoto shots do the opposite. Therefore, zooming in from a wide shot to a close-up changes the depth relationship and focus. The result is much less realistic looking to the viewer than a dolly where depth and focus relationships are maintained. The dolly, therefore, provides a more realistic shot and makes the viewer feel more like he or she is there in the space of the frame. However, because focus is relative to camera-to-subject distance, a dolly can result in loss

Figure 3.15 A dolly is a movement toward or away from the talent. A truck is a movment to the left or right. An arc moves right or left in a curved line.

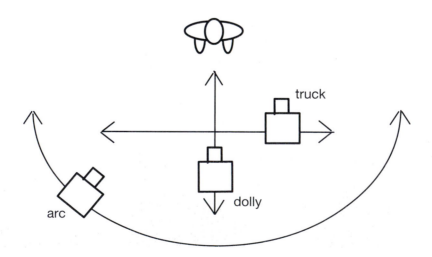

of focus. To avoid this, you must shift the focus while moving or have enough depth of field to accommodate the movement. On a professional shoot, a camera assistant is usually responsible for *pulling the focus*. (See the *Depth Through Blocking and Camera Placement* activity on the book's companion website for examples of different camera movements.)

MOVEMENT THROUGH EDITING

If we define movement within the frame as a way of changing what the viewer sees and hears, editing is part of movement too. The subject can move within the frame, changing what the viewer sees from a long shot to a tighter shot, or the subject can exit the frame altogether. The camera can move, panning with the subject as he or she moves or dollying in on a subject until all we see is his or her eyes, or the camera can stop and move to another vantage point or a whole new location, either keeping the subject the same or changing to a different subject. In this way, the viewers have experienced a shift to a different point of view, regardless of whether or not they saw the movement happen. For example, a woman and a man are talking. First we see and hear the woman from over the man's shoulder. Then we see and hear the man from over the woman's shoulder. As viewers, we have moved to the other side of the room, though we did not witness the transition. The movement occurred when the two shots were edited together (Figure 3.16). The movement can also be more dramatic. An editing transition can move the viewer across the street or across continents. (Editing, or structuring, will be covered more extensively in Chapters 8 and 9).

shot #1   shot #2

Figure 3.16 Editing transitions can provide a sense of movement. Perhaps the audience does not see the movement take place, but they experience the change in vantage point that results from moving the camera to another position.

MOVEMENT CONSIDERATIONS IN DIFFERENT MEDIA
MOVEMENT AND THE LONG TAKE

Go to the Source—
André Bazin

André Bazin (1918–1958) was an influential French film theorist and critic. Cofounder of the important film journal, *Cahiers du Cinéma*, Bazin helped define film as a topic of serious discourse. In his writings, he supported realism and the use of the long take and deep focus in film. Some of Bazin's best-known articles and essays are published in *What Is Cinéma*, Volumes I and II (1967 and 1971, respectively).

The terms *take* and *shot* both refer to an uninterrupted piece of film or video recording. A take is the result of turning on the camera and turning it off again. Some filmmakers prefer the use of **long takes** to the use of editing shots together in order to construct a story. By its nature, the long take rejects editing as a means of movement and relies on subject and camera movement. Although it is possible to have a static long take without any movement, it would be difficult to engage the viewer with such an approach. Proponents of long takes in filmmaking claim that the long take is the way to utilize cinema's aesthetic and political potential (Go to the Source—André Bazin). Some claim that long takes impart more realism to a scene and that editing is a dishonest manipulation of time and the viewer's point of view. Long takes allow the camera to move within a scene, more like the viewer would if present him- or herself.

Long Takes in Fiction Narratives

Long takes allow actors to build dramatic tension through an entire scene, as opposed to shooting out-of-sequence shots and putting them back together in the editing room. Long takes lend themselves to virtuosic camera moves, such as the sweeping crane shots down the Harlem street and outside the protagonist's house at the beginning of Spike Lee's *Jungle Fever* (1991) or the 360-degree pans around the pool table in Martin Scorsese's *The Color of Money* (1986). Interestingly, though, these long takes work against Bazin's idea of film realism. Dramatic camera movements, while impressive, call attention to themselves and the inherent manipulation involved in the process of filmmaking or video making.

Long takes also encourage blocking the talent to move through the frame, giving them motivated reasons to change their facings and positions. In *Rope* (1948), Alfred Hitchcock constructed the film from a series of long takes to appear as one long take unfolding in real time. (He accomplished this by, for example, masking the edit points by having a character pass by the camera lens and completely obscure the lens for a split second with the sleeve of a black jacket.) Within the movie, which takes place within the single set of a New York City apartment, the two main characters are kept busy setting the table, moving books, and pouring drinks. This *business* motivates their blocking and the blocking of the camera by giving them believable reasons for moving toward the camera and creating a close-up or walking into the kitchen and causing the camera to dolly behind them. The subject and camera movement are incorporated into the story to keep it from being static.

Long Takes in Documentaries

In documentaries or nonfiction media, long takes allow the viewer to see a subject's behavior unfold in real time without the filmmaker taking information out of context. Long takes lend themselves to an approach to documentary filming called *observational* or **direct cinema**, which relies on the observation of behavior as opposed to a third-person voiceover narrator or interviews (Go to the Source— Direct Cinema). Some filmmakers believe that this approach of being "a fly on the wall" is less manipulative and therefore represents the documentary subjects more accurately. Media scholars have long debated whether or not long takes are really a more "honest" and less manipulative approach to filmmaking and video making. Some argue that real time is maintained and that the filmmaker has fewer opportunities to skew the truth by omission or reconstruction of elements. The other side would argue that the appearance of a less manipulative approach is dishonest in itself and that any mediation of reality is highly subjective and manipulative. The maker decides where to put the camera, when to turn it on, which long take to use, and what order to put the takes in. In addition, the effect of the presence of the camera on the subject's behavior can further distort reality. Other makers would say that documentarians should not even aspire to objectivity and that open subjectivity that acknowledges the maker's biases and the inherent manipulation of the media-making process results in more honest work. This approach can be called **reflexivity**. In a reflexive documentary, the maker would not hide his or her involvement in the process through techniques, such as appearing in sound or image in the documentary or intentionally showing lights or microphones in the shot. Thus the audience would be reminded of the manipulation inherent in the media making.

Budget Considerations

You might think that shooting in long takes is more economical than other shooting choices because it reduces the editing that must be done or eliminates the need for several cameras to shoot from several different vantage points at once. Certainly in some situations this is true. Generally, though, the use of long takes increases production time, and "time *is* money." Shots that rely on choreographed subject and camera movements take longer to rehearse and shoot. Often more takes need to be done to get the camera movement, performances, and technical conditions just right for the entire length of the take. Long takes are considered more cinematic, even though they can be used in video, because they are done on larger budget productions, which typically use film instead of video for its better image quality.

Documentaries that rely on observational long takes often require a longer production phase as well. Waiting for subjects to reveal themselves through their behavior tends to take longer than asking them to explain their situation in an interview, and it definitely takes longer than having a voiceover narrator provide the needed information. Thus there is usually a larger **shooting ratio** (the comparison between the amount of film or video shot and the amount that is

---

Go to the Source— Direct Cinema

Direct cinema is an approach to documentary filmmaking that was first used during the 1960s in the United States. It is characterized by observational shooting, that is, by being a "fly on the wall." Direct cinema avoids the use of narration or interviews to tell the story. Instead, the filmmaker relies on the subject's behavior to reveal the truth of the situation. Direct cinema became possible with the introduction of lightweight, portable 16 mm film cameras, faster film stocks that allowed proper exposures with available light, and portable sync sound audio recorders, such as the Nagra.

Direct cinema is similar to the cinema verité approach that was developed in Europe at the same time. However, cinema verité often includes the presence of the filmmaker as questioner or provocateur. Direct cinema works to minimize the intrusion of the filmmaker into the filmmaking process. Proponents claim that with time and proper technique, the subject becomes used to the camera's presence and reacts as if it is not there.

Prominent early direct cinema filmmakers include Robert Drew, Albert and David Maysles, Richard Leacock, and D. A. Pennebaker, who often collaborated on films. One of the best-known documentaries of this genre is *Primary*, directed by Robert Drew, which chronicles the 1960 presidential primary campaign of John F. Kennedy.

actually used in the finished product) in a documentary that is observational and uses long takes. That means more time (more personnel and location costs), more film or tape stock, and more time spent logging and transcribing (making written records of what is seen and heard in the footage).

ANIMATION AND MOTION GRAPHICS

Illusion of movement can be created with photographic representations of the real world or through **animation**. Animation uses drawings, paintings, cutouts, and 2D or 3D computer images or models (such as clay figures). Animation can be as simple as a flip-book or as complex as a feature film or video game. It relies on breaking down a movement into increments. The key positions of the movement are created as *keyframes*. *Tweening* is the term for the creation of the in-between frames that are necessary to convey a convincing sense of movement. The more in-between frames, the smoother the movement. The extreme is the creation of one image for each frame of film or video, but that is not always necessary. It depends on the speed of the animated movement and the smoothness desired. Many hand-drawn animations use only 12 images per second—each one printed on two frames of film. The *Persistence of Vision* activity on the companion website illustrates a very simple 2D animation.

There are many methods of animation, too many to detail here. In traditional *cel* animation, drawings are made on sheets of clear acetate, laid one by one over a painted or drawn background and filmed. When projected, the drawn subject seems to move in front of the background. *Stop-motion* animation uses clay figures or other models that are painstakingly manipulated to show the stages of movement.

Computer animation techniques have revolutionized the practice. Adobe Flash software is used extensively for 2D and 3D animation, especially for the web. It is discussed further in Chapter 10. Autodesk Maya software allows for the creation of realistic or abstract three-dimensional worlds. You can model an object, creating the shape. Then you can create a texture to cover the model—metal, cloth, fur, etc. Backgrounds are created and the scene is lit, complete with shadows. Then the object is animated. Tweening, in computer animation, mathematically renders one image per frame (Figure 3.17).

Motion graphics is the term generally used for the animation of text and other graphic elements, which are commonly used for title sequences and other text-based moving media. Adobe's AfterEffects is a primary tool for creating motion graphics.

The development of **motion capture** technology is bringing together the worlds of animation and live action. Motion capture allows real performers to wear markers on their bodies and have those markers tracked by software that can then create those same movements for an animated figure.

Figure 3.17 Autodesk Maya software is used to create 3D animation. (Image courtesy of the artist, shun Liang, and by permission of Autodesk.)

CONCLUSION

The concepts of depth and movement apply to all media, including audio and still images. With moving pictures, however, depth and movement are the two big illusions that define the medium. In actuality, film and video are two-dimensional and made of still images. Creating convincing and dynamic moving pictures with a sense of depth is the magic.

PUTTING IT INTO PRACTICE
OBSERVING

Watch for the use of movement in movies and on TV. Be able to name camera movements when you see them. Watch for approaches to talent blocking and actors' business. Try to discern between dollies and zooms. Watch for the use of long takes.

WRITING AND DOING

Create a story involving at least two characters that can be acted out in two minutes or less. Videotape three versions of the same story—all long takes. That means no stopping the camera until the story is over. You may, if you wish, tape multiple takes of the same version.

Version #1—Keep the actors and camera static. Create an illusion of depth through placement of talent and props.

Version #2—Emphasize talent movement. Keep the camera in one spot. Try putting small pieces of gaffer's tape (a kind of adhesive tape that is easily removed without damaging surfaces) on the floor so actors know where they need to be. You will need to rehearse the talent so they will "hit their marks." Give the actors business to motivate their movements. Coordinate movement with plot and dialogue.

Version #3—Emphasize camera movement, but avoid zooming. Be creative in finding ways to smoothly move the camera on a low (or nonexistent) budget. Wheelchairs and skateboards are two possibilities. Make the viewer feel that she or he is a participant in the action through the lens of the camera.

KEY CONCEPTS

animation	phi phenomenon
blocking the talent	rack focus
crane	reflexivity
direct cinema	shooting ratio
directed tension	tilt
dolly	track
illusion of depth	tripod
long take	truck
motion capture	vectors
motion graphics	x-axis
pan	y-axis
pedestal	z-axis
persistence of vision	zoom
perspective	

CHAPTER 4

Light

THE IMPORTANCE OF LIGHT

Media production is based on the reproduction of different forms of energy that travel in waves. Visual media starts with light energy. As discussed in Chapter 2, our eyes see because waves of a certain form of electromagnetic energy called visible light reflect off of physical objects and into the cornea of the eye. Bright objects reflect most of the light and absorb only a little, whereas dark objects absorb most of the light energy and reflect only a little (Figure 4.1). Light is then focused on the retina, which converts the light energy into electrical impulses that are read by the brain as visual information. A camera in media production does much the same thing. The lens gathers the light and focuses it through the aperture onto the image plane, where either an electronic or chemical process converts it to information that can be saved and reproduced.

Light shows us the world. It reveals the visual details of familiar and strange surroundings. It creates the patterns of light and shadow that make order out of our chaotic world—the slashes of light and dark on a wall as the sun shines through the venetian blinds or the dappled pattern of leaves on a sleeping face under a tree. It creates the high contrast of the noonday sun on bare trees in a snowy landscape or the monochromatic low contrast on a day of steady rain. It gives us the information we need to know about an object's texture without having to touch it. We can see the rough ridges on the tree bark or the glossy slickness of washed fruit as revealed through light and shadow.

Lighting conditions indicate the time of day, time of year, and part of the world—the rosy, soft glow of dawn; the harsh, golden light of October; the unambiguous, revealing light of the American Southwest. Light can cause us to feel a certain mood. It lends a tone to a place or experience—the soft romantic glow of a candle; the unexpected, unknown shadows of night; the cool, melancholy dimness of winter twilight.

Light is the basis for visual media. It has the following two main tasks: *technical* and *aesthetic*. Technically, light provides the energy that allows us to reproduce an image. Aesthetically, light, along with composition, reveals truth and lies and creates beauty and ugliness within the frame.

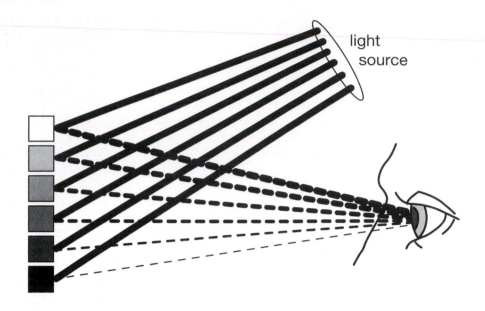

Figure 4.1 Light-colored objects reflect most of the light waves that strike them. Dark objects absorb most of the light, reflecting only a little.

UNDERSTANDING LIGHT

We consider the issues of light by studying the quantity, quality, direction, color, and sources of light.

QUANTITY

Exposure

When we discuss quantity of light, we are mainly referring to light's technical task. Every type of camera and image-making material (e.g., film, tube) needs a specific amount of light in order to optimally reproduce an image. We already know that the lens can control the amount of light that enters the camera through *aperture* and *shutter speed* controls. We know that film stock, tubes, and CCDs have varying *sensitivity* to light. These are the factors that contribute to **exposure**. Exposing an image-making material means letting light strike it. To accurately reproduce an image, the frame must be properly exposed by receiving the correct quantity of light (Figure 4.2). Underexposure and overexposure are sometimes errors of miscalculation, but they can also be conscious effects. A slight underexposure might help reinforce the look of nighttime lighting. Overexposure can erase detail in the highlight areas, lend a glamorous effect to a close-up, or give a scene an otherworldly tone. Such effects must be done carefully. Image-making materials have a limited range of exposure. Go too far in either direction and you have no image at all. Any special effects should be part of a consistent style that reinforces the content of the overall piece of media.

Quantity of light is measured in **foot-candles**. This unit of measurement comes from the amount of light produced by a candle at a distance of one foot. Because, like any form of wave energy, light weakens, or

attenuates, as it travels, the closer a source of light is to an object, the more intense the light will be.

Foot-candles can be measured by a *light meter*. Light meters can be either handheld or built in to the camera (Figure 4.3). They are designed to measure light either through a reflected or an incident light meter (also called an *ambient meter*) reading. An **incident light meter** reading measures the light striking the subject; a **reflected light meter** reading measures the light bouncing off of a subject (Figure 4.4).

An incident light meter is a handheld device with a small glass disk or dome that reveals a light-sensitive material and a scale that mechanically or digitally displays foot-candles. To take an incident reading, the meter is held at the subject's position and aimed toward the camera. When the dome attachment is used, the meter measures the overall amount of light from all sources falling on the subject. Incident readings can also be used to compare the brightness of one source of light to another. To do this, you use the flat disk attachment and aim the meter at a specific light source. The reason for comparing the brightness of light sources will be discussed later in the section on light direction.

A reflected light meter reads the intensity of light reflected off an object or scene. Built-in meters are reflected meters because they measure the quantity of light reflected off the subject that the camera sees through the lens. Some built-in meters average the brightness of the entire scene,

A

B

C

Figure 4.2   Too much light results in an overexposed image that is too light overall, with no detail in the highlight areas. Too little light results in an underexposure that is too dark overall and has no detail in the shadows. **A**, Overexposed image. **B**, Properly exposed image. **C**, Underexposed image.

A

B

Figure 4.3   **A**, A Sekonic analog light meter. **B**, A digital light meter. (Courtesy of Mamiya America Corporation.)

Figure 4.4 **A**, An incident or ambient light meter reading measures the quantity of light falling on a subject and is determined by the strength of the light source and its distance from the subject. **B**, A reflected light meter reading measures the light reflecting off a subject and is also affected by the brightness of the subject.

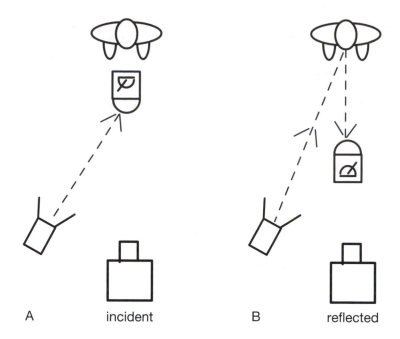

A   incident   B   reflected

whereas some are designed to weigh the center of the frame more heavily, assuming that is where the most important subject will be. A *spot meter* is a special type of reflected light meter for measuring reflected light off specific objects within a frame because light-colored objects reflect more light than dark ones in the same lighting conditions.

Contrast

Comparing spot meter readings can help you determine differences in contrast within your frame. **Contrast** is the comparison between the brightest and darkest elements in the frame. A *grayscale* chart illustrates contrast by representing the gradations of tone between pure white and pure black (Figure 4.5). A high-contrast image has strong blacks and whites that reproduce the extremes of the grayscale. A low-contrast image is made up of tones that fall close together on the grayscale.

A *contrast ratio* numerically compares the luminance, or brightness, reflected off the brightest and darkest surfaces in a frame. If the lightest object in the frame reflects 200 foot-candles and the darkest reflects 10 foot-candles, the contrast ratio is 20:1. This is important because different media can accurately reproduce different contrast ratios. The human eye can handle a contrast ratio of close to 1000:1. That means we can look at a scene on a bright, sunny day and recognize the details of light and dark objects in the sun and the shade simultaneously. Film can handle a contrast ratio of over 100:1; standard definition video, only 30 or 40:1.

Figure 4.5 A grayscale shows the gradations of tone from black to white. Taking a shot of the grayscale can show you how broad your contrast range is.

If the contrast ratio within your frame exceeds the capabilities of your medium, proper exposure becomes tricky. If you expose the frame so your brightest (or highlight) areas are properly exposed, the shadows will lose detail. Not only will the black areas appear black when reproduced but so will dark grays and maybe even medium grays. If you expose for the shadow areas, you will lose detail in your highlights.

The range of brightness within a video image can be demonstrated by looking at a *waveform* or graphic representation of an image's signal (Figure 4.6). The range from 7.5 to 100 represents the range of darkest to brightest objects within the frame.

Figure 4.6 The waveform displays the brightness range of your signal. The desired range is 7.5 IRE to 100 IRE. The waveform also displays the presence of chroma or color (color burst) and the sync signal, which provides a timing pulse. Many nonlinear editing systems have simulated waveform monitors as part of the software.

Waveform monitors are commonly used in video production. A waveform monitor is a cathode-ray tube (CRT), like a television, with a display screen. A video signal can be fed into the waveform monitor to display several of its characteristics. A properly exposed signal will have a black level of 7.5 Institute of Radio Engineers (IRE) units, called *reference black*. Reference black relates to a subject that is reflecting approximately 3% of the light striking it. Highlights should peak at 100 IRE units or *reference white*. Reference white is created by approximately 90% of light being reflected off an object. A scene that ranges from reference black to reference white is taking advantage of video's full contrast range.

Waveform monitors are used to set levels for video cameras, especially in situations where several cameras are being used together, so that desirable levels are consistent. If a waveform monitor is used to set the exposure for a video camera, the black level is set to 7.5 IRE units, then the iris is opened until the highlights peak at 100 IRE. If the black level is too low, shadow areas lose detail. If the highlights extend above 100 IRE, detail in the bright areas is lost. If the signal does not extend for the entire range, the image will have limited contrast. Most video editing software now has a graphic display that, although not a true waveform monitor, can show the brightness levels your images.

QUALITY

Light striking a subject can be *hard,* producing distinct highlights and sharply defined shadows, or light can be *soft,* producing subtle highlights and shadows with a less defined edge (Figure 4.7). This is a separate issue from exposure and contrast, which relate to the overall quantity of light supplied to the camera and the relative amounts of light reflecting off objects within the frame. The hardness or softness of a source of light defines its quality. It has more to do with the aesthetic effect of light—the look and mood of the image.

The quality of a light source has to do with how the light waves travel. If they travel in straight lines from the source to the lit object, they are reflected back to the lens of an eye or camera in similarly straight lines. This produces light that is **hard**, **direct**, or **spotted**. The light energy covers a relatively small area but maintains maximum intensity or brightness. Direct light emphasizes texture. Highlights, caused by the light striking light-colored surfaces, will be harsh, contributing to increased contrast. Shadows are dark and hard edged. The sun produces direct light on clear days. Hard light can create a dramatic

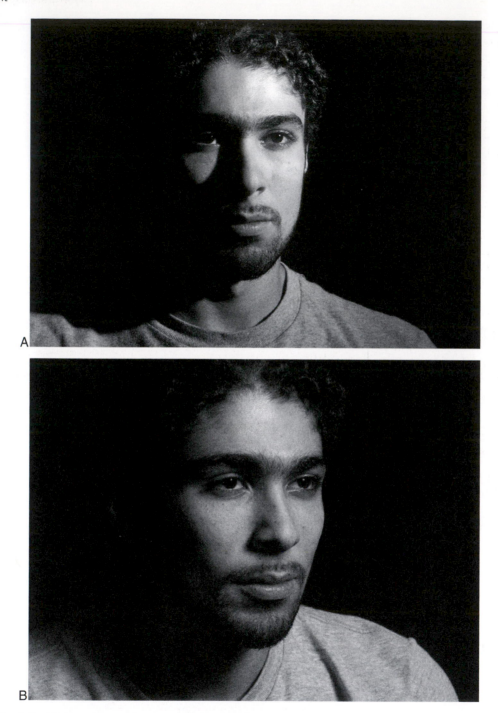

Figure 4.7 **A**, Hard light produces intense highlights and dark, hard-edged shadows. It reveals an object's texture well. **B**, Soft light produces less intense highlights and lighter, softer-edged shadows. Detail and texture are less obvious. For that reason, it is usually a more flattering light for human subjects.

look, often suggestive of nighttime because many of the sources of night lighting, such as street light and headlights, are direct.

All light starts out as direct, but if the waves of light bend or bounce off of another surface, they travel in several simultaneous directions and find their way to the lens in a less direct way. This produces light that is **soft**, **diffused**, or **flooded**. A diffused light source will cover a larger area but be less intense or bright than the same initial amount of direct light at the same distance from its subject. Highlights and shadow still occur, but they are more graduated and soft edged (Figure 4.8). Soft light is pretty, calming, and flattering to the human face.

Light can be diffused in many ways. Cloud cover or fog diffuses the direct light of the sun. A hard light pointed at a reflective surface like a white wall or a textured silver umbrella results in a softened light. *Diffusion material,* sheets of flexible, textured heat-resistant material, can be placed in front of lighting instruments, held by a metal frame or clothespins. *Soft boxes* are large fabric diffusers on frames that fit over light instruments (Figure 4.9).

DIRECTION

A photograph, a film, a video, and a computer screen are all two-dimensional media. A frame has height and width but no depth. Yet so often these media present convincing representations of the three-dimensional world. What is it about these two-dimensional portrayals that cause them

Figure 4.8 **A**, Hard light travels in straight unbroken waves, creating a stronger reflection. **B**, Soft light, caused here by light reflecting off an umbrella, bends and scatters the light rays.

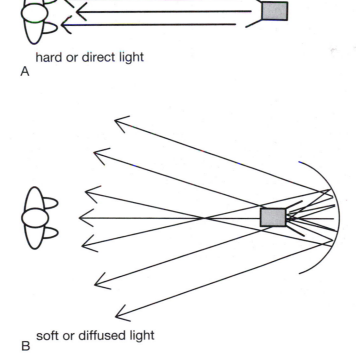

hard or direct light
A

soft or diffused light
B

Figure 4.9 Methods of diffusing light include (from left to right) an umbrella, diffusion material (attached to a gel frame), a soft box, and, in the background, a reflector.

to be convincing reproductions of our three-dimensional reality? What contributes to the **illusion of depth** within a two-dimensional medium? Several ways of creating an illusion of the third dimension were discussed in chapter 3. Lighting is yet another way.

Light casts shadows when it falls on a three-dimensional object. Shadows help the viewer visually define the shapes of objects. They function as visual proof that an object has three-dimensional shape or depth. Therefore, the presence of shadows within a two-dimensional frame contributes to the illusion of depth. Lighting students often think of shadows as the enemy and seek to eliminate them. Shadows help communicate depth, mood, time, and place, but they must be carefully controlled. Lighting, in fact, can be defined as *casting and controlling shadows*.

The classical formula for lighting is an approach called **three-point lighting**. As you will quickly discover, three-point lighting has its limitations, but it is a good starting point and helps clarify the function of light coming from different directions. Three-point lighting is made up of a **key light**, a **fill light**, and a **backlight**. Each has its own purpose.

The purposes of the key light are to provide the basic illumination (fulfill the technical role of lighting) and to cast shadows (providing the illusion of depth). Lighting placement is always relative to the position of the camera because that is the view that will fill the frame. The effect of a lighting instrument will change dramatically when seen from different points of view. A key light is generally placed at an angle of 30 to 45 degrees from the camera/subject axis and positioned to strike a subject at a 45-degree angle from the floor (Figure 4.10). The angle from the camera is important for the casting of shadows. Generally, a somewhat spotted or direct light is used as a key, but if the highlights are too harsh, the key light is diffused (Figure 4.11).

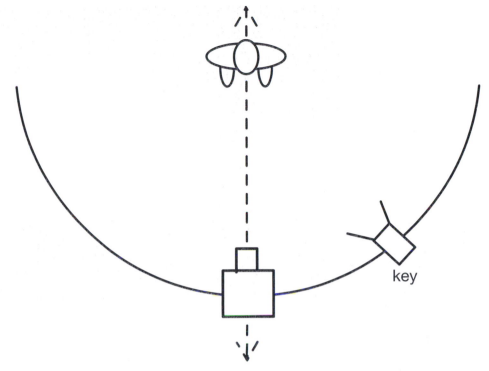

Figure 4.10   The key light for classical three-point lighting is placed 30 to 45 degrees on either side of the camera/subject axis.

Figure 4.11   Key light provides general illumination and produces modeling, the casting of shadows.

A light placed on the same axis as the camera will still illuminate the subject and will, in fact, still cast shadows, but those shadows will fall directly behind the subject and not appear in the frame. The effect of a camera-axis key light is an evenly lit subject, lacking visible shadows and therefore lacking depth. This is called **flat lighting** (Figure 4.12). We often see it on the news or in paparazzi photography because the light or flash is mounted on the camera. This is a convenient practice, allowing the cameraperson to be mobile, but it does not produce aesthetically pleasing lighting.

Sometimes, though, "bad" lighting is exactly what you want. The flat, hard light of a camera-mounted flash, because it is used by paparazzi photographers, can lend a tone of immediacy and gritty realism to an image. It is not pretty, perhaps, but it might be the appropriate aesthetic for your particular content. This is a perfect example of knowing the rules but breaking them with control and understanding of the aesthetic implications of your choice (Figure 4.13).

Often, shadows created by a key light are harsher and darker than you want. Fill light is used to soften, but not eliminate, the shadows from the key light. A very soft light is used for fill so that it does not create competing shadows on the key side of the subject (Figure 4.14). You can fill with a very diffused lighting instrument or even by bouncing the key light back with a white surface or *reflector* (Figure 4.15). Reflectors provide a very natural-looking fill light and reduce the number of lighting instruments needed.

The brightness relationship between the key and fill lights is called the **key/fill ratio**. The ratio can be determined by aiming the incident or ambient light meter directly at the key light from the subject's

Figure 4.12 Key light on the camera/subject axis produces flat lighting without dimension. Flat lighting can also occur when your key light and fill light are equal in intensity.

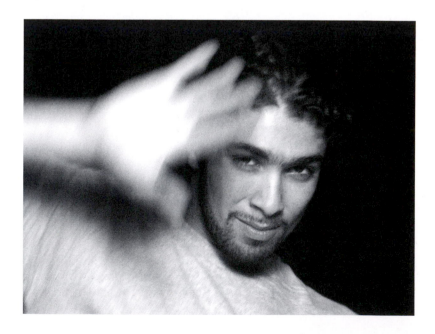

Figure 4.13 Flat lighting, such as that produced by a flash unit or lighting instrument mounted on the camera, can produce a "paparazzi" look, perhaps a desired aesthetic.

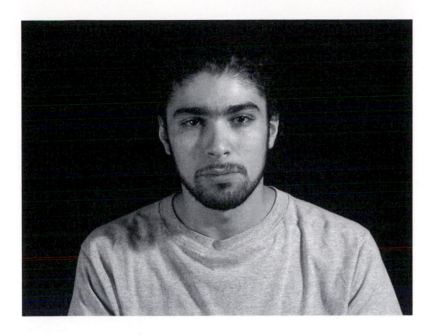

FIGURE 4.14 Fill light softens shadows created by the key light.

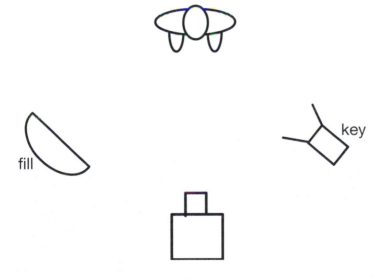

Figure 4.15 The fill light is placed on the opposite side of the camera/subject from the key light.

position, then directly at the fill. Then determine the ratio between the two readings. If the key light reads 300 foot-candles and the fill, 150 foot-candles, the key/fill ratio is 2:1. This would be called **high key lighting** and is a common look for studio sets on TV or typical daytime, upbeat lighting. A ratio any lower than this (with the fill light any closer to the value of the key) starts to become flat lighting, which is similar to the effect of a key light along the camera-axis.

A higher key/fill ratio (4:1, 8:1, 16:1, or more) results in an effect called **low key lighting**. Low key lighting is dramatic and moody, with the fill side of the subject falling into shadow. Nighttime lighting is often low key, with singular sources of light that cast shadows but little ambient light to fill those shadows (Figure 4.16). The lighting exercise on the text's website allows you to experiment with key and fill light positions and ratios. If the key/fill ratio starts to approach the contrast ratio of the medium, you risk losing detail in either your key or fill areas.

A

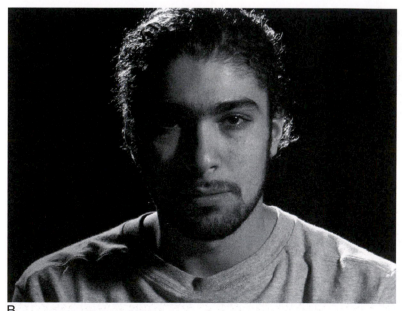

B

Figure 4.16   **A**, High key lighting has a key fill ratio or 2:1. **B**, Low key lighting has a key/fill ratio of 4:1, 8:1, or even more.

The key/fill ratio differs from the contrast ratio because it is based on incident, rather than reflected, light readings. It measures only the quantity of light coming from the key and fill sources, not the reflected luminance, which is affected by the relative lightness or darkness of the subject. While an incident reading of a key light might measure 150 foot-candles, that same light reflected off a dark coat might yield a reading of 10 foot-candles.

Backlight, like key light, helps provide the illusion of depth. A back-light is a source of light aimed directly at the back of the subject (Figure 4.17). (This is not to be confused with background light, which is any light used to light background objects or set pieces.) The best way to see what backlight does is to start with just a backlight on a subject. In the absence of key or fill, the backlight creates a silhouette effect (Figure 4.18). This outline of light produces separation between the subject and the background, which emphasizes the fact that they exist on different planes of depth from the camera.

Backlight is particularly important when some or all of the subject is similar in color or brightness to the background. Without the backlight, the subject can disappear into the background, and look flat.

Classical three-point lighting, with the key light to one side of the camera, the fill to the other side, and the backlight directly behind the subject, is a standard for **presentational lighting**. This includes portraits and talking head shots (e.g., news anchors, talk shows) where the subject is addressing or looking at the camera. In a presentational situation, there is no illusion that it is anything other than a construction for the camera. The three lights perform the important aesthetic tasks of casting shadows, controlling the intensity of the shadows, and

Figure 4.17 Backlight is aimed at the back of the subject.

Figure 4.18 Backlight creates a visual separation between the subject and the background, helping to create the illusion of depth.

creating separation between the subject and the background. If using artificial lights, these tasks can be done with three lighting instruments or two. A reflector can be used to bounce key light back as fill. If natural separation of foreground and background exists because of differences in color and brightness, perhaps no backlight is needed. Sometimes a *kicker* might replace a backlight. A kicker is a light to the side of and behind a subject that highlights hair and gives a glamorous look. A direct side light might do the job of a backlight, allowing for a diffused key light closer to the camera (Figures 4.19 and 4.20). There are many ways to light; three-point lighting is a good starting point.

Figure 4.19 Two lights are used to light this subject—a key light from the side and a fill near the camera.

key

Figure 4.20 Three-point lighting is just a starting point. Another approach might be a key light from the side, providing modeling and some separation from the background. A fill light near the camera axis would provide soft, flattering illumination.

 fill

However, when filling your frame, you are often trying to re-create a scene from the real world. You want the scene to look natural, not like something lit for the camera. You are then working with a **representational lighting** situation. Creating a natural look with lighting is not always simple. As we know, film, video, and digital imaging respond to light differently than the human eye. So even if you want to re-create the look of the location in which you are shooting, simply using the existing light is often not enough. Lights need to be emphasized, diffused, or maybe cheated on a little bit. If you are trying to re-create a lighting effect on a set or in a different location, you are building it from scratch.

The best way to learn how to create representational lighting is to observe the light quantity, quality, direction, and color in real situations. In doing so, you soon realize that the light in the world around you is not the result of key, fill, and backlights placed at classical angles. To re-create situations realistically, you need to have **motivated lighting**. Every source of light in your frame must *seem to* come from a real source. Sometimes the source of the light is seen within the frame, often not. (Seeing the source of light, though, reinforces the motivation.) What becomes important in these situations is not the precise placement of the lights in three-point lighting but the purposes of the light—casting shadows, filling shadows, and creating separation from the background. Overhead lighting fixtures key light a subject from above, requiring fill from a lower angle. The light coming in a window might provide the main illumination on a subject. If keying from the side, a fill light closer to the camera that softly illuminates the front of the subject would be required. A subject outdoors might have key light from the sun overhead and fill from the sun's reflection off of snow. A car's dashboard lights could provide the illumination for a low angle key light, while a strong backlight could be provided by the headlights of the car behind the subject. Separation is sometimes provided by color or tonal differences between the subject and the background, making a backlight less necessary.

Lighting is an art mastered by keen perception of the world around you and much practice. Lighting is also one of the key factors that separates amateur-looking visual media from that of professional or artistic quality. See the *Light Direction* activity on the book's companion website books.elsevier.com/companions/9780240809076, where you can experiment with changing placement of different lighting sources.

COLOR

The visible light spectrum that allows us to see is also referred to as *white light*. We can see, when light waves travel through a prism and are separated into their components, that white light is the combination of a full spectrum of colored light waves. Red, orange, yellow, green, blue, indigo, and violet light together form the radiant energy that allows us to see and reproduce visual images. Visible light is energy with a range of **wavelengths**. A wavelength is the measurement of one full cycle of a wave. Red waves have the longest wavelength in the visible light spectrum; violet has the shortest. These differences are only a few millionths of a meter, but those differences are crucial. Visible light is just one type of radiant energy called **electromagnetic energy**. Energy with wavelengths shorter than violet and longer than red light exist, but they cannot be seen by the human eye (Figure 4.21).

We see color because receptors called **cones** in the retina of our eye respond to energy with certain wavelengths. There are three types of cones, each responding primarily to red, green, or blue light. An object appears red to us because when light strikes it, it absorbs all the wavelengths of the spectrum except for the red ones. The red wavelengths reflect off the object onto the retina of our eyes, where the red-sensitive cones receive it and convert it to the electrical impulses that can be perceived by our brains as sight. Light reflected off a white object equally excites all three types of cones. A yellow object would excite the green and red cones but not the blue. There are other receptors in the retina called **rods**, but they react primarily to low levels of light, not specific colors, and help the eye see at night.

When describing color, we often use the characteristics of **hue**, **brightness**, and **saturation**. Hue refers to what color it is (blue, red, orange—where in the color spectrum it falls). A color's brightness refers to how much light is reflected and how close to complete reflectance or complete absorption it is. Brightness can be measured by comparison to a *gray card*, a graphic representation of the grayscale, discussed earlier in the chapter. Saturation is the intensity of the hue. Is it a bold red or a diluted pink? Both could be the same hue but differ in saturation of that hue (i.e., the pink being mixed with white). See the *Brightness, Saturation, Contrast and Color* exercise on the companion website books.elsevier.com/companions/9780240809076.

Reproducing Color

In Chapter 2, we discussed reproducing a visual image through the conversion of light energy using the chemical process of film or the electronic process of video or digital imaging. At that point, we talked in terms of black-and-white imagery, but most image reproduction we see is in color. The process by which the image's color information is gathered by the lens, gets read, and is stored is a key part of media making.

Two systems are used to reproduce color—**additive color mixing** and **subtractive color mixing** The system of color on which video cameras,

Electromagnetic Spectrum
From shortest waves and highest frequency to longest waves and lowest frequency

Gamma rays
X-rays
Ultraviolet (UV)
Visible light
Infrared light
Radar
Microwaves
Radio (FM, TV, shortwave, AM)

Figure 4.21 The electromagnetic spectrum includes many kinds of radiant energy, each with a specific range of wavelengths.

digital cameras, and monitors are all based is additive color mixing. It is similar to the process described previously that takes place in the retina of the eye, where different types of cones respond to light of varying wavelengths. It is based on the three additive primary colors—*red, green,* and *blue*—that when mixed together make white. Additive secondary colors are perceived by mixing the primaries. The secondary colors are *magenta, yellow,* and *cyan*. Magenta is formed by mixing red and blue, yellow by the mix of red and green, and cyan by the mix of blue and green. (See the *Additive Color Mixing* activity on the book's companion website books.elsevier.com/companions/9780240809076 to see how the additive primaries combine.)

The other approach to color reproduction is subtractive color mixing. It uses the same principles but comes at them from the other direction. If you take the additive secondary colors—magenta, yellow, and cyan—you can define them by the two additive primaries that mix to form them, or you can say that they are white light minus a primary color. So magenta is either the combination of red and blue or it is white light minus green. Therefore, if you take white light and filter out certain wavelengths, all the colors can be formed. No filtering results in white. Filtering all the primaries results in black because no light is allowed to pass. Subtractive color mixing is the basis of color film exposure, processing, and printing. (See the *Subtractive Color Mixing* activity on the book's companion website books.elsevier.com/companions/9780240809076 to see how the subtractive primaries combine.)

Color Temperature

Light is produced by many different sources, such as the sun, an incandescent light bulb, or a fluorescent fixture. Most light sources produce light that is a combination of all the wavelengths of the color spectrum (red, orange, yellow, green, blue, indigo, violet), but they mix the colors in varying proportions. Some have more of the reddish hues; some are more blue. The specific proportion of the wavelengths determines the light's **color temperature**. Color temperature is measured in a unit of measurement called the **kelvin (K)**. Color temperature is related to thermal temperature ($K - 273 = {}^\circ C$), and usually you can say that the color temperature is the color of the light given off by a hypothetical object (theorized by Lord Kelvin) when it is heated to that thermal temperature. In other words, something that glows blue when burning has a higher thermal temperature and a higher color temperature than that same object glowing red. Higher color temperature in kelvins means that more waves from the blue end of the spectrum are contained in the light.

We say daylight has a color temperature of 5400 to 5600 K because that is a good average on a sunny day at noon. The color temperature of daylight actually varies tremendously. Daylight is a mixture of longer reddish waves that travel rather efficiently through the atmosphere (*sunlight*) and the shorter blue waves that are diffused and scattered by the atmosphere (*skylight*). The scattered blue wavelengths bounce off the atmosphere, giving the sky its blue color. Clouds block sunlight, causing the skylight to dominate and subsequently raising the color temperature. Overcast days can produce light with a color temperature as high as 25,000 K.

At sunrise or sunset, the longer red waves can penetrate the atmosphere when coming from such a sharp angle and the color temperature can drop to under 2000 K (Figure 4.22). Color temperature changes throughout the day and throughout the year with the moving angle of the sun and varying atmospheric conditions.

Artificial light is more consistent. Different types of artificial light have different color temperatures, however. A standard incandescent or tungsten light bulb has a color temperature of 2900 K when new, though the temperature drops a little as it ages. Quartz light bulbs, used in media production lighting instruments, rate at 3200 K, which makes both tungsten and quartz closer to the reddish end of the

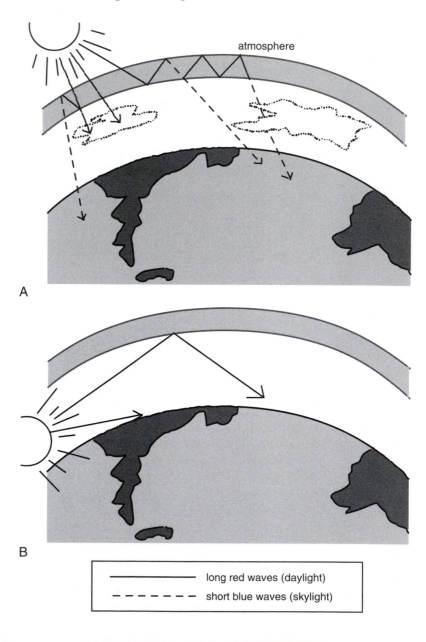

Figure 4.22 **A**, Overcast days and twilight produce light with a very high color temperature (more blue). **B**, During sunrise and sunset, the angle of the sun allows more of the sun's longer red waves to penetrate the atmosphere, producing light with a lower temperature (more red) for a short time.

long red waves (daylight)
short blue waves (skylight)

spectrum than daylight. Quartz bulbs retain a consistent color temperature throughout their lives. There are many types of fluorescent bulbs, with varying color temperature. The most common fluorescent tubes (cool white) measure about 4000 K, in the greenish range. Flash bulbs used for still photography and some lighting instruments that are used for film and video are rated at 5600 K, the same as daylight (Figure 4.23).

Why does color temperature matter? When using our eyes, it rarely does. The human eye does not notice a difference in color unless it is extreme or someone has trained himself or herself to notice such things. We can have a lamp on in a room and light coming in the window and see the combined lighting as all white light. If you look for the differences, you can see them, though. Walking home at dusk (when the light is very blue), the light from our window at home looks so "warm" and inviting. This is largely due to the reddish cast to that lamplight and to the psychological effect of warm colors. (Notice that psychological temperature is opposite of color temperature. "Warm" colors like red, orange, and yellow have lower color temperatures than the "cool" colors of blue, indigo, and violet.)

When we move to the reproduction of visual images, color temperature differences matter a lot. Film, video, and digital imaging systems are less forgiving of color temperature differences than our eyes. A film stock is balanced to reproduce either daylight or tungsten (quartz) light. A video or digital camera has settings to reproduce daylight or quartz light accurately. So film choices and camera settings need to be accurate or the color reproduction will be off. (See the *Color Temperature* activity on the book's companion website

Color Temperature *

incandescent light bulb	2900K
quartz bulb	3200K
cool white flourescent	4000K
direct sunlight flash HMI light	5600K
overcast daylight	10,000–20,000K

* All except quartz are approximate values.

Figure 4.23   Color temperature chart.

books.elsevier.com/companions/9780240809076 to see the difference film choice and color temperature settings make.)

When daylight and quartz light are combined in the same frame, one of the settings should be changed to match the other, or the quartz areas will look reddish and the daylight lit areas blue. Mixed lighting situations are handled by the use of *gels*. Gels are a tinted, translucent, plastic material. Blue gels can be placed in front of quartz light to add more bluish waves to the light and cause it to match the daylight. Orange gels can be placed over windows to add the appropriate color to the daylight and have it match the quartz light. (*Important note:* This is an "either/or" situation; don't do both or you will only duplicate your problem in reverse.) If all the light sources match and the appropriate film stock or camera setting is used, color representation should be accurate.

There are times when accurate color is not your goal. An image can be intentionally given a blue cast, to imply coldness and starkness and lend a grim institutional pallor to the subjects. A nostalgic romanticism can be reinforced by a golden or sepia tone. Sometimes these effects are produced by intentionally reproducing inaccurate color. Often, they are effects of postproduction, accomplished after the fact. The advantage of postproduction techniques is that you can change your mind. Once the image is reproduced inaccurately, it is difficult or impossible to change it back later.

SOURCES OF LIGHT

Sources of light can be **existing light**—both daylight and artificial light already present in your location—or **added light**—lighting instruments used in a studio or location setting. Understanding and controlling the existing light may be all of the lighting that you need to do. If the existing light is not enough, understanding the quantity, quality, direction, and color of the light around you is the key to reproducing natural-looking lighting effects with added instruments.

Daylight

The most common and varied lighting instrument is the sun. Direct sunlight can provide so much light that the iris of your camera needs to be as closed as it can get, and twilight can provide just enough light to get an image with the iris wide open. Direct sunlight is very harsh, producing dark, hard-edged shadows. Sunlight filtered through clouds or bounced off a reflector or white wall can produce soft, almost shadowless light. Noonday sun can come from straight overhead; afternoon or morning sun can shine sideways through a window. With a color temperature of approximately 2000 K, sunrise or sunset light can lend a golden glow, whereas twilight lends a ghostly blueness.

Often, either by choice or necessity, the sun is your only source of light. The biggest challenges in working with sunlight are the lack of control and the extreme contrast created by direct sunlight. When using sunlight, there is much time spent waiting for the sun—waiting for the right time of day to get the effect you want or waiting for a cloud to pass across the sun. Daylight conditions can change quickly, so often you need to work fast to ensure that lighting conditions remain consistent.

Because film, video, and digital media cannot accurately reproduce a range of tones as broad as the human eye can see, contrast becomes a concern. While your eye can clearly see the face of someone with the sun to her back as well as the brightly lit scene behind her, the camera cannot. The scene may exceed the contrast range of your medium. Using a reflector to bounce some of the sunlight back onto the face of your subject might be enough to adequately lower the contrast ratio. An artificial lighting instrument could be used, but then color temperature differences become a concern. You would need to put a blue gel on an instrument of 3200 K, use a special type of light with the color temperature of daylight, or use a flash (which is balanced for daylight) if you're taking a still image.

Existing Artificial Light

It is tempting to try to use existing light in order to create a natural lighting effect. Sometimes this works, but because of the differences between how the eye sees contrast and color and how the visual media reproduce light, existing light alone is often not the best solution. Indoors, existing light can either be all artificial lights or a combination of light fixtures and sunlight through windows or doors. The problem of mixing artificial light and daylight has already been discussed. Another problem is that although existing light may be natural, it is not always aesthetically pleasing. It does not always perform the functions of casting shadows, filling shadows, and creating depth through separation of subject and background. Much light in our homes and places of business come from tungsten or fluorescent overhead fixtures. The lighting is designed to be soft and even or flat—good for seeing but not very pretty. The overhead direction creates unflattering shadows under eyes and chins. Many times, you want light that looks natural, only better.

Added Lights

There are more types and brands of lighting instruments than we could possibly cover in this book. We can discuss, however, the four main type of instruments used by media makers:

1. flash,
2. quartz light,
3. arc lamps, and
4. specialized fluorescents.

Flash provides light in short bursts and only when the exposure is taking place. Flash units come in many forms, ranging from those built into consumer still cameras to large units that can power several different heads or light sources and recycle very quickly for rapid shooting. Flash, by its nature, is suitable only for still images. Because the light is only on during the exposure, not as much power is used and not as much heat is generated as other types of lighting. The color temperature of flash matches daylight so combining flash and daylight is no problem.

Professional flash units have modeling lights, which are low-power bulbs that allow you to see the direction of the light during setup.

Quartz lights are the standard of film and video production. As previously discussed, quartz bulbs have a color temperature of 3200 K. Instruments vary greatly and include large studio lights that are designed to hang from overhead grids and small portable instruments that mount on a collapsible light stand. Some are designed to be spotlights; some are floods or soft lights. Some, like the studio or portable *Fresnel*, have knobs to adjust the light emission to be either direct or diffused (Figure 4.24). Further diffusion can be achieved with umbrellas, diffusion material, or soft boxes.

Arc lamps (HMI) are portable lighting instruments designed to match the color temperature of daylight. Often powered by portable generators, the light from the arc lamps can be easily mixed with daylight. If the sun is providing light that is too high in contrast, an arc lamp can be used as fill (Figure 4.25).

Specialized fluorescent lights are a relative newcomer to film and video production. The greenish cast and flicker of a standard fluorescent bulb made it unacceptable for production. Technical advances have gotten rid of the flicker and allowed color temperatures that match either daylight or quartz bulbs. Power efficiency (amount of light produced per watt of electricity) and low heat generation make

Figure 4.24 Fresnels are spotlights with glass lenses that can be partially diffused. Some Fresnels are made for studio use or, like these, for location work as well. (Courtesy of Arriflex Corporation.)

Figure 4.25 Some lights (HMIs) are made to balance the color temperature of daylight. (Courtesy of Arriflex Corporation.)

fluorescents a viable option. They work well when an even, flat light is desired. (Figure 4.26)

With any lighting instruments, safety issues are crucial. Power needs to be adequate and properly balanced between circuit breakers. Make sure light stands are properly extended and stable. Power and extension cords need to be properly secured to avoid someone tripping over them. *Gaffer's tape*, a wide adhesive tape that doesn't tangle easily or damage surfaces, is often used to tape cords to the floor. Obviously, outdoor use of any electronics requires care around dampness and precipitation. In the studio, take care when climbing ladders to adjust lights. Use safety cables to keep lighting instruments from falling from grids when moving or adjusting instruments. If touched with a bare hand, the glass of quartz bulbs can weaken, which reduces bulb life and may even make them explode. Bulbs and the surrounding instruments get very hot and can cause severe burns. (Wear gloves!)

LIGHTING CONCERNS OF DIFFERENT MEDIA
FILM

Whether using still or moving picture film, there are several issues of light and color unique to the chemical process of reproducing film images. We've already mentioned that film can reproduce a higher contrast ratio than video or digital images. Although still far less sensitive than the human eye, film has the ability to retain detail in a highlight

A

B

Figure 4.26 **A**, Fluorescent fixtures for film and video. **B**, Large fluorescent figures lighting through silk diffusion create the look of north light for the TV movie, *Shackeltan*. (Courtesy of Kino Flo Lighting Systems.)

that is over 100 times brighter than the darkest object in the frame. Therefore, it is possible to use light with a higher key/fill ratio (low key lighting). The reality that most movies eventually are seen on a television screen, however, often keeps lighting directors from fully utilizing the contrast range.

Color Reproduction

Film color is reproduced through subtractive color mixing. As explained before, this means looking at each reproduced color in terms of which colors need to be filtered out of white light in order for the desired color to remain. For example, magenta is white light minus green wavelengths. Color negative film (still and motion picture) is coated with multiple layers of emulsion, all containing silver halide particles. Each layer is treated with dyes to make it sensitive to red, blue, or green. When struck by light reflected off a red object, the red-sensitive layer forms black silver crystals. A negative image is formed. Light reflecting off a yellow object exposes particles in both the red and green layers, since yellow is the complement of blue. Light reflected off white objects forms particles on all layers (since white light is a combination of red, blue, and green wavelengths), resulting in a black area on all three layers of the negative. Black objects (reflecting little or no light) cause reactions in none of the layers, leaving the film clear.

In color film processing, the silver halide crystals are dyed the color that is complementary to the color that produced them. The crystals in the red-sensitive layer are dyed with red's complement, cyan. Crystals in the green-sensitive layer are dyed magenta and the blue layer, yellow.

However, creating the cyan, magenta, and yellow negative is only half of the process. A still color negative must be printed on paper, and motion picture color negatives are printed onto a positive type of film stock. The negative is exposed to white light. The layers of the positive stock react similarly to the negative stock. When the white light is shined though the cyan areas of the negative (formed by red areas in the original scene), it forms crystals in the green and blue layers of the positive stock. (Cyan is white light minus red.)

In the developing of the print (paper or film stock), the crystals of the green and blue layers are dyed their complements, magenta and yellow. Magenta and yellow form red on the final print (Figure 4.27).

With transparencies (photographic slides) and color reversal film for motion pictures, a process similar to that for color negative film takes place. The original piece of film only goes through two processing stages (exposure and developing). The result is that the final slide or film print can be reproduced without losing quality. Negatives can be printed many times and still maintain consistent quality.

Color Temperature and Film Stocks

Because film stocks are not as forgiving as the human eye when it comes to the color temperature of light, different stocks are formulated to deal with light sources of different color. Film is classified as either **tungsten film** or **daylight film**. Tungsten film is balanced at 3200 K, the color of a quartz bulb. Daylight film is balanced at approximately 5400 K, but remember that 5400 K is just an average of the sun's color temperature. Fine tuning of color negative film can be done during shooting or printing, through the use of colored filters. **Filters** are translucent, colored pieces of glass or plastic that absorb

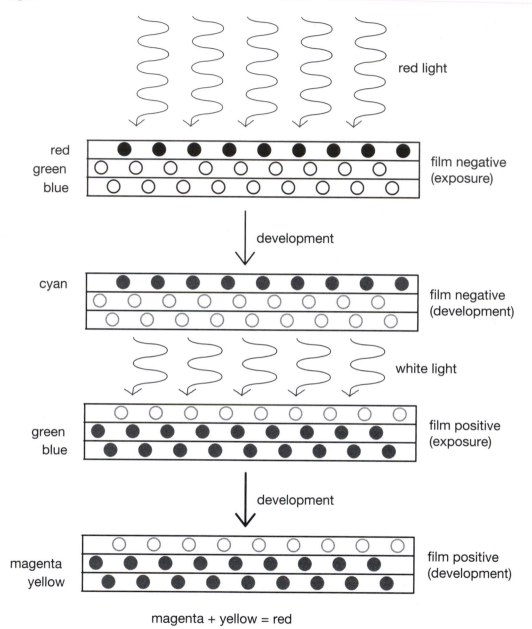

Figure 4.27 Color film is separated into layers with silver halide crystals that are sensitive to one primary color. Red light coming through the camera exposes crystals in the red layer. In developing the negative, the red crystals are dyed cyan, red's complement. When light is projected through the negative onto positive stock, the cyan exposes crystals in the green and blue layers of the positive stock, since cyan is the combination of green and blue. When the positive is developed, the green and blue crystals are dyed their complements, magenta and yellow. Magenta and yellow make red, so when light is projected through the developed positive, a red object is seen.

some of the filter's complementary colors, making the white light closer to the color of the filter. Filters are not only used during the printing process; a filter that is placed over a camera lens can change the color of the light entering the camera. With an orange filter, tungsten film can be used in daylight. With a blue filter, daylight film can be used with quartz light. Keep in mind, though, that the use of a filter decreases the amount of light coming in the camera (and will, therefore, decrease your depth of field).

VIDEO AND DIGITAL IMAGES

For standard definition video and digital images, the difference in contrast ratio can mean a different approach to lighting. Traditionally, we think of video as demanding flat lighting, which means avoiding bright highlights and deep shadows. Whereas black on film renders a clean, solid black, shadow areas on video appears somewhat washed out and the *noise* of the electronic signal becomes apparent. Noise is the unwanted information in the video signal and is analogous to grain in film. It appears as little, shifting specks of light in the image. On the other end of the spectrum, areas of video that exceed the contrast ratio "blow out" and create a glowing area, devoid of detail. Both extremes are generally unaesthetic and may cause the video to be technically unacceptable for broadcast. Contrast is kept lower by controlling lighting ratios and avoiding high-contrast sets and costumes.

High-definition (HD) digital imaging is changing things. HD rivals and even exceeds the resolution or sharpness of 35 mm film; it also has comparable contrast range. Though the technical specifications of the HD image rival film, it does have what some consider disadvantages. Many lighting directors have to work to avoid overexposed areas or "hot spots" when working with HD. The hyper-detail of HD can create unattractive close-ups where every flaw is visible. Softer lighting can help. The increased sensitivity of HD over most film stocks also makes the use of available light and minimal added light a viable option.

Color Reproduction

Whether you're talking about an old tube video camera, a digital still camera, a television, or a computer monitor, all of these technologies are based on additive color mixing to reproduce color. Equal amounts of red, green, and blue light mix to make white. By varying the amounts of those three color primaries, any color can be made. Black is the absence of color. Light entering the lens of a video or digital still camera is separated into red, green, and blue wavelengths by a prism or **beam splitter**. Professional-quality cameras have three chips (also known as charge-coupled devices or CCDs) or tubes (in old analog cameras) that are covered with light-sensitive pixels. Each CCD receives one color component of light (red, green, or blue). Less expensive consumer cameras often have only one chip with red, green, and blue striped filters placed in front of it. The filter accomplishes the same purpose with less quality but lower cost and increased portability. Each color light

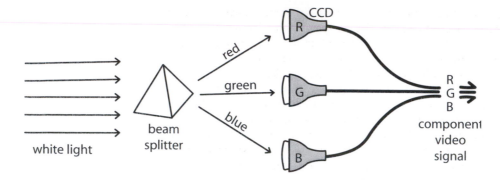

Figure 4.28 In a three-CCD camera, white light is broken down into its red, green, and blue primaries by the beam splitter. One electron beam reads each CCD, encoding the chrominance information for that color. The chrominance and luminance are then transmitted as a combined signal or kept separate, traveling on separate cables. Chapter 9 has more information on different types of video signals.

striking the chips is read, encoded, and amplified into a usable signal (Figure 4.28). The color information or **chrominance** is separated from the brightness or **luminance** signal. The color components of the signal are reunited when the signal is displayed on a television monitor or receiver. Three separate electron guns beam their signals to the face of the picture tube or flat-screen TV. The monitor's screen is made up of groupings of three pixels, each one sensitive to red, green, or blue. They glow in response to the strength of the signal that reaches them, thus reproducing the hue, saturation, and brightness of the original subject (Figure 4.29).

Accurate Color

Knowing that the color of light sources differs, how do video and digital still technology handle those differences? Accurate color reproduction is accomplished through a process called **whitebalancing**. During whitebalancing, a sensor in the camera evaluates the color temperature of the light coming through the camera and shifts the strength of the red, green, and blue signals to make the white in the frame reproduce as a neutral white. If white is really white, all the other colors will fall into place. In order for this to work best, the camera has to be pointed at a pure white object. White cards are made for this purpose. (Be careful because what may appear to be white, such as a wall or clothing, may have a tint of color that will throw the whitebalancing

Figure 4.29 Each pixel block on the TV monitor is actually a grouping of a red, a green, and a blue pixel. If the signal being delivered to a certain part of the frame is of a red object, the red pixel will glow. If the object is yellow, red and green will glow. If the object is white, all three will glow.

off.) Many cameras (and all consumer cameras) have an auto-whitebalancing function that will take care of this by itself, without a white card, by simply averaging the colors in a frame and calling it white. Consumer cameras usually have a manual override that allows more accurate whitebalancing with a white card. All professional video cameras allow manual white balancing. Many cameras also have color presets, usually indicated by an icon of the sun, a light bulb, and a fluorescent lamp. Presets are different from manual or auto-whitebalancing in that they do not read the lighting conditions present but adjust for the standard daylight, tungsten, or fluorescent settings. **Neutral density** filtration is a common video camera option and is sometimes combined with a daylight preset. Neutral density filters, called ND filters, are neutral gray and do not affect color temperature, but they do decrease the amount of light coming into the lens. They can be used to reduce depth of field in brightly lit situations.

CONCLUSION

Control of the technical and aesthetic properties of light is a major difference between amateur- and professional-level image production. Whether it's erecting an elaborate lighting setup in a studio or having the eye and patience to capture the perfect natural light, lighting is a science and an art that takes years of practice to master.

PUTTING IT INTO PRACTICE
OBSERVING AND WRITING

Train your eyes. Analyze the lighting conditions around you. Notice whether light is hard or soft. Observe the shadows and direction from which light is coming. Watch for observable differences in color temperature, especially at the beginning and end of the day. Record your observations in your notebook. Sketch scenes, indicating lighting source placement.

DOING

Choose an exterior scene. Photograph the same scene six different times, under different lighting conditions. Analyze the differences in mood.

KEY CONCEPTS

added light	contrast
additive color mixing	daylight film
attenuate	electromagnetic energy
backlight	existing light
beam splitter	exposure
brightness	fill light
chrominance	filters
color temperature	flat lighting
cones	foot-candle

KEY CONCEPTS   *cont'd*

hard/direct/spotted light

high key lighting

hue

illusion of depth

incident light meter

kelvin

key light

key/fill ratio

low key lighting

luminance

motivated lighting

neutral density

presentational lighting

reflected light meter

representational lighting

rods

saturation

soft/diffused/flooded light

subtractive color mixing

three-point lighting

tungsten film

wavelengths

whitebalancing

CHAPTER 5

Sound

THE IMPORTANCE OF SOUND

In some ways, mediated sound is entirely different from the visual media experience. Images, whether still or moving, produced chemically or electronically, are dependent on light and our sense of vision. Our aural sense engages a different part of our brain and is not triggered by light waves but by physical vibrations of the air.

Audio media, such as radio and audio CDs, can stand alone or be combined with visuals in movies, television, websites, and other interactive media, changing and enriching the experience of visuals alone. Sound by itself encourages us to imagine visuals in our minds, creating a unique experience for each listener. Audio is sometimes the "ignored child" of media production and theory. There are volumes of critical writing on the aesthetics and cultural impact of movies and television, but in comparison, little has been written on radio. In the writings on film and TV, the visual aesthetic tends to dominate, even though a movie or television program without sound (unless designed that way) is only half the experience, at best. The dialogue or narration of most movies is crucial to understanding the story. Television has been called "radio with pictures." Although this is sometimes considered a derogatory phrase, referring to the unimaginative use of visuals on TV, it illustrates the dominance of the audio track in most TV genres. It is much easier to understand what's happening on television when you're only hearing it rather than when you're only seeing it.

Sound allows us to hear what people are talking about, and hearing their voices, as opposed to reading their words, can give us information about their attitude, mood, geographical origin, and age. The same words can mean different things when shouted and whispered. A slight inflection or emphasis can imply sarcasm or doubts that are not evident in the printed word. Environmental sound can set location, time of day, or year and give information about who or what is present. Lapping water, the yell of gulls, children's voices, and the bell of an ice cream truck create a clear sense of location, whether there is an image accompanying the sound or not. Even if there is a visual component to the media work, sound can imply the presence of people or things not present in the visual frame. The sound of a shot fired off screen can be an important but unseen aspect of the story. Music creates an emotional impact by itself or as accompaniment to other sounds or images.

At the same time, our understanding of sound is similar to that of light, which is the basis of reproducing images. Sound is energy that travels in waves, like light. Sound has both technical and aesthetic roles in making media and can be described in terms of quantity, quality, and direction, just like light. Sound waves are converted to electronic signals, as in the electronic reproduction of images. We can speak of the audio "frame," that definition of what, when, and from what location you hear sound. Sound has depth and perspective. Sound, like images, can be structured in various ways by both abrupt and gradual transitions. The methods of editing audio are quite comparable to those used for picture editing; indeed, in the new world of digital postproduction, the approaches are almost identical. Sound is a powerful tool of expression, both alone and in combination with images.

UNDERSTANDING SOUND
SOUND WAVES

Sound is created by physical vibrations that set molecules in motion, creating sound **waves** that travel through the air. When a sound is made, the molecules in the air surrounding it are displaced and then pull back slightly, creating a pressure followed by release. The maximum pressure is the **crest** of the sound wave; the release is the **trough** of the wave (Figure 5.1). As with any type of energy that travels in waves, the waves are characterized by their speed and their size. The speed or **velocity** of sound remains constant, at least at the same temperature and altitude. Sound travels at 1130 feet per second at sea level and at 70°F (21°C). This changes somewhat as altitude and temperature change but not a lot. What varies much more are the size and rate of the waves.

The size of a sound wave is measured in terms of length and height. As discussed in Chapter 4, the measurement of one cycle of a wave is called its **wavelength** (Figure 5.2). A cycle measures a single vibration of the air—a compression and release of the air molecules. Sound waves have longer wavelengths than those of visible light. Sound waves vary from a fraction of an inch in length to approximately 60 feet. The wavelength of a sound wave is related to its rate or frequency.

Figure 5.1 The crest of a sound wave represents the maximum air pressure produced by a sound. The trough represents the release of that pressure.

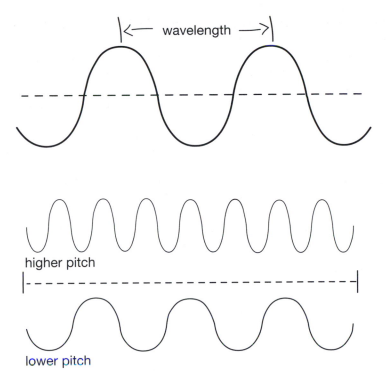

Figure 5.2 Wavelength is the measurement of the distance from one crest to the next.

Figure 5.3 The speed of sound stays constant, so the length of a wave is related to its frequency. More short waves will travel through a given point in a second than long waves.

Frequency is the number of cycles that the sound wave travels in 1 second. Because the speed of sound stays constant at a given altitude and temperature, the length of the wave determines how many cycles travel through a given point in 1 second (Figure 5.3). Therefore, wavelength and frequency are closely aligned. The longer the wavelength is, the fewer cycles that are able to pass through a point in a second and the lower the frequency. The shorter the wavelength, the higher the frequency. Frequency is measured in cycles per second (cps). The equation for determining wavelength or the frequency is

$$\text{wavelength} = \frac{\text{velocity (speed of sound)}}{\text{frequency}}.$$

Frequency determines the **pitch** of a sound—how high or low it is. A human ear with excellent hearing can hear frequencies that range from 20 to 20,000 cps; most of us hear a bit less. A wave with a rate of 7000 cps has a frequency of 7000 **hertz** (**Hz**) or 7 *kilohertz (kHz)*.

The height of a sound wave is called its **amplitude**. Variations in amplitude are caused by variations in the loudness of a sound. A loud sound produces a stronger vibration, causing more air molecules to be displaced. That larger vibration is represented by a taller sound wave (Figure 5.4). Amplitude is measured in a unit called a **decibel** (**dB**). A sound at 1 dB can barely be heard; 150 dB and above will permanently damage your hearing.

louder

softer

Figure 5.4 The louder the sound, the greater the air pressure created. This produces a wave with a greater distance between its crest and its trough—greater amplitude.

Once created, sound waves travel outward in all directions, like ripples when a rock is thrown into water. However, they don't travel equally in all directions. When you speak, you project stronger sound waves in front of you than behind you (Figure 5.5). Like all waves, sound waves get weaker, or attenuate, with distance.

If a sound stays at a constant loudness and pitch, its wave also remains the same. Most sound, however, such as speech, music, and most environmental noise, contains variations of both frequency and amplitude (Figure 5.6).

THE EAR

The creation of the sound wave is just half the story. To be heard, it has to be received and perceived (unless you'd like to argue the other side of the "If a tree falls in the forest, and no one is there to hear it, does it make a sound" argument).

Figure 5.5 Sound waves travel in all directions, though not necessarily evenly. The waves attenuate as they travel.

Figure 5.6 A sound wave with variations of amplitude and pitch.

Figure 5.7 The sound waves travel through the ear and are converted into electrical impulses that reach the brain.

The human ear is made up of the *outer, middle,* and *inner ear.* The outer ear funnels the sound through the ear canal to the middle ear in which the eardrum, or *tympanic membrane,* is located. The sound waves cause pressure on the eardrum that is then amplified (made stronger) by three small bones (*ossicles*) that act as a lever. The vibrations then travel to the *cochlea,* a fluid-filled coil that holds small hairs (*cilia*) that attach to nerve cells (Figure 5.7). Here the vibrations are converted into electrical signals that travel to the brain via the auditory nerve. The brain reads these impulses as sound in a process that is similar to how the brain reads the impulses from the optic nerve as sight.

REPRODUCING SOUND

Reproducing sound for media production follows a similar process to that of sound transportation in the human ear. Transmitting sound from one location where it is created to another where it is heard or to saving that sound for playback at a later time requires another step. The sound waves created by the vibrating voicebox of someone speaking, an instrument playing, or a knock at the door need to be converted from one form of energy (sound waves) into another (electronic signal). The conversion of one form of energy into another is called **transduction**. The transducer for sound is a microphone. The microphone creates a signal that contains all the variations of amplitude (loudness) and frequency (pitch) produced by the sound source. The electronic signal can travel along a microphone cable to a loudspeaker, recording device, or mixing console. A mixing console allows you to input several microphones and other audio playback equipment and combines them into

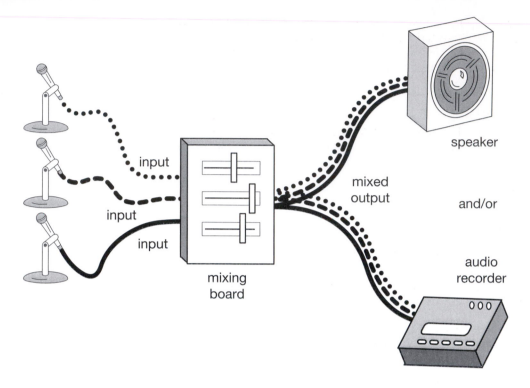

Figure 5.8 A mixing board allows multiple inputs to be combined into a single mixed output. The mixed output can be sent to multiple locations, such as both a recorder and a monitor speaker.

a mixed signal to be recorded for future playback, played back live, or transmitted via wires or **radio frequency** to another location or locations (Figure 5.8). When you play back a recorded signal, the process is reversed. The signal is transduced by a speaker into physical vibrations that travel to the ear to be received by the eardrum and perceived as sound by the brain (Figure 5.9).

When a wireless microphone is used or sound is transmitted via radio, a second stage of transduction occurs in which the electronic signal is converted into radio-frequency waves. Radio waves have a much

Figure 5.9 Two stages of transduction: **#1**, Microphone converts vibrations into an electronic signal. **#2**, The speaker converts the electronic signal back into vibrations of the air.

higher frequency than sound waves and are even higher than those of visible light. This characteristic allows radio signal information to travel long distances without wires. Received by an antenna, the radio waves are converted back to an electronic signal and then to sound waves to be heard by the listener.

MICROPHONES

There are many different kinds of microphones and several ways to classify them—by the type of transducer, their impedance, the way they pick up sound, and how they are used.

Using Microphones

Knowing which type of microphone to use requires the consideration of many factors:

- What kind of sound are you reproducing—speech, singing, instrumental music, or background sound?
- Where is that sound being recorded—a sound studio or a busy city street?
- What else is going on? Is the speaker moving? Is a visual image also being captured?
- How will the reproduced or recorded sound be heard—through a small television speaker or through high-quality surround sound speakers?
- What kind of microphone can you afford? Quality and price vary considerably.
- What is the production situation? Are you a one-person crew, recording sound and picture, and perhaps conducting an interview all at the same time, or is this a high-budget production with many microphones available for use?

Understanding how microphones vary can help you make a good choice.

Transducer

All microphones convert sound vibrations into an electrical signal, but transducing elements inside the microphone vary. When referring to transducing elements, most microphones you come across will be either **dynamic** or **condenser**. A dynamic microphone works on the principle of magnetism. A small, metal coil is placed near a magnet, which generates energy called a *magnetic field*. When the coil receives the sound vibrations, it moves. Movement of the coil within the magnetic field creates electric energy or **voltage** that retains the information about amplitude and frequency of the original sound wave (Figure 5.10). Another type of magnetic microphone is a ribbon mike, which has a small strip of metal instead of a coil. Ribbon mikes are sometimes classified as dynamic mikes and sometimes considered a separate category.

Condenser mikes, also called *capacitor mikes,* work a bit differently. They have two plates, one fixed and one moving, one with a positive charge and one with a negative charge. Voltage is created as a result of the proximity of the positive and negative charges. The moving plate moves toward and away from the fixed plate in response to the sound vibrations. The closer it moves, the stronger the voltage. The variation in the voltage matches the variation in the sound waves, and it is encoded into the electronic signal (Figure 5.11). The voltage created in a condenser or capacitance microphone is very weak, so it needs to be amplified

Figure 5.10 A dynamic microphone works by means of a metal coil within a magnetic field. Magnets convert vibrations to electrical energy.

Figure 5.11 Condenser mikes create electrical energy by the proximity of two plates with opposite charges. The closer they get, the stronger the signal.

before it leaves the microphone. This amplification is powered by power voltage, which is different from the polar voltage created by the charged plates. The preamplification is accomplished by a battery or externally provided circuit called **phantom power**. Phantom power is often supplied by the wiring in a sound or TV studio or can be present in the circuitry of a audio mixer, camcorder, or other device. A common type of capacitance microphone, called an *electret,* has permanently charged plates that require only a very small battery for preamplification.

The different transducer types have some general characteristics, but the microphone quality can vary greatly. When we compare one to the other, we are comparing microphones of similar quality. Generally, dynamic microphones are the most rugged and the least susceptible to damage if bounced around. This makes them an excellent choice for field mikes. Condenser microphones are a little more fragile and more susceptible to interference. They are better for music reproduction because they tend to have a wider **frequency response** than dynamic mikes do. They also need preamplification so they must be turned on and have appropriate power before use. Ribbon microphones tend to be larger than other mikes and very fragile, hence not suitable to field use, but they have a rich sound and excellent reproduction of lower frequencies, which makes them an excellent choice for speech (especially low voices). Having said all this, though, these are generalizations. Some dynamic mikes need preamplification. When used with a little bit of care, many condenser mikes perform very well in the field. Newer ribbon mikes are smaller and less susceptible to interference. Ultimately, you need to experiment with microphones to see which has the sound and performance that works for you.

Pick-Up Patterns

Sometimes you want a microphone to pick up sound equally from all directions. Often you want the mike to favor a certain sound source over others. Microphones are designed with different **pick-up patterns** to suit varying needs. Pick-up pattern means the area around the microphone in which sound will be clearly reproduced. The three main classifications are **omnidirectional**, **bidirectional**, and **unidirectional**. An omnidirectional mike, as the name implies, has sound sensitivity all around the microphone, except for right behind it (Figure 5.12).

omnidirectional

Figure 5.12 Omnidirectional mikes pick up equally from all directions, except for some falloff directly behind them.

Omnidirectional microphones are good for recording **ambient sound**—the overall sound of a particular location. They are also fine for picking up the sound of one speaker *if* that speaker can be placed very close to the microphone. Generally, you don't want the speaker too close to the mike, but omnidirectional mikes are less sensitive to unwanted vocal noise than other types of microphones.

Bidirectional microphones are sound sensitive in two directions (Figure 5.13). They are not very common, but they have the capability to receive sound from two different sources in opposite positions. This type of mike allows you to cover two speakers facing each other with one microphone without having to move the mike.

Unidirectional mikes are sensitive in one direction, but it's not quite that simple. Even if a mike is designed to receive sound from one position (directly in front of the mike), it will inevitably have some degree of sensitivity along the sides of the mike and behind the mike, as well (Figure 5.14). Pick-up will be strongest and clearest in front of the microphone. This is the desired **on-axis** range for quality recording. Sound picked up from the side or back of the microphone will be weaker and relatively muffled, but it is still present. This degree of side sensitivity can vary.

Unidirectional mikes are also called cardioid mikes. **Cardioid** describes the heart-shaped pattern of sensitivity that unidirectional mikes have. Sometimes the heart is quite wide. Mikes that are characterized as simply cardioid have a wide area of sound pick-up in front of the mike and a good bit of side sensitivity. A mike with less side sensitivity and a narrower pick-up pattern is known as a *supercardioid*. *Hypercardioid* mikes have even less side sensitivity and an even narrower pick-up area. Unlike a cardioid mike, supercardioid and hypercardioid microphones also have an area of sensitivity directly behind them (Figure 5.15).

Unidirectional microphones are used to record sound that emphasizes a particular source. Someone is speaking. You want to hear some background sound, but you want to hear the speaker clearly above the

bi-directional

Figure 5.13 Bidirectional mikes pick up in two opposite directions, good for interviews if you only have one mike.

uni-directional

Figure 5.14 Unidirectional mikes are designed to pick up a narrow range of sound. However, they do have some side and back sensitivity.

Figure 5.15 A, Cardioid mikes are basically unidirectional but vary in terms of their side sensitivity. **B,** Supercardioid mikes have a narrower range and more side and back sensitivity than a cardioid. **C,** Hypercardioid mikes have an even narrower range and even more side and back sensitivity. The narrower the range, the more selective the mike in its ability to cleanly pick-up the sound created within its pick-up pattern and minimize the sound outside of it.

background. Your ability to do that is based on three considerations: the pick-up pattern, the distance between mike and speaker, and the relative volume of the background noise compared to that of the speaker.

The louder the background sound is, compared to the speaker, the closer the mike's pick-up pattern needs to be to the speaker so the speaker's sound will be favored. Many cardioid mikes are designed to be used close to the source of the sound.

If the microphone cannot be very close to the speaker because getting it there is impossible, impractical, or unacceptable, you need to make sure the angle of sound sensitivity is narrowed and side sensitivity is lessened. You do this by using a supercardioid or hypercardioid mike. Such mikes are designed to be used anywhere from 1 foot to approximately 15 feet from the source of the sound. They will work at a distance because the narrow pick-up range and reduced side sensitivity screen out much unwanted sound from the background. However, you do need to ensure that the mike is accurately pointed at the source of the sound, keeping the speaker in the on-axis range. You may have to use a mike at such a distance to avoid seeing it in the shot and therefore having to back it out of camera range, which makes unidirectional mikes a common choice for film and video use.

Microphone Usage Types

Microphones are also characterized by their usage. Some common types include handheld mikes, lavalieres, and shotguns.

Handheld microphones are just that—designed to be held in your hand. They can also be attached to desk stands or floor stands (Figure 5.16). They can be condenser, dynamic, or even ribbon. A ribbon handheld is usually used on a stand to avoid interference from a moving hand. Many handheld

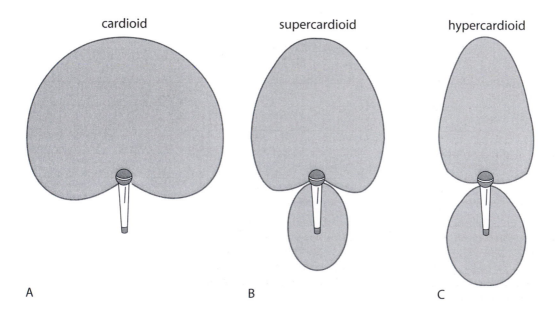

cardioid   supercardioid   hypercardioid

A   B   C

Figure 5.16 Handheld mikes can be just that—held by hand—or placed in a desk or floor stand.

mikes are made to be used close to the speaker's mouth and are widely used by singers, narrators, and field reporters. The advantage of this type of microphone is the level of control. For example, a talk show host uses a handheld mike when standing out in the audience, and as long as she keeps hold of the mike, she can choose who speaks and for how long. A reporter in the field can turn an omnidirectional or cardioid handheld away from himself and capture the sound of live events. He can then turn the mike to himself and, by placing the mike close to his mouth, have his voice heard clearly above any background noise.

Unfortunately, handhelds have a limited range of pick-up and can be rather obtrusive. Because they are either omnidirectional or cardioid, they cannot be used successfully more than a foot or two from a primary sound source. They either need to be used for picking up environmental sound from a distance or be very close to the source. Having a microphone in your face is not a problem for professionals, but it can be intimidating for interview subjects. Also, if images are being captured with sound, the microphone will likely be in the frame with the primary sound source. This is acceptable in a news report, talk show, or other presentational type of program but is not desirable in a representational piece such as a fiction film.

Lavalieres, or *personal mikes,* are small, unobtrusive mikes that are designed to clip onto an individual's clothing. They are generally condenser mikes, which require a battery, so the small mike is connected by a wire to a power pack that can be clipped to a belt or tucked in a pocket. Lavalieres, sometimes called *lavs,* can be wired or wireless. A wireless lav has a radio-frequency (RF) transmitter that sends the signal to a receiver, which converts the RF back to an electronic signal to be transmitted or recorded.

Figure 5.17 Lavs should be placed on the side the subject is facing, but its omnidirectional pick-up pattern allows for some movement.

Lavalieres are usually omnidirectional but are intended to pick up one speaker and little ambient noise. This works as long as the lav is clipped close to the speaker's mouth (approximately 6 inches away). The omnidirectional pick-up is an advantage if the speaker turns his or her head. The lav should be placed in the direction the talent is speaking, however, to ensure the cleanest recording (Figure 5.17). A lav will appear in the picture, but because of its small size and position, it does not draw much attention. Lavalieres work well for interview subjects, getting a clear signal of the voice without being intimidating. However, they are susceptible to wind noise and the sound of clothing brushing against them. A wired lav limits the subject's movement. A wireless lav allows more freedom of movement, but it can pick up other services that also use RF (e.g., radio stations and pagers, especially in urban areas).

Shotgun microphones are so named because of their gun barrel–like appearance and their need to be properly aimed in order to be useful. They are designed for use at a distance from the primary source of sound—from 1 to maybe 15 feet away. However, the further a shotgun mike is used from the primary sound source, the more ambient sound will be heard. They are not used often for audio-only productions, except when it is impossible to get close to the sound source. They are very useful, however, in film and video when you don't wish to see the microphone in the shot. Seeing the microphone in the frame creates a visual distraction, especially in a fiction piece where you want the viewer to get lost in the story, not think about the mechanics of making it. Occasionally, such reminders to the viewer of the production process are acceptable in a nonfiction program, like a documentary. The audience accepts that a subject or narrator is speaking directly to them. A microphone in the shot reminds the audience that this is a process where the information is communicated through mediation.

Shotguns can be dynamic but are usually of the condenser type, which gives them a good frequency response and requires preamplification. They generally have a supercardioid or hypercardioid pick-up pattern. The narrow range of sensitivity is necessary in order to be able to pick up a primary source of sound from a distance while minimizing other sounds in the environment. Because the range is narrow, it is important to make sure the microphone is on the proper axis to record the sound you want (Figure 5.18).

Figure 5.18 Proper aim is important when using a shotgun mike.

Shotguns can be mounted in several ways. You don't want to hold them because even slight hand movements can cause unwanted noise. Pistol grips can be used. Placing the shotgun on a boom or a handheld boom pole (or fishpole) allows closer placement to the subject, but it is still out of the frame (Figure 5.19). Cardioid handheld mikes are also put on booms when a larger pick-up area is desired. You only want to do this if there is little background noise, because the cardioid will pick up more of it. Many video cameras have mounts for shotgun mikes. This can be convenient if you are a one-person production crew, recording both sound and picture, but the camera is rarely the optimal position for good sound recording. Additionally, the mike is apt to pick up some camera noise.

Figure 5.19 Mounting equipment for microphones ranges from (**A**) pistol grips to (**B**) handheld boom poles or fishpoles to (**C**) studio booms mounted on wheels.

ANALOG VS. DIGITAL RECORDING

Recording audio involves electricity and magnetism. The microphone converts sound waves into an electronic signal that contains all the variations of sound. When that electricity comes in contact with the magnetic particles on the surface of the audiotape, the particles rearrange themselves to mirror the information encoded into the electronic signal. When played back, the pattern of magnetic particles on the tape creates an electrical signal that matches the original signal created by the microphone. A loudspeaker converts that signal back to sound waves.

Recording of an audio signal is done through both analog and digital means. Although digital methods of recording and postproducing audio are standard practice in the media production field, analog recording still takes place and is preferred by some. Each method has its own advantages and disadvantages.

In analog recording, the reproduction of the sound wave is a one-to-one transfer. All of the variations of amplitude and frequency are included in the transfer.

Try this analogy to explain the difference between an analog and a digital process. You want to have a shoe custom made so it fits your foot exactly. An "analog" method of fitting that shoe might be to have a plaster casting made of your foot. The shoe could be constructed on the mold of your foot. The leather would be cut according to the size and shape of your foot. There is a direct relationship between your foot and the shoe. Your foot might move in the wet plaster or the plaster might have lumps in it, adding something to the model that was not part of the original foot. And if you made copies of the plaster mold, by using the plaster "foot" to make a second mold, there's a good chance that those imperfections would multiply. A "digital" method would be to measure the length, width, and curvature of your foot and use those measurements to cut the leather and make the shoe. The more measurements that were taken of different dimensions of your foot and the more detailed the measuring device—millimeters as opposed to centimeters—the more exact the fit would be. Once those measurements were taken, many pairs of shoes could be made from them, each as exact as the other. To make a second pair of shoes, you wouldn't have to measure the first pair, you'd just use the original measurements.

In the analog recording process, that direct relationship between the sound waves and the recorded signal results in the recording of a **continuous wave** (Figure 5.20). This may be an advantage of analog recording, resulting in a richness and naturalness of sound that digital recording lacks. However, a disadvantage of the analog recording process is its susceptibility to the addition of interference or noise

Figure 5.20 The variations of frequency and amplitude are reproduced in their entirety when sound is recorded by analog means. Copying analog signals causes generational loss.

soundwave

analog signal recorded on tape

sampled sound wave

10011010001001011101010101001100110101110110101100101

digital signal recorded on tape

(unwanted sound) such as machine hiss. That noise gets worse if you make a recording from the recording, such as dubbing or copying a tape, a situation called generational loss. Each generation (i.e., each copy of a copy) worsens the signal degradation.

In the digital recording process, the wave is measured or *sampled*, and the information is converted to mathematical units or **quantized**. The information is stored as a series of ones and zeros that describe the characteristics of the wave. The more often the wave is sampled (its **sampling rate**), the more fully the wave is reproduced (Figure 5.21). The more detailed the measurements (its **bit depth**), the more accurate its re-creation. Sampling should be done at a rate at least twice the frequency of the sound wave for high-quality recording, resulting in common audio sampling rates of 44.1 or 48 kHz (more than twice the highest frequency of human hearing, which is 20 kHz). A bit depth of 16 results in 2^{16} or 65,536 pieces of digital information per sample. That's enough for high-quality reproduction, but a bit depth of less than 8 or greater than 16 bits is sometimes used.

Digital recording avoids the discernible noise of analog recording when the bit depth is high enough (16 bits). In analog recording, noise comes along with the signal in the recording process. In digital recording, just the signal is sampled and quantized so, virtually, only the signal is re-created. The result is a cleaner sound.

The digital recording process is essentially free from generational loss, but only if the process is digital all the way through. This is because you're not actually copying one recording; instead, you are using the same digital measurement to re-create the signal again. An unlimited number of recordings can be made from the original data with no degradation of quality. Digital recording has its own pitfalls though. Dropouts, resulting in a pop or brief gap in sound, can occur from imperfections in a digital tape. Also, degradation of the sound can occur if a digital image is compressed.

SOUND VARIATIONS

Sounds, obviously, are not all the same. The variety of sounds is tremendous—loud or soft, high or low, muffled or clear, organized into speech and music or a chaotic cacophony. We can start to understand the possibilities of sound by considering the following characteristics:

Figure 5.21 In digital recording, the sound wave is sampled. The more often it is sampled (sampling rate) and the more precise the measurement (bit depth), the more accurate the reproduction. Sampling allows a reduction of unwanted sound or noise. Copies can be made without quality degradation.

the quantity, quality, and direction or placement of sound, and how to record it.

QUANTITY OF SOUND

Quantity of sound refers to its amplitude, which the ear perceives as loudness or volume. As discussed earlier, a sound wave's amplitude constantly adjusts to the strength of the vibrations being produced. To be heard, sound waves must be strong enough to be registered by the ear. To be recorded, the amplitude of the wave must be strong enough to vibrate the transducers in the microphone, creating the electronic signal or voltage.

Amplitude of recorded sounds can be measured by different types of meters, the most common being **VU meters** and **LED meters**. A volume unit (VU) meter measures and displays the amount of voltage passing through it. This voltage corresponds to the strength of the sound wave being captured by the microphone. VU is a measurement of signal strength. Most VU meters measure amplitude in two ways, in volume units (from −20 to +3 VU) and as a percentage of modulation (0% to 100%). The values are displayed on a mechanical meter with a needle (Figure 5.22). Zero VU is equivalent to 100% and represents the strongest sound desirable. Light-emitting diode (LED) meters have a row or column of lights that light up in proportion to the strength of the signal. The lights change color (usually from green to red) when the signal becomes too strong (Figure 5.23).

When **monitoring** a captured sound, the needle will move or the lights will illuminate in response to the varying loudness of the sound. A properly recorded primary audio signal should **peak** at 0 dB or 100% (the highest point). If the signal exceeds 100%, you risk the possibility of **overmodulation** and subsequent distortion. Digital recording

Figure 5.22 A VU meter usually displays both volume units and percentage of modulation. The signal should be kept below 0 units or 100%.

methods are much more sensitive to overmodulation than analog ones. To be heard, a signal needs to be above 0%, at approximately −20 dB.

An audio recorder or a mixing console inputs multiple audio signals and outputs a single, mixed signal and allows you to control the levels of the incoming signals to ensure high-quality recording. You can preset the levels before recording or mixing, and if the levels change during recording, you can **ride the gain** or adjust them as you go.

Signal-to-Noise Ratio

The **signal-to-noise ratio** is the comparison between the sound you want and the noise you don't want. The term, used strictly, applies to the difference between the voltage of the audio signal and any electrical interference with that signal. A high signal-to-noise ratio indicates clean sound. The signal-to-noise concept, though, is also useful in comparing different sound sources within your signal. A meter reading tells you what your overall volume level is, but it doesn't tell you if you're capturing the particular sound that you want. You might want to hear the voice of an interview subject on the street with the sounds of the city low in the background, but you might be getting loud traffic sounds with a barely perceptible voice. Maintaining a good signal-to-noise ratio is dependent on proper microphone choice and placement. In the example above, a lavaliere mike used a few inches from the subject, a handheld cardioid held close to the subject's mouth, or a very accurately aimed shotgun a foot or so away from the subject could all give you a clearly recorded voice.

Generally, you want to record your primary audio sources as a strong foreground sound with your ambient sound well in the background. More ambience can always be added in postproduction. The sound mixing exercise on the companion website illustrates how this works. To determine that you are actually getting the sound you want, you need to listen to or monitor the sound. A signal can be split and sent to multiple locations, such as a recording or mixing device and a headset jack or speaker, so you can hear what's being captured. Monitors also have volume level controls that you can adjust for comfort, but changing the level of the monitor does not affect your recording or mixing volume. That needs to be adjusted separately, according to the VU meter.

QUALITY OF SOUND

When we speak of a sound wave of a particular amplitude and frequency, we mean a single wave at a particular volume and pitch, but sound is really more complex. A piano playing a musical note (say, middle C) sounds very different from another instrument playing that same note or a voice singing that note. The **timbre** or tone quality of each sound is different. Each sound is actually made up of a group of frequencies or **harmonics** that distinguish one sound from another.

The shape of the sound wave also makes it distinctive. This is called the sound **envelope**. How quickly does a sound wave peak at its maximum amplitude (*attack*)? How quickly does it back off from that peak (*initial decay*)? How long does the sound last (*sustain*) before it drops out of hearing (*decay*)? Differences in the sound envelope contribute to varying sound quality (Figure 5.24).

Figure 5.23 An LED meter is small and inexpensive, but not as accurate as a VU meter. Higher-quality plasma meters work in same way as LEDs but are more costly.

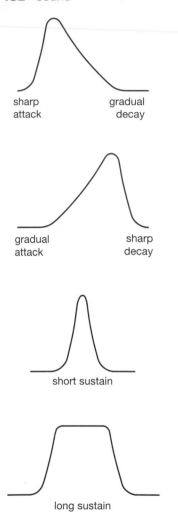

sharp
attack

gradual
decay

gradual
attack

sharp
decay

short sustain

long sustain

Figure 5.24 Quality of sound is affected by how quickly it attacks, how long it sustains, and how quickly it decays.

Reverberation

Sound waves (like all energy waves) can be absorbed or reflected by different surfaces. The walls of a room, for example, will absorb some sound and reflect some. A hard surface like tile will reflect more sound waves; whereas, fabric drapes will absorb more waves. The multiple sound reflections off all the surrounding surfaces create the effect of **reverberation** or *reverb*, which is somewhat like an echo but not as distinct. A *dead space* has little to no reverb. A *live room* has a lot. Reverb can be added to a recorded sound signal electronically to change the sound quality.

Presence

The term **sound presence** defines the subjective closeness the listener feels to the sound. A recorded voice with a great deal of presence sounds close to your ear with little background noise. It has a sense of intimacy. A recorded voice with little presence sounds distant with a good deal of air and background sound mixed in. It has little to do with volume but can be manipulated by choice of microphone and placement of that mike in relation to the source of sound. A lavaliere clipped to the talent's chest or a handheld mike with excellent frequency range held close to the talent's mouth will deliver great sound presence. A shotgun at a distance of 5 feet will have less presence, even if properly aimed with a strong level. You usually want to match sound presence with shot size, if shooting visuals. A close-up matches strong presence. A long shot should sound further away.

DIRECTION OF SOUND

Our ears hear sound from all around us. We have **binaural hearing**. The **sound perspective**, or perception of placement of the sound in space, comes from many clues. We can tell which side of us a sound is coming from—it reaches one ear before the other and is louder in that ear. We can tell how close a sound is by its volume and its presence. Sound waves bouncing off the walls reflect back to our ears, giving us a sense of placement and of the size of the room (Figure 5.25).

Figure 5.25 Our ears hear binaurally. Our brain receives clues about the placement of sound from how direct and reflected sound waves reach our ears at different strengths.

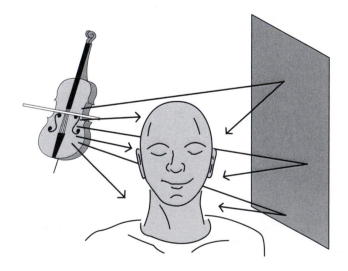

Recorded sound is different. A single microphone records one input of sound. One-channel playback, or *monaural playback,* of all the sound comes to our ears from one direction. **Stereo** recording, done by using two microphones, each recording the sound from slightly different locations (somewhat like your two ears), can then be played back through a right and left speaker. While providing an effect with more perspective than monaural playback, stereo does still not provide the 360-degree effect of the human ear. *Surround sound* comes closer, using four or more speakers placed around the listening area. Sound can be panned (or moved) from one speaker to another. An effect even closer to human hearing is possible with special binaural microphones and headset playback. This is the next stage of realistic sound playback.

Moving Sound

Chapter 3 concentrated on the concept of visual movement, but sound can move through the space of the frame as well. By shifting the presence (the perception of proximity) of the audio, the sound seems to be moving closer to or farther from the listener. An increase in presence of the foreground sound is usually accompanied by a decrease in volume of the background audio. With visual media, sound movement is usually matched by visual movement. If a shot is tighter (and therefore the viewer feels closer to the subject), the presence should increase as well. Matching sound presence to shot size and establishing a sense of where the sound is coming from creates a realistic **sound perspective**. Sound perspective is achieved naturally by the use of a boom microphone. As the shot gets wider, the microphone needs to be farther from the subject to avoid being seen in the frame. A tighter shot allows a closer microphone, causing more presence. This holds true whether the change in shot size is the result of subject movement, camera movement, or editing.

Stereo, as mentioned earlier, is a method of recording, mixing, and playing back the audio on two separate channels or tracks. Stereo speakers are used to the right and left of the listener (and also the screen if used with images). By mixing the audio so it *pans* from one channel to the other, the sound moves from one side of the listener to the other, creating movement within the audio frame that can correspond with movement in the visual frame. To record for stereo, at least two microphones, facing different directions, must be placed far enough away from each other to avoid causing interference (Figure 5.26).

channel 1   channel 2

Figure 5.26 Recording stereo audio requires at least two microphones recording the sound from different positions. If they are too close to each other, electronic interference will result.

Surround sound takes this idea further. Although different systems are in use, surround sound employs multiple speakers—front, side, and back—to place the listener within a three-dimensional sound environment. Sound can travel in all directions, once again corresponding with visual movement. Movie theaters and HDTV are increasingly taking advantage of this technology.

RECORDING CLEAN SOUND

There are many tricks to recording good sound. Generally, you want to record the *cleanest* sound possible (high signal level, low noise level), leaving any special effects, such as reverb or additional ambient sound, until postproduction. Sound recording should always be *monitored* by listening through good-quality headphones. A test recording should be done and played back to catch any interference caused by bad electronics. Interference can also occur when a microphone cable runs parallel to an electrical cord. (Run them perpendicular.) Local radio signals can sometimes be picked up in your recording when ungrounded connections or wiring acts as an antenna. (Change the mike cables or unplug from the wall AC circuit and run off batteries.)

Recording studios are constructed to minimize unwanted noise and reverb. Anywhere else you record audio, you'll be faced with the challenge of controlling ambient sound. Sometimes, ambient sound is desirable. Every space has its own unique ambience or room tone. The *room tone* helps to establish a sense of place in your audio recording. If your audio is going to be edited, you should always record some extra room tone with no one talking or moving to fill in between pieces of audio.

However, ambience can overpower your audio and needs to be managed. Hums from air conditioners, refrigerators, or fluorescent lights can create unpleasant background noise. They should be turned off, if possible, or the noise at least reduced by pointing the microphone away from the source of the hum and as close to the desired source as you can.

Clean sound recording often requires patience. If you are recording a situation you can control, such as a scripted scene or narration, you can wait for the airplane to fly over or the truck to drive away. An uncontrolled situation requires careful monitoring, careful mike placement, and the realization that your audio might be unusable during the sound of the siren.

The handling, placement, and quality of your microphone are key to clean recording. Better mikes have low **impedance** (as opposed to high impedance). That is, they have less resistance to the signal and therefore create less noise and interference. Better mikes also tend to have a greater frequency response and are sensitive to a greater range of low to high frequencies.

The desired proximity of the mike to the source of sound is dependent on the design of the mike, as previously discussed. Some microphones, such as handhelds, can be a couple of inches from a speaker and get a clean signal that is free of pops and sibilance ("s" sounds).

A lavaliere is best used approximately 6 inches from the speaker. A shotgun is designed to be used at a distance of at least a foot, which is handy when you can't get close to the sound source or want to create the effect of a faraway voice with minimal presence. If you are hand-holding the microphone or using it on a boom or fishpole, careful handling is important to avoid interference.

Recording Formats

Sound can be recorded onto many different devices. Earliest sound recording was done onto a wax disk, much like a phonograph record. Later, a magnetic coated wire was used. During World War II, the Germans perfected audiotape, which remained the standard until recently. Audiotape originally was a strip of metal, now usually made of polyester, one side of which has the magnetic coating that records the signal. Audiotape can come in various widths and is distributed in different forms.

Analog Formats   Although digital audio formats dominate the field today, analog equipment is still used and even preferred by some who find digital recording "too clean." The first audiotape was *open reel,* which is still in use today, in both analog and digital formats. A supply reel holds the raw tape; a take-up reel spools up the tape after it is recorded. The tape travels through an erase head, a record head, and a playback head. The erase head makes sure the magnetic particles are neutrally aligned, the record head aligns the particles with the incoming signal, and the playback head allows the signal to be monitored during recording and after playback (Figure 5.27). Reel-to-reel tape can be 1/4 inch, 1/2 inch, 1 inch, or 2 inches. The 1/4-inch size is more portable and is used for field recording. The wider tape formats are used in recording studios because they allow room for more tracks of audio. Varying the tape speed during the recording process affects the quality of the sound. A faster speed allows more information to be recorded and subsequently better frequency response and a lower signal-to-noise ratio but obviously allows less recording time on a tape.

Analog audiotape has been put into different housings as well. The *audio cartridge* is a self-contained device that loops tape through and

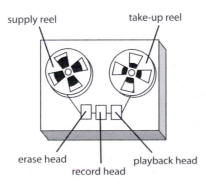

supply reel   take-up reel

erase head   playback head
record head

Figure 5.27   An open reel audio recorder. The tape leaves the supply reel, travels through the erase head, record head, and playback head, then wraps around the take-up reel.

can be easily inserted into and removed from a playback machine. The consumer version (eight-track tape) has been obsolete for many years. Audio cartridges or *carts* of short duration are still sometimes used for promos, commercial spots, and sound effects in radio and TV stations because of their ability to recue themselves, but they are rapidly being replaced by digital versions with disks instead of tape.

Analog *audio cassettes* house 0.15-inch tape in a convenient form and have had wide use over the years in both professional and consumer formats. However, they, too, have become rare. Their sound quality is quite low, compared to other options (Figure 5.28).

Digital Formats Many digital audio formats are in use today. Each seems to have its own advantages and therefore a niche in the market. The sampling rate and bit depth of a digital recording determine the recorded sound quality. The common sampling rates for audio are 32 (digital broadcast standard), 44.1, 48, and 96 kHz. Sampling rates are commonly 16 or 24 bit, with 24 bit being better.

Digital audiotape, like digital videotape, is somewhat of a hybrid. The audio signal is sampled and stored as bits, thus preventing digital audiotape from experiencing the noise and generational loss inherent in analog processing. Tape, though, is a linear format, so digital tape does not have the random access capability associated with digital technology. You still need to play or fast-forward the tape from the beginning to get to the end. Digital audiotape is available in a variety of open-reel formats.

Figure 5.28 Analog audio formats have changed over the years. Although analog is still used, all forms of analog are giving way to the many and also changing digital formats. Below are an audio cart, an open reel of 1/4-inch tape, and a cassette tape.

Some have stationary heads, like analog recorders, that require fast tape speeds. Some have rotary heads, which spin and increase the ability of the recording head to encode information on the tape. This is called *helical scanning* and is used by videotape recorders as well. Consequently, tape speed can be much slower, allowing more recording on a tape.

Digital audiotape (DAT) is the most common digital cassette format. The tape and the cassettes are very small and produce extremely high-quality recordings. DAT is used in both field and studio recording.

Disc-based formats have the advantage of random access. Also, the recorded information is a bit more stable, and less susceptible to wear and damage. *Audio compact discs* (CDs) were introduced in the 1980s and became the dominant audio distribution form in the 1990s, replacing phonograph records, eight-track tapes, and analog cassettes. CDs are losing favor to digital music players such as iPods. Regular CDs allow playback only. *Recordable CDs* (CD-Rs) allow recording, but only once. You cannot rerecord. *Rewritable CDs* (CD-RWs) allow CD use for mixing and editing because you can go in and make changes by rerecording over a section of the disc. However, the different CD formats are not completely compatible. CD-RWs must be played in their own drives or a special CD-ROM drive, not on a standard CD player. *Digital versatile discs* (DVDs) are sometimes used in audio production in addition to video, because of their much expanded storage capacity.

Mini discs (MDs) are similar to CD-RWs—digital quality and random access—but use a magnetic recording system, somewhat similar to tape. MDs were introduced as a consumer format and have two different disc types. One is for prerecorded audio, and one is for recording. High quality and portability made MDs a popular professional format, but one that is losing ground to digital audio recorders, which are discussed next.

Digital Audio Recorders Digital audio recorders that record straight to computer memory are quickly replacing other digital audio devices (Figure 5.29). The recording can be to a hard drive or to flash memory (such as a CompactFlash card). The capacity of flash memory continues to grow while the prices come down, but at this writing, a hard drive gives you more storage for less money. Flash memory is less susceptible

Figure 5.29 Digital audio recorders, such as this portable model manufactured by Marantz, record digital audio files directly to a removable Compact-Flash card. Files can also be transferred to a PC by a USB cable. (Courtesy of D&M Professional, a D&M Holdings US Inc.)

to movement so is a better choice for portable devices and is quickly and easily erased and reformatted. Both types allow downloading to a PC.

TYPES OF AUDIO MEDIA

Audio recording is part of a great variety of media forms that are distributed in many ways. This includes those that are purely audio and those that are sound in conjunction with image. The sound/image relationship is further explored in Chapter 6.

RADIO

Radio is the transmission of audio signals through the air. The electronic signal is transduced into high-frequency radio waves that travel a distance and are received by an antenna. The antenna transduces them back to the electronic signal that can be transduced to sound waves by the radio speaker. **Broadcasting** is transmitting of radio waves point to multipoint, reaching to many receivers from one transmitter (Figure 5.30). Like television signals, radio can also be distributed through cable systems or via satellite. Within the past few years, most broadcasters have also begun to program simultaneously on the Internet. This involves converting the radio signal to digital information that can be sent through the phone lines or larger types of cable that

radio
transmitter

Figure 5.30 Radio broadcasting sends the signal from a transmitter, through the air, to be received by radio receivers in the transmitter's range.

carry Internet service (like a cable modem or ISDN line) and listened to on your home computer speaker. Because an audio signal requires much more digital information than does text or graphics, *streaming* is required. Streaming sends the audio information in a small, steady flow that can start to play while the rest of the information is still being sent, as opposed to one large piece of information that could take a long time to download to the computer. Radio is also now transmitted via satellite. Providers offer national programming to listeners for a monthly fee. As with satellite TV, this type of service often bypasses the local broadcaster and, therefore, local news and public affairs programming.

In the so-called "Golden Age" of radio broadcasting during the 1930s and 1940s, there was a great variety of original programming, ranging from dramas to situation comedies to variety to news to music. When television came along, virtually all of the dramatic and comedy programming migrated to TV, which left radio with news and music. Most radio programming is now prerecorded music with disk jockeys or hosted talk shows. News, sports, traffic, and weather punctuate both types of programming. Public radio offers some additional program types—commentaries and the occasional radio drama or acoustic art. Some programming is nationally syndicated. Increasingly fewer corporations own a larger and larger percentage of radio stations, but most radio is locally produced, which gives it a regional flavor missing from most other types of media today.

PODCASTS

The term **podcast** gets its name from the Apple iPod and refers to a radio broadcast or audio blog that can be downloaded or streamed to a personal computer. It can be listened to from the computer or downloaded to an iPod or other portable media player. Often listeners subscribe to a podcast, enabled by a group of web formats called RSS that allow for automatic updating. Podcasts are created by large media outlets and individuals alike, ranging in topic from major news events to esoteric special interests. A recent search of newly created podcasts included rock band interviews, religious services, and a podcast created by a class of fifth graders.

MUSIC RECORDING

Recorded music makes up a large portion of the audio-related media that we consume. The format we purchase and listen to has changed more than any other media form. Phonograph records gave way to eight-track cartridges, then cassettes, CDs, and now, digital music, downloaded off the Internet and stored as compressed digital files on a tiny handheld digital storage device that can hold thousands of songs. Downloaded music off the Internet has been the subject of legal battles, pitting those who want to protect the recording artist and record companies' right to profit from their music against those who claim the right to obtain it without charge. The courts have upheld the rights of artists and record companies, but as with all the technologies that allow easy reproduction of creative property, copyright is difficult to protect.

MP3 is the dominant format that takes digital audio files (such as those recorded on an audio CD) and compresses the amount of digital information required without losing audio quality. MP3 and other file formats are discussed further in Chapter 10.

Music recording is integral to the sound design of movies and television, and music videos revolutionized TV programming and film and video editing styles. Most music recording is done under controlled conditions in studios and heavily remixed and postproduced. Live recording and mixing are also done, albeit in less controlled environments.

ALTERNATIVE AUDIO

Though music recording and radio programming, hosted by disk jockeys, dominate sound-only media, other programming types do exist. Documentaries based on interviews, field recordings of actualities (ambience and sound effects recorded in the field), and narration explore issues and sometimes obtain access to people and places that film or video cameras could never get. Radio dramas still challenge our imaginations to visualize action, setting, and characters just as they did in pretelevision days. Occasionally you can hear a documentary or drama on public or alternative radio.

Sonic or acoustic artists use sound as a medium of expression like paint or light or the human body (Go to the Source—John Cage). Sonic art can stand alone, performed in concert or broadcast on alternative radio outlets. Some sonic artists exhibit their sound art in installation form, creating listening experiences for museums, galleries, and public art spaces. Sound can also combine with dance, performance, or visual arts in a multimedia expression.

CONCLUSION

Mediated sound is a big part of our lives—alone and in combination with images. Music, voice, and environmental sound inform us, entertain us, and move our emotions. Despite our culture's visual dominance, effective communication through sound is a powerful media tool.

PUTTING IT INTO PRACTICE
OBSERVING AND WRITING

Go to a location that will provide an interesting mix of sounds and where it is safe for you to sit and listen awhile. Listen and write in your journal. How many distinctive sources of sound can you hear in a 20-minute period? Where are those sounds coming from? How do they compare in terms of amplitude and frequency? Are there sounds that start as background sound and become foreground sound or vice versa? If you heard these sounds blindfolded, without knowing where you were, would you be able to identify your location?

DOING

Using the audio recording equipment and microphones available to you, create a sound collage that defines a particular location and com-

---

Go to the Source—
John Cage

John Cage (1912–1992) was a musician and composer, best known for his willingness to redefine our concept of music. He used found sound, silence, and what some would only consider noise to create his musical compositions. One piece called *Water Music* (1952) was written for piano, radio, whistles, water, and a deck of cards. He often collaborated with choreographers (especially modern dance icon Merce Cunningham), filmmakers, sculptors, and painters to create performance pieces. He also published essays, including a book called *Silence* in 1961.

municates a sense of place. This can be the place you visited and wrote about in the "Observing and Writing" activity on the previous page or a different one. This is not an edited exercise, so you will need to think about the order and duration of your recordings. Combine voice and environmental sound. Think about foreground and background sound. Think about presence created by microphone placement. The final piece should be no more than 5 minutes in length.

KEY CONCEPTS

ambient sound	peak
amplitude	phantom power
bidirectional	pick-up pattern
binaural hearing	pitch
bit depth	podcast
broadcasting	quantized
cardioid	radio frequency
condenser	reverberation
continuous wave	ride the gain
crest	sampling rate
decibel (dB)	shotgun microphone
dynamic	signal-to-noise ratio
envelope	sound perspective
frequency	sound presence
frequency response	stereo
handheld microphone	timbre
harmonics	transduction
hertz (Hz)	trough
impedance	unidirectional
lavaliere	velocity
LED meter	voltage
monitoring	VU meter
omnidirectional	wavelength
on-axis	waves
overmodulation	

CHAPTER 6

Sound and Image

A + B = C

Some forms of media production are solely visual or solely aural. Chapter 2 discusses still photography. Chapter 5 discusses radio and acoustic art. Many websites have only visual content—text and graphics. Much of our media consumption, however, involves simultaneous sound and image. Even before sound film came along, live music accompanied silent films in theaters. "Talkies," or films with sound, once thought by some to be the death of film art, were actually a natural and enduring addition to the reproducing of our visual world through film. Television brought us radio with pictures, giving visual dimension to many of the same characters and programs that had been so popular on radio. Sound has increasingly become an important aspect of computer-based media, though the full understanding of sound's role on the Internet or other interactive applications is still being discovered. The dual experience of seeing and hearing is so natural to most of us that we only notice when one is missing, not when both are there. For that reason, silence in a film or a black TV screen with sound can be very attention grabbing.

The combination of sound and image can be straightforward and descriptive. It can be convoluted and symbolic. We can hear exactly what we're viewing or something very different from what we see. To a perceptive observer, however, every combination of sound and image yields more than just the sum of its parts. A + B is not just A and B. The two components of the experience, sound and image, inform each other and form a new level of understanding. It's not just A and B but a distinct entity of its own, C.

For example, a young man is telling a story about his experience climbing a mountain. If we are looking at him as he tells the story, his verbal account may tell a tale of bravery and endurance—man vs. nature. If his body language includes fidgeting hands, darting glances, or a defensive posture, the sound and image together tell a story of a young man struggling to be brave despite his insecurities—man vs. himself (Figure 6.1). If instead we see the young man delivering his story to a young woman who is obviously bored, the story becomes one of the man's attempt to impress a woman, only to be rejected—man vs. (wo)man. If we see the birth of a baby while we hear about climbing the mountain, the story of reaching the mountaintop might become a

Figure 6.1 The visual image can contradict what is being said.

metaphor for the creation of a new life. The A + B = C exercise on the companion website books.elsevier.com/companions/9780240809076 further illustrates this concept.

Although we have already acknowledged the primacy of visual media in our culture, we should realize that artful **sound design** is equal in importance to visual composition in creating effective audiovisual media. Sound design is the combination of sound elements, how they work together as part of the soundtrack, and how they work with the visual to tell the story.

ELEMENTS OF SOUND DESIGN

What are your options when creating a sound design? What are the pieces that can be woven together?

Dialogue is integral to most fiction pieces of media. Conversations between characters make up a large part of many movies and are even more central to television drama and comedy. With its radio parentage and smaller screen size, TV has always been more talk based and character driven than movies, which tend to be more action based. Dialogue is also an important element in some documentaries that observe subjects conversing with each other. A subject being questioned by an interviewer (who may or may not be heard) can be considered dialogue as well.

Narration is similar to dialogue, except the narrator is speaking directly to the audience, not to someone else on screen. A narrator may either appear on camera or only on the soundtrack. Narration that is only heard is called a **voiceover**. Voiceover (VO) can be written and spoken in the third person by an unidentified voice that is generally accepted as an expert. VO can also be first person, the voice of the maker or a participant in the story, identified explicitly or implicitly. The narrator might introduce himself, or his identity might become clear through what he says or through voice recognition.

Ambience, as described in Chapter 5, is the sound of the space where the story takes place. Ambient sound is part of the sound recorded on location. Sometimes different or additional ambience is mixed into the soundtrack later.

Sound effects are extra sounds that can either come from things seen on the screen or be mixed into the soundtrack. Sound effects can replace the actual sound recorded for a screen event to increase the dramatic emphasis. A punch performed on the set may not sound hard enough for the demands of the story, so a sound effect of a sledgehammer striking a cabbage is inserted (Figure 6.2). Sounds of unseen sources can be inserted to enhance the atmosphere or mood of the scene portrayed on screen. Sound effects can be birdcalls, lapping waves, footsteps, gunshots, clinking glasses, or screaming crowds. Sound-effect libraries are sold with hundreds of sounds to choose from, but a **foley** artist, or sound effects creator, can produce sounds more tailored to a specific image.

Automatic dialogue replacement (**ADR**) is a technique used especially in the production of fiction film or television production. Because it is often difficult to record high-quality sound on location, the soundtrack

Figure 6.2 Sound effects are created to enhance the power of an on-screen event or to suggest off-screen action.

is essentially rebuilt from scratch. Actors are brought into the studio for ADR or *looping*—watching their image on a screen while respeaking their lines. These cleanly recorded dialogue tracks are then mixed with ambience tracks and sound effects to recreate the original sound—only better.

Music that is used as part of sound design is such a common and accepted part of media storytelling that often we don't even notice it. Music sets the tone, triggers changes in mood, creates suspense, and lets us know when the story is going to end. **Scoring** is composition of music specifically for certain visuals. Sometimes the music comes first and the visuals are created to illustrate or complement it, such as a music video or montage of Olympic moments.

Ultimately all these sources will be combined together, forming the *sound mix*. The technical process will be discussed in Chapter 9. Creating a good sound mix is a true art. The subtleties of variation in sound level and quality are very important to the success of a film, video, or other media project using sound.

(See the *Sound Mixing* activity on the book's companion website books.elsevier.com/companions/9780240809076 to experiment with combining dialogue, ambience, and sound effects.)

SOUND/IMAGE COMBINATIONS

The relationship between sound and image can exist in several ways.

Synchronous sound is sound that matches the action and is recorded at the same time as the picture. The character's lips are moving while we hear her words. The door shuts, and we hear the slam. Synchronous sound is recorded as the image is acquired; it is the sound of what we're seeing. Recording clean synchronous or *synch* sound can be a challenge on location because unwanted noise or too much ambient sound may be present. However, when the sound and image match on screen as they do in reality, it contributes to a sense of authenticity. ADR, as described earlier, would be an example of post-synchronized sound.

Nonsynchronous sound is any sound that was not recorded with the image and does not match the action. Nonsynchronous or *non-*

synch sound can be *wild sound*, which is audio recorded in the field but not simultaneously with the picture. It can also be music, narration, dialogue happening off screen (off-screen sound), sound effects, or any combination. Nonsynch sound can be descriptive; for instance, it may accompany a shot of a couple silently drinking coffee while we hear conversations from unseen patrons in the shop and the clattering of dishes back in the kitchen. The sound/image relationship is realistic, but the sound was likely recorded in a different time and place. A less realistic use of nonsynchronous sound would be created by the same shot with the soundtrack of the couple arguing the night before with a crying child in the background.

Related to but somewhat different is the distinction between **diegetic** (sometimes spelled *diagetic*) and **nondiegetic** sound. Diegetic sound is sound that is part of the story—sound that characters in the story can hear. Diegetic sound can be synchronous or nonsynchronous off-screen sound. The term is often used to describe the relationship between the music and the story. For example, music coming from a car radio on the screen or played by a piano player in the corner of the bar where the scene takes place is diegetic music. Music that only exists on the soundtrack and is not heard by the characters on screen is nondiegetic. Voiceover narration is nondiegetic also. It is heard by the audience but not by the characters. For example, we see a young boy riding his bike through a 1980s suburban neighborhood, but we hear the character as an adult talking about the lost innocence of youth.

The relationship between sound and image can shift from scene to scene. We hear the voice of a schoolteacher talking about the Revolutionary War while we see exterior shots of a one-room schoolhouse. We then cut to inside the school and see the teacher addressing her students. The narration is diegetic because it is part of the world of the story, but it started as off-screen nonsynchronous sound and became synchronous. In another example, music might at first seem to be a nondiegetic score that does not exist in the world of the characters. A young woman sits thoughtfully on the beach as we hear a melancholy tune. The camera then zooms out to reveal her car parked next to her with the radio playing. The song ends and the disk jockey speaks. She can hear the music; it is diegetic after all.

The ability to layer sound and image, shifting the dynamic between them, is an integral part of media art. Sound and image can match, sound can contradict image, or the juxtaposition of sound and image can create meaning neither could on its own.

SOUND RECORDING FOR DIFFERENT MEDIA
FILM SOUND

Film and film sound are usually captured at the same time (synchronous sound) but use separate pieces of equipment to do the capturing. Shooting film is a mechanical and chemical process that takes place in the camera, whereas audio recording is electronic. In order for the sound and image to be precisely synchronized, the audio recorder must work at the exact same speed as the camera. Even very slight differences can result in *out-of-synch* sound, such as the sound of the voice or a door slam that is heard just before or just after the image.

When portable 16mm filming and synch sound capabilities were first developed in the 1960s, camera/audio recorder rigs were connected by a cable to make sure the motor of the camera was the same speed as that of the recorder. Later, oscillating crystals in the camera and recorder regulated the speed of the recorder to match that of the camera and made the cables unnecessary (crystal synch). Now that digital audio recording and transfer of film to video for digital nonlinear editing are the norm for film production and editing, timecode synchronization is most common. Described more thoroughly in Chapter 9, timecode is an electronic signal recorded onto tape that identifies each frame or the audio equivalent of the recording. Whether synchronized by crystal synch or timecode, there needs to be a way to match up the shot of film with the piece of synchronous audio that goes with it. This is done by slating. A **slate**, or *clapper*, is the recognizable rectangular object with the hinged top (called *clapsticks*), which is snapped shut right before the director yells, "Action" (Figure 6.3). Slates are made to be written on with chalk or dry erase markers. The shot, take number, and date are then visually identified for each take. An electronic or "smart" slate has a timecode counter that can be aligned, or *jam synched,* to match the timecode on the digital audio recorder. Slates without clapsticks are used to identify shots when recording video. If the slate is used at the beginning of each shot, it's possible to match the frame of film with the point on the audio where the sound begins. If the film and sound were recorded in synch, they will stay synchronized after that beginning point is found. Each shot needs to be synched before editing can begin.

Figure 6.3 Each film shot with synch sound needs to be slated so the frame of film where the clapper first makes contact with the slate can be matched to the first frame of sound.

Different types of audio recorders are used for film. For many years, the Nagra, a high-quality, rugged, analog open-reel recorder, which uses 1/4-inch tape, was the standard for location shooting. As digital recording has come to dominate, digital multitrack recorders, DAT cassette recorders, and disc-based recorders are also widely used. All digital recorders used for synch film production include timecode capabilities that provide acceptable synchronization.

Editing film and film sound is discussed in detail in Chapter 9, but, in short, once recorded, the sound must be transferred for editing. When editing the film itself (cutting apart shots and taping them together in the proper order), the sound is transferred to *magnetic stock* (or mag stock), a type of audiotape that is the same size as the film (16 mm or 35 mm). The shots of film are matched up with the correct pieces of sound and stay together through the editing process (Figure 6.4). If editing is done digitally (now the norm), sound is digitized directly from its original format into the editing software.

Once the editing process is complete, the sound must be physically put onto the film for theatrical distribution. Several methods are available for doing this, the most basic being an optical stripe on the film, in which sound is read by a light beam in the projector. In addition to the optical stripe, digital enhancements, such as Dolby, can be added to the film.

Figure 6.4 This flatbed editor allows for two tracks of magnetic or *mag* stock to play in synch with the 16 mm film. (Courtesy Steenbeck GmbH.)

VIDEO SOUND

Unlike the double-system method of recording sound with film, video uses a single-system method where sound and image are recorded together onto the same material. (A single-channel film system exists, but it is essentially obsolete.) Videotape is divided into separate sections for different pieces of information, including the video signal, timecode, and audio information (see Chapter 9). Different formats of video put information in different places, but on any format there will be at least two channels of audio. When you record sound for video, you can usually direct your microphone signal or signals to record on either channel or both. Some consumer camcorders allow only one microphone input with right and left stereo channels. If you don't have enough microphone inputs, you can input the mikes into an audio mixer, which comes in field versions that can run off of battery power, and feed the output of the mixer into the camcorder. Mixers are also used with audio recorders for film. One warning—first, make sure that the mix is the way you want it when recording. Mixing is live editing. Once the different mike sources are mixed, you can't "unmix" them.

Despite the fact that video sound is recorded with the image, it is not uncommon for people to record sound separately as well, on a flash or DAT recorder. It allows for more control in monitoring and setting levels—separating those functions from the camcorder operation. This is especially true with fiction projects on video but true in nonfiction work as well where there is a large enough crew and the desire for high production values. A slate like that used in film production can be used to allow synching the sound and image in postproduction, but if the audio recorder has a timecode function synching the footage is easier.

When editing video, the sound and picture are generally digitized into the editing software together. Other tracks of sound, such as voiceover, music, and sound effects, can be added to the track or tracks of live audio. It is also possible to delete live tracks if you like. At the end of the editing process, all the tracks are mixed into a final soundtrack that accompanies the picture onto the release tape. Television sound has traditionally had a reputation for poor quality. The limited frequency response of audio on analog videotape and the small mono speakers on most TV sets supported this reputation. However, with the advent of digital videotape with its digital-quality audio recording capabilities and the use of stereo speakers and even surround sound in consumers' home entertainment systems, television sound can be produced and experienced at a high-quality level.

AUDIO- AND COMPUTER-BASED MEDIA

As we have seen, producing and editing sound for film and video is increasingly taking place digitally. Once audio has been digitized into a sound file on a computer, it can be used for any digital media piece. Audio is becoming an important aspect of both web-based and DVD distributed interactive programming.

For audio to be usable in computer-based multimedia, it needs to be digital and in a usable format. The computer needs to have enough storage to hold the application, enough memory (RAM) to run it, and a fast enough processor to play it back smoothly without interruption.

Digital audio creates files that are larger than text, but smaller than video. One minute of uncompressed CD-quality stereo audio has a file size of 10 megabytes, which is the same as approximately 1000 pages of text. (In comparison, 1 minute of uncompressed standard definition video has a file size of 1.5 gigabytes.) The file size of digital information has always been an issue. Initially, trying to save large files on a personal computer's hard drive was a problem. This is no longer the case. Hard drives are hundreds of gigabytes in size. One tiny flash drive holds a gigabyte or more, and most personal computers have built in CD and DVD burners. CD-Rs hold 650 megabytes, and the most common format DVDs hold 4.7. gigabytes. HD DVDs hold 15 gigabytes; its competitor, the Blu-ray Disc (BD), holds up to 50 gigabytes. And the storage capabilities just keep increasing. The increased availability of broadband Internet service, as opposed to connecting through a telephone line, means that downloading or streaming audio (and video) files is less often a problem. Techniques are available that help make it possible to distribute audio and multimedia via the Internet. One is compression, or making the size of the digital file smaller. Compression will be discussed more thoroughly in Chapter 9, but simply, compression takes out unneeded information and by doing so, reduces file size. Some compression reduces quality (lossy); some does not (lossless). Common methods of audio compression include RealAudio and a variety of Motion Picture Experts Group (MPEG) formats, including the popular MP3. MP3 is able to produce digital quality sound with a small file size by removing audio information that is outside human hearing.

Reducing the sampling rate, for example, from 48 kHz to 32 kHz, will reduce file size, as will using mono sound as opposed to stereo, but both of these will reduce the quality. **Streaming audio** is an important technique for using audio and video over the Internet. It eliminates the need to download the entire file onto your computer before hearing and/or seeing it. Streaming allows a gradual download that can be accessed while it is playing.

CONCLUSION

The symbiotic relationship of sound to image that exists in movies and television has yet to be fully explored in multimedia. Often audio on websites or as part of disc-based interactive programming seems to be an interesting but unnecessary add-on, such as sound effects or background music. Or the audio is the programming, as with streaming radio stations. The power of the sound/image relationship in all media forms is there for you to discover—a challenge for a new generation of media makers.

PUTTING IT INTO PRACTICE
OBSERVING AND WRITING

Find specific examples of synchronous, nonsynchronous, diegetic, and nondiegetic sound in films and TV programs. Describe two examples of each in your journal. Describe how the combination of sound and image in each example creates a meaning that is different from that of the sound or image alone.

DOING

1. Experiment with the *Sound Mixing* and $A + B = C$ exercises on the book's companion website books.elsevier.com/companions/9780240809076. *Sound Mixing* allows you to take different sources of sound—ambience, dialogue, and sound effects—and adjust their relative volume. $A + B = C$ demonstrates how changing soundtracks can effect the meaning of the visuals.

2. Choose a scene from a favorite film. (The helicopter air attack scene from Francis Ford Coppola's *Apocalypse Now* [1979] is a good choice.) Watch it without sound. Then watch it again with sound. Try to identify all the different tracks of audio that went into the final sound mix. Listen for changes in background/foreground relationships. Watch for uses of nondiegetic sound.

KEY CONCEPTS

ambience

automatic dialogue replacement (ADR)

dialogue

diegetic

foley

narration

nondiegetic

nonsynchronous sound

scoring

slate

sound design

sound effects

streaming audio

synchronous sound

voiceover

CHAPTER 7

Time

TIME AND SPACE

All art and media experiences have both **temporal** and **spatial** aspects. It takes time to experience them, and there is a physical object needed for the experience to occur. Often, one aspect dominates. A sculpture is spatially dominant because it exists in three dimensions and has mass, but it is experienced temporally when a museum visitor walks around it. A film in a theater is a temporally dominant experience because the viewer sits for two hours, but the film, projector, and screen have a spatial presence. Watching that same film on your iPod as you carry it with you introduces another spatial element to the experience. A communal public space is replaced by a changing personal space. We experience television as a stream of disrupted time. We jump from program to commercial to promo and back to program, but it is all presented as continuous "TV time." The TV set, however, is a spatial presence in our homes, one with considerable cultural importance.

Most audiovisual media experiences are temporally dominant. With traditional forms—radio, movies, and television—time is controlled by the media maker or the controller of the media outlet. A movie, a television program, and a song on the radio are designed to be experienced from beginning to end in a time frame determined by the maker. They are **linear** in how they tell the story, as discussed in Chapter 1. These pieces of media have a beginning, middle, and end and are intended to be experienced from beginning to end in real time. The linear nature of a media experience is most evident when someone other than the viewer or listener controls the means of distribution, such as with a television or radio broadcast or a movie in a theater. True, you can walk out of the theater or change the channel or station, but someone else controls the program scheduling. When the viewer controls the scheduling and operation, such as with a film or recorded program on DVD, which allows the use to stop, start, search, rewind, and fast forward the film, the concept of linear programming is obscured. It becomes less linear in the traditional sense when a movie is viewed on a DVD or when television programming is viewed with a digital video recorder, which allows pausing and instant replays of live programming.

153

Movies or television programs, though, are still essentially linear. The story is designed to be experienced in one direction. Film, videotape, and audiotape are linear media tools. Even though they can be paused or fast forwarded, you have to pass through each inch of film or tape to get from the beginning to the end.

Interactive media programming, distributed through the means of the Internet or on a DVD, gives the user control over the order in which the material will be seen and heard and the length of time required to experience the program. Interactive programming on websites and DVDs are inherently **nonlinear** in that they are dependent on the user to navigate through multiple options. Digital means of distribution allow **random access**, which means that the user can jump from one spot in the program to another. You don't need to start at the beginning and go the end. There are many possible paths and destinations. The experience is still a temporal one, the time frame is just less prescribed. The length of the experience and the pace at which the user experiences it are under the user's control. Surfing the web also has a spatial component, though. The model of the *web* and the concept of *cyberspace* imply that the information exists in a certain place and is traveling through space to your computer screen. The computer itself and the mouse, keyboard, or game controller have a physical presence that is part of the experience.

TV remote controls, audio CDs, digital video recorders, and on-demand television services are examples of nonlinear means of distribution that are designed to be used with linear programming types. They allow viewers to control linear, time-based experiences.

FROZEN TIME

Time is the fourth dimension of the frame. A frame has height, width, and the illusion of depth. Even when we use the frame analogy applied to sound, the audiospace is defined top to bottom, right to left, foreground and background, revealing depth. Time defines our experience with the frame. Is the frame a single frozen moment in time, such as a photograph or digital still? Or do we see thousands of frozen moments projected in quick succession, giving the illusion of movement and time unfolding—a movie?

Henri Cartier-Bresson, a French photographer of the early 20th century, described his photographs as examples of the **decisive moment** (Go to the Source—Cartier-Bresson). When trying to express your message through just one single visual image, it becomes very important that you choose the right moment to freeze. The composition, the light, and the expression and position of subjects must all be right and work together. Capturing that perfect moment takes great skill and, sometimes, a bit of luck.

SERIES

Individual media works are often grouped together for purposes of exhibition or distribution. This could include several photographs hung on

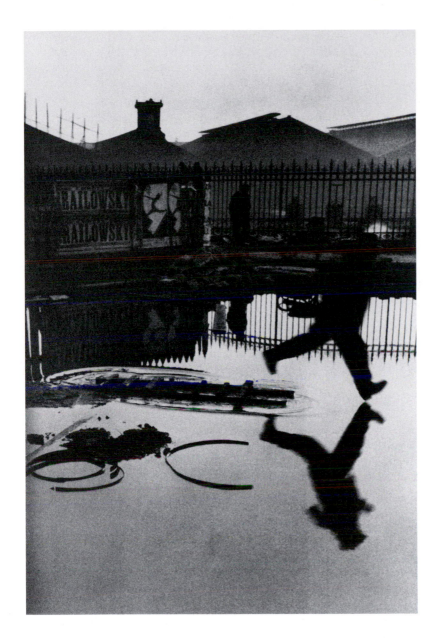

Go to the Source—
Cartier-Bresson

Henri Cartier-Bresson (1908–2004) was a French photographer best known for his "street photography." Cartier-Bresson did not like to pose subjects; he waited for the "decisive moment" to occur. He has said the camera is "an extension of the eye." Cartier-Bresson published several books of his photographs and writings on the art of photography, including *The Decisive Moment*, which was published in 1952. Much of his work was done in France, but he worked extensively as a photojournalist all over Europe and Asia. (Photograph by Henri Cartier-Bresson, Place de L'Europe, Paris, 1932. By permission of Magnum Photo.)

a gallery wall in a one-person or group show or a book of photographs. An audio recording (CD, most likely) is a series of individual songs. A website can contain many **series**—an image gallery, audio interviews, or video clips—from which a user can choose. The pages of an interactive program can be seen as a series itself. A television magazine format show, such as NBC's *Dateline*, provides a series of story segments, connected by the anchor's transitions and introductions. What qualifies these as series is that the individual pieces can stand on their own. Though they may be united by a common theme, style, or timeliness, each piece is a complete media statement within itself.

Great thought may go into deciding the order in which the pieces are presented (as with a book of photographs), or that control might be given to the user (as with surfing a website, wandering through an art gallery, or listening to a CD with a skip button on the remote control). If you pull out one web page, visual image, or song, it can stand alone and have meaning.

Sequencing and duration of time are the two factors at work here. Still images give the user control over the sequence (the order in which they view the experience) and duration of time spent with each image. This is true whether the images are in a book, on a wall, or on a website. The audio CD, though laid out in a linear order on the disc, allows the user to control the sequencing but not the duration. The random access capability of the means of distribution lets you listen straight through or program your favorite songs first. Sure, you could alter the duration by listening to only part of the song, but that would not really be participating in the full media experience as intended. (You can close your eyes and plug your ears during the movie, too, but then what's the point?) The only way to get the full experience of a song is to listen to it in real time. A news magazine show on television embeds linear segments within a linear distribution form. You can't control sequencing or duration of the segments unless you record the show and view it later. Even if you did, the show would still be considered a series of stories because the individual stories stand alone and could be understood and appreciated in any order of presentation.

SEQUENCE

Sometimes, the order of the individual parts is crucial to the appreciation of the work. The intended meaning is communicated only when experienced in a certain order. Like the chapters in a novel, still images in a certain order can tell a story. This is sometimes called a **sequence** in the world of still photography (Figure 7.1). In the sequencing exercise on the companion website, you can sequence still images in order to tell a story.

Similarly, a sequence in film and video terminology refers to a series of *shots* put together in a specific way to tell a story or express a logical message. (A **shot** is a continuous piece of film or video, from camera starting to camera stopping.) Even a single shot, though, can be considered a sequence. Each frame is a still image, the sequencing of which is crucial to the process of persistence of vision that allows us to see the shot as a moving image.

With a photography sequence, the order is determined but not the duration. The viewer can spend as much time with each image as he or she wants. With a film or video sequence, the maker determines both order and duration. With a nonlinear media work such as an interactive game, many sequences are possible because the structure is branching, as opposed to linear. The user controls both sequence and, to a large extent, duration. (These concepts will be discussed in detail in Chapter 10.)

Figure 7.1 A sequence of still images can tell a story.

SOUNDS AND IMAGES EXISTING IN TIME
REAL TIME

The moving images of film and video provide us with a primarily temporal media experience. The linear nature of the frames of picture and sound, recorded or exposed in quick succession, are both captured and experienced in **real time**. Unless you manipulate a film camera to shoot in slow or fast motion, the time it takes to capture a scene of fictional dialogue or an interview is the same amount of time it takes to replay it. There is a one-to-one time relationship between recording or shooting time and playback time. This, of course, does not take into account preparation or preproduction or the manipulations of time that can happen in postproduction.

Certain types of media experiences maintain this real-time relationship. **Live programming**, by its very nature, happens in real time and is experienced in shared real time by the user. Film cannot be experienced live because of the processing and printing parts of the process that take substantial time in themselves to accomplish. Audio and video can be experienced live by broadcasting, cablecasting, satellite casting, or webcasting. All of these means of distribution take the sound or light waves, transduce them into electronic signals, and either transport these signals by wire or transduce them again into radio frequencies that are received by antennas or satellite dishes (Figure 7.2). The time used to make the live transmission is the same duration of programming that is received by the listener or viewer. Most radio programming is live (though it often includes prerecorded inserts such as CD cuts or recorded commercials and promos). Televised news, morning shows, and sporting events are examples of live TV, but they may have portions of prerecorded material too. Streaming webcams or audio feeds provide live programming on the Internet.

Live programming can be produced by a single source (e.g., camera or microphone) outputting an unbroken stream of information or by mixing multiple sources through an audio mixer or video switcher. These different production configurations will be discussed further in Chapter 11.

Another example of a real-time media experience would be a gallery or museum installation where sound, image, and sculptural elements are presented in combination. Though primarily a spatial experience, installation work provides a real-time experience for those who visit, lasting for the time of their visit (Figure 7.3).

RECORDED REAL TIME

Live-on-tape programming maintains a real-time relationship between production time and replay time but is experienced by the user sometime later. Live-on-tape programming is produced as if it were being transmitted live but is recorded on audio- or videotape. Still, the time it takes to record the program is the same as the playback time. It looks and sounds like it could be live. Game shows and talk shows are live-on-tape programming. Typically, live

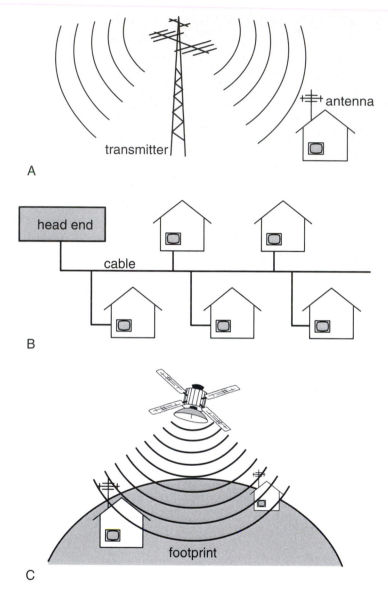

Figure 7.2 Audio and video signals can be transmitted live in several ways. They can be broadcast as radio frequency waves from an antenna. **A**, Both VHF (very high frequency) and UHF (ultra high frequency) waves are used. VHF is less susceptible to interference but UHF travels farther. They can be sent to a cable head end then distributed through a cable system to individual users. **B**, Signals can be transmitted to a communication satellite, using a form of electromagnetic energy with frequencies even higher than UHF. **C**, Communication satellites stay within a geosynchronous orbit (22,236 miles or 35,785 km about the equator), which keeps them in sync with Earth's rotation, and they seem to hover over the same location on Earth. Programming is downloaded to satellite receivers within the footprint or coverage area of the satellite (approximately one-third of Earth's surface). These methods can be combined, such as when cablecasters receive feeds from national cable networks via satellite, then distribute them through their cable system.

Figure 7.3 Sonalumina-13 (2004), a computer-driven installation featuring sound, light, and sculpture. This site-specific installation is based on the resonance and materials of the Art Interactive gallery space in Cambridge, Massachusetts. (Courtesy of the artist, Jeff Talman.)

programming is simultaneously taped for purposes of archiving or future reruns.

Uninterrupted shots by a single film or video camera also maintain a real-time capture/replay relationship. It is rare, though, that an entire program be a single shot. An example at a very low production level would be a camcorder taping a city council meeting from start to finish or a single microphone broadcasting a live press conference nonstop. Film is limited in the length of its takes by film reel length (somewhere from 3 to 11 minutes). The long take, as discussed in Chapter 3, is a cinematic device used by many directors to emphasize a moving camera or to pull the viewer into the scene as though seeing through the eye of the camera. The aesthetic of the long take and its use in fiction narrative and documentary film and video making are discussed in Chapter 8.

ILLUSION OF REAL TIME

Many media programs we see, especially scenes from fictional movies and television programs, appear to be taking place in real time. This is called the **illusion of real time**. The car pulls up to the house. Out jumps the detective. She knocks at the door. A man inside opens the door, sees who it is, and slams the door. The detective kicks the door open. The man escapes through the back door and runs down the alley. The detective calls for backup, runs out the back door, and sees the man climbing a fence. She runs, catches him, pulls him to the ground, and handcuffs him. In real life it would take two minutes. On the screen it takes two minutes; on the set it took two days. Twenty minutes of film were shot. There's a real-time relationship between story time and screen time, but production time is very different.

That's because of the production approach that was chosen. The story was shot with a single camera, not as a long take, but as a series of shots, each taken from the camera position and chosen by the director as the best vantage point for that particular piece of the action. In postproduction, the pieces of film are reassembled to look like one seamless, two-minute piece of time. It's an illusion of real time that is a part of **continuity editing** (Figure 7.4), which is discussed further in Chapter 8.

ELLIPSIS OF TIME

In the next scene of our movie, backup assistance has arrived, and the man is being placed in the squad car. In the next scene, the detective is arriving at the babysitter's to pick up her young child and take him home. We follow what is going on, but the real-time relationship is broken. The boring parts have been taken out. We don't need to see the backup arrive and take the man to the car. We don't need to see the woman return to the station, pack up for the day, go the parking lot, get in her car, turn the key, and so on. Time has been compressed.

Figure 7.4 When edited together, **(A)** the wide shot of the man exiting the truck and **(B)** the closer shot appear to be a continuous action, happening in real time, even though they were taken at different times. (Courtesy of the film-maker, Roberto Carminati, from his film *A Fronteira*.)

It's how a story can span days, weeks, and years within a two-hour movie. The story moves ahead logically and often chronologically (except for flashbacks and flash forwards), but through editing, time can be highly manipulated. **Ellipses of time** are an accepted convention of media storytelling.

Most narratives are told as scenes of illusion of real time with an ellipsis of time happening as the scenes change. Two defense attorneys discuss a case in their office (illusion of real time). Cut to the courtroom where the trial is in progress. The time it took the lawyers to get to court and start the proceedings has been dropped. The closing arguments give the illusion of real time. Cut to the lawyers' office as they sit with the client and await the call that the jury is back. Several hours may have been dropped. Time within the scenes may have been compressed as well. Within the closing arguments, there may have been some minor time compression to streamline the storytelling; that compression of time is not obvious to the audience, which is intent on the dramatic impact of the story. The shots may cut from the prosecutor's final statement to the first statement of the defense attorney. As an audience, we accept the fact that we didn't see the prosecutor sit down and the defense attorney rise, organize her notes, and begin to speak. A subtle ellipsis of time has occurred.

DEFYING TIME

Some media experiences break the real-time relationship and make no attempt to hide it. Documentaries often jump through time and space to create their story and logic out of the structuring of concepts, not out of the unfolding of chronological events (Figure 7.5). A documentary about education reform might jump from a classroom in Chicago taped two months ago, to an interview in Washington from last year, to a graph of standardized test scores all to make a point about the importance of small class size. A music video might go from live performance footage to the artist romping in the ocean in slow motion to scenes of the band on the road. The "sense" of the piece is less

Figure 7.5 Two images from the documentary *Pure Chutney*, which uses narration to create a logical flow from images that jump through time and space. (Courtesy of the filmmaker, Sanjeev Chatterjee.)

Figure 7.6 Images from *Fisherman* (16mm, 1998) in which disparate images are combined to create meaning. (Courtesy of the filmmaker, Robert Todd.)

logical, more visceral and abstract, dominated by the music and not rooted in chronological time. This is a technique that is also used by many experimental films and videos, where implicit messages are valued over explicit storytelling or information presentation (Figure 7.6).

Surfing the web or using other types of interactive programming allows a similar defiance of time but one that is user controlled. There is a real-time relationship as the user decides where to go, when, and how long to stay, but one can jump freely through time. The live streaming webcam might provide you with a real-time long take, but you probably won't wait for the shot to end.

CONCLUSION

Unconventional portrayals and manipulations of time are being used more often by some directors. Films like *Pulp Fiction* (1994), directed by Quentin Tarantino, and *Memento* (2001), directed by Christopher Nolan, defy our expectations of chronological and logical storytelling. *Pulp Fiction* jumps around in time as the audience continues to redefine their sense of what happened first to the two hit men. *Memento* moves backward in time, unveiling a murder mystery in the direction opposite of the norm.

The FOX TV series *24* (2002) has met with mixed critical response but is interesting for its approach to time. The show uses the premise that each of the season's 24 episodes will portray—by illusion of real time—one hour in the life of an agent (Kiefer Sutherland). In the first season the agent attempts to save the life of a presidential candidate and rescue his own kidnapped family in 24 hours. What was first considered experimental is now becoming mainstream (a common occurrence). More and more wide-release theatrical films and television series are telling stories by manipulating our senses of past and future.

PUTTING IT INTO PRACTICE
OBSERVING AND WRITING

Analyze movie, television, radio, and computer media experiences in terms of their relationship to time. Are the story time, production time, and experience time the same or different? Look for examples of illusions of real time. Look for examples of ellipses of real time. Record your observations.

DOING

1. Take a series of six still images that are related in theme but not reliant on a specific order to communicate your message.
2. Take a sequence of six still images that tell a sequential story.

KEY CONCEPTS

continuity editing

decisive moment

ellipsis of time

illusion of real time

linear

live-on-tape programming

live programming

nonlinear

random access

real time

sequence

series

shot

spatial

temporal

CHAPTER 8

The Theory of Linear Structure

PUTTING THE STORY TOGETHER

The way your sounds and images get pieced together is key to the effectiveness of your storytelling. *Editing* might be another word for it, but editing implies that the work is done in the postproduction, or last stage, of the production process. The decision about the structure of your piece—what gets placed in what order and how long it lasts—is a process that permeates all stages of production. Editing implements the structure, but if you don't think about the final structure until you're editing, it may be too late to create the piece you want.

Linear structuring is the process of putting things together—one following the other—so that the final product unfolds in a straight line through time. Examples of linear structure are found in the familiar realms of movies, TV shows, and radio programs. There is a prescribed beginning, middle, and end. *Nonlinear structuring* occurs in the realm of digital interactive media. Instead of a straight line, there is a branching structure and multiple options for progressing through the information. Nonlinear structure is discussed in Chapter 10.

Let's think in terms of sequencing units of media. These can be still images, pieces of audio, or shots of film or video. When you put these units in combination, you are manipulating all of the following:

1. The *content relationship* between units. Are you building meaning in a logical way, with each step taking us a little farther along a clear path? Or are you creating meaning out of the juxtaposition between the units?
2. The *formal relationship* between units. Do the directions of movement, volume, tempo, and color flow seamlessly to the next unit? Or does the audience have to adjust to the change?
3. The *order* in which you put the units. Which unit is revealed first, second, third, or last? What has the audience already heard or seen that creates the context for new information to be presented?

4. The *duration* of each unit. Variations in the length of each unit help create rhythm and pacing. Units of similar duration or repeated patterns of duration assembled together can create a sense of calm and stability that can either reinforce your message or bore your audience. Units of sustained duration can build suspense. Quickening units can create excitement.

Consciously or not, every time you assemble units of media, you are making decisions about content relationship, formal relationship, order, and duration.

ISSUES OF STRUCTURE IN PREPRODUCTION

Structuring begins when you write the script. Various script formats are used for the various media, as discussed in Chapter 1. Scripts are written at different times in the production process. A narrative fiction script is written before shooting begins. A documentary script is often not written until the sounds and images in the form of interviews, observational footage, or archival material have been gathered. Scripts are written documents, of the visualization (or audio equivalent) process that goes on in the mind of the maker.

As you visualize your piece, you are sequencing or mentally editing the material you plan to obtain. You see and hear your heroine brandishing her weapon and the villain cowering in pain and defeat in your mind. You are making decisions about content and order. You see the heroine from below (emphasizing her power). She looks downward. Then you see the villain from above. He reaches his arms upward, shielding himself from the heroine's wrath (Figure 8.1). You are making decisions about the formal relationships between shots. If you see the static shot of the villain interspersed with increasingly tighter shots of longer duration of the triumphant heroine, you are making decisions about rhythm and pacing and are building excitement.

In films and videos, the written material in the script is usually visualized with drawn or computer-generated storyboards. The storyboard breaks the action down shot by shot. The visuals are drawn, and the audio portion (e.g., dialogue, sound effects) is described beneath the image (Figure 8.2). You don't need to be a gifted artist to draw a storyboard, but the more accurate and thorough your drawings are, the more helpful they will be. If the idea of

Figure 8.1 The heroine looks toward the bottom of the frame. In the next shot, the villain gestures upward. We have established a relationship between the two without ever seeing them in the same shot.

Shot 1

Anna: I just don't love you anymore.

Shot 2

(Will sits silently...)

Camera pans right (... then runs out.)

drawing seems impossible to you, investigate some of the computer software applications that generate the storyboard forms and use drawing tools and clip art to ease the process. Storyboards can make your vision clear to other people who are involved in the production and help you figure out camera setups.

Documentaries can be a bit harder to visualize and are story-boarded less often. Although some documentaries start with a script that is written before shooting takes place, most don't. Those that are pre-scripted tend to be based on a voice-over narration and visuals that illustrate the narration. This approach lends itself to historical documentaries, such as the work of Ken Burns, or documentaries that are educational or informative in nature (Go to the Source—Ken Burns). Documentaries that explore current issues or feature real-life subjects are often approached quite differently. As a maker, you start with a premise or story to explore. Preliminary research, such as reading about the topic or interviewing subjects, is done. Then it's time for the production stage when sounds and images are captured. You don't know exactly what people will say or how an event will play out until you are in production. However, an outline of topics, a list of interview questions, and a sense of the other material that could support your vision of the piece can create a framework from which to work. This can keep you more focused and organized, even if there are changes from your original vision (which there inevitably will be).

Some people are naturally better "visualizers" than others, but it is a skill that can be developed through practice. It's not easy, though, and many beginning media makers think they are making it easier for themselves by planning to just go out, see what material they can get, and figure out how it fits together in the editing room. The bottom line is that the more you can visualize in the preproduction stage, the more accurately you can help others share your vision, the more efficient your production and postproduction processes will be, and the closer your final product will be to what you wanted to make.

Figure 8.2 Storyboards help you visualize the action. Generally, one frame is used for each shot. If the shot changes considerably, multiple frames, connected by a line, illustrate a single shot.

Go to the Source—
Ken Burns

Ken Burns (born 1953) is known for his highly researched histori-cal documentaries broadcast on PBS. His films have explored American institutions, events, and people. Some of his best known works are *Brooklyn Bridge* (1982), *The Civil War* (1990), *Baseball* (1994), *Lewis and Clark* (1997), and *Jazz* (2000). *The Civil War*, a nine part, 11–1/2-hour series, earned PBS its highest ratings ever. A true independent filmmaker, Burns generally acts as producer, director, cinema-tographer, and, often, writer. His films bring history to life through archival materials, interviews, oral dramatizations, and music. Burns lives and works in New Hampshire.

APPROACHES TO STRUCTURING FILM AND VIDEO

The overarching structure of a film or video can almost always be classified by one of the following three approaches: continuity style, montage, or a verbally driven structure. These conceptual approaches to structuring linear moving media (film and video) have been developed over the years. Each approach lends itself to a different subject matter. Other film and video texts will vary in their classifications, perhaps using different terminology to describe the conventions of editing that we see daily, but whether editing approaches are divided into two categories or three and regardless of the exact terms, the techniques described in the following subsections are generally recognized by everyone from textbook authors to media professionals to movie and television viewers.

Putting sound and images together in certain ways helps viewers recognize the information or emotional content of your production. Part of the reason that viewers accept the conventions of editing is that they have been conditioned to do so. Years of watching TV and movies have taught us how to understand a story through certain patterns of shots. These conventions are also based on valid theories of perception that were developed by psychologists and implemented by filmmakers.

The approaches described next are *not* the only ways to structure film and video. It is important to realize, though, that following the conventions is one way to make your editing, and thereby your story, easily accessible to your audience. Conventional editing formats do not generally call attention to themselves—they allow the subject matter or story to speak for itself. That may or may not be your goal. By breaking the conventions, you call attention to the process of media making itself. Emphasizing the artifice and inherent manipulation of the film, audio, and video making process may be just what you want to do, but you run the risk of confusing your audience and putting them a bit on edge. Once again, creating a sense of uneasiness may be exactly your goal. But remember, to break the rules effectively, you must know and understand the rules you're breaking and the implications of your deviations from the norm.

CONTINUITY STYLE

A continuity approach to making film or video is used to tell a story in a way that is logical, linear, and usually chronological. (Although *continuity editing* is a term associated with the visual media of film and video, you'll see that many aspects of continuity sequencing apply to audio projects as well.) A continuity approach employs a set of conventions that were developed in the early 1900s by filmmakers, such as D. W. Griffith, and are accepted by audiences (Go to the Source—D. W. Griffith). These storytelling conventions are so accepted that they are practically invisible, leaving the viewer to concentrate on the plot and characters, not on the mechanics of the video or filmmaking process.

D.W. Griffith directing the 1914 film, *The Avenging Conscience*. Courtesy of the Library of Congress, LC-USZ62-115719.

Go to the Source—
D. W. Griffith

D. W. Griffith (1875–1948) was a silent film director who worked in Hollywood, and he is often credited with developing the approach to structuring films that we call *continuity style*. Although maybe not the first to use all of the techniques, his combination of using close-ups, crosscutting between characters, and making screen acting less theatrical advanced the technique of Hollywood style continuity. In addition to directing hundreds of silent short films in the early 1900s, Griffith directed many features, working with the era's best actors, such as Mary Pickford, Douglas Fairbanks, and the Gish sisters, Lillian and Dorothy. His best known film, *Birth of a Nation* (1915), is also his most controversial. Griffith's portrayal of post–Civil War Southern society includes the glorification of the Ku Klux Klan and stereotypical depictions of African Americans. The film resulted in outrage at the time of release and has tarnished his legacy.

Often referred to as *Hollywood narrative style*, continuity is the primary style of commercial narrative films and dramatic television series. Continuity techniques are also used in documentaries and other types of nonfiction media.

Continuity, as the name implies, means a continuous sense of *something* as we move from shot to shot. Continuity is a fluid concept that applies to editing styles, shot selection, camera placement, and consistent props and costuming. When we are creating continuity, we are creating a sense of real time and space. A long take has natural continuity. The viewer sees one time and place from an unbroken vantage point. Shooting an ongoing scene with multiple cameras has natural continuity of time and place, but the point of view is changed as we cut (either live or in postproduction) from one camera to another. Breaking a scene down into shots and shooting them one at a time with a single camera (often out of sequence) is the way most fiction feature films and prime-time TV dramas are made. There is no natural continuity in that process. Time is disrupted, there is no guarantee that one shot is in the same location as the next, and point of view can be altered at will. The result, though, is a thoroughly comprehensible telling of a story that unfolds logically in the mind of the viewer. Here is an example of a TV narrative, structured in continuity style:

Scene 1: (morning) (hospital emergency room) The nurses move about the emergency room, discussing work schedules and gossiping about the doctors, particularly the marital problems of one of the surgeons until she walks into the scene. They quickly stop talking. Paramedics bring in a bleeding patient. (This scene takes

1 minute, 8 seconds of screen time and 2 minutes of story time. It is made up of 7 shots.)

Scene 2: (a few minutes later) (operating room) The surgeon is struggling to save the life of a gunshot victim. She yells at the nurses in frustration. (1 minute, 30 seconds, 19 shots)

Scene 3: (that afternoon) (hospital emergency room) Residents and nurses discuss the surgeon's outburst and loss of the patient. (40 seconds, 9 shots)

Scene 4: (late that night) (bedroom) The surgeon argues with her husband, who claims that she has no time or interest in their relationship anymore. (57 seconds, 7 shots)

If you analyze the sense of time here, you find that you have scenes of seeming continuous time (*illusion of real time*) and missing time (*ellipsis of time*) between the scenes, as discussed in Chapter 7. This is extremely common in fictional narrative storytelling. Audience members are given all they need to know to follow the storyline, are unaware of the disjointed manner in which the various shots were produced, and don't tend to think about what's missing in the ellipses of time between scenes.

If you want your story to be told in chunks of continuous time, moving forward in a logical way, you need to create that sense of continuous time out of the shots you have gathered. This approach can be used in nonfiction storytelling as well, such as a documentary about an up-and-coming female boxer. The story starts with a scene in the gym with the main subject sparring in the ring. The boxing was shot as a long take, documenting a real-life event. But a 10-minute bout might be edited down to a 2-minute scene, with reaction shots of the fighter's manager cut into the long take to mask the points at which footage was removed. The end result is a scene with an illusion of real time in which a logical, forward-moving part of the story is communicated. From there, we cut to a scene of the boxer on a date with her boyfriend. There is an ellipsis of time, but the viewer is comfortable with the transitions, assuming this scene takes place later that day or someday soon and that nothing necessary was left out.

As a media maker, how do you create that sense of real time and space out of shots that were created hours, days, weeks, and miles apart? What are the rules or conventions of sequencing that audiences accept so readily and that allow their attention to focus on story and character? Many conventions that were developed by past filmmakers are accepted (or sometimes rejected) by current makers. They include maintaining a sense of continuous action; the order of shot sizes that you structure together; and issues of lighting, audio, costuming, prop use, and screen direction. When an edit breaks the rules of continuity, it's called a **jump cut**.

To preserve continuity, every element—action; shot size sequencing; props, costumes, hair, and makeup; lighting and sound; and screen direction—must follow the rules of continuity.

Action

One challenge of sequencing in continuity style is maintaining the sense of continuous action, even when that action is shown as a series of shots taken at different times from different camera positions. You have several options if you are shooting the following scene: An actor gets up from a chair, walks to a door, opens it, and walks through the doorway into another room. You can shoot it as a single shot with a single camera, either from a static camera position or with the camera following the actor. In this example, the sense of continuous time is intact because a real-time relationship was maintained.

Another option is to shoot the action with cameras on either side of the door. With multiple cameras, you can cut between the two camera angles as the actor steps through the doorway, changing the camera angle but not interrupting the movement and the sense of continuous time that it conveys. The transition from one camera's point of view to the other can be done either live or in postproduction with video. For film, it would have to happen during postproduction because film needs to be processed, making it impossible to edit live.

What if you are shooting with a single camera and want the camera angle to change when the actor steps through the door? This would be accomplished by shooting two separate shots with two separate camera positions, each with its own lighting and microphone setup. Shot 1 might show the actor approaching the door, turning the knob, and stepping through into the other room, and shot 2 might be shot from the other side of the door when the actor turns the knob, opens the door, steps through into the other room, and crosses the room to the window (Figure 8.3).

The shots are done separately, maybe even on different days, probably shooting more than one take of each shot. Then the two shots need to be edited together. To combine the shots and give the sense of one continuous action, the edit must take place exactly at the right point. In both shots, you need to identify the frame that represents the same moment in the action seen from two different vantage points. That's the

Figure 8.3 From both camera positions, the actor opens the door and walks through the doorway. In shot 1, the actor starts in the chair and stops inside Room B. In shot 2, the actor starts by opening the door and stops at the window.

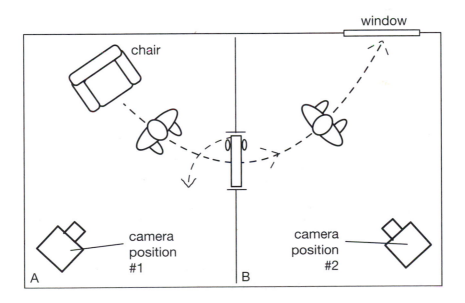

Rules for Good Matched Cuts:

1. Overlap action.
2. Cut on movement.
3. Change shot size—but not too much.
4. Don't cross the 180° line.
5. Change camera angle—more than 30 degrees but without crossing the 180° line.
6. Match the eyeline of subjects.

edit point. This type of edit is called a **matched cut** (see the rules for making good matched cuts in the margin). To execute a matched cut, the action in shot 1 must overlap that of shot 2. This means that you allow shot 1 to continue beyond where you know the edit point will be before you yell "Cut." Likewise, begin shot 2 well before the edit point. This allows the movement to be fluid in both shots, so the action flows from one shot to the next.

Cutting on movement is another hint for creating a smooth matched cut. The movement masks the edit somewhat, making it less noticeable.

When continuity editing, adjoining shots need to be different enough from each other to warrant making a change in camera position, but not so different that they confuse the viewer. Because continuity style is about giving the information needed for the viewer to follow the story and avoiding calling attention to the editing itself, cuts should only occur when there is a reason to make them. They should be **motivated edits**. Therefore, if you change the point of view of a single subject, such as cutting from one shot of a child playing to another shot of the same child, the shot size should change. If starting with a medium shot of the child piling up blocks, cut to a long shot when the tower tumbles or a close-up of the child's frustrated expression. The change in shot is motivated by the action or emotion, and it helps the viewer understand what's important.

Along the same lines, there is a rule that calls for a change of camera angle. If you imagine a circle of 360 degrees around the subject, the camera's position on that circle should change at least 30 degrees (Figure 8.4) (but without crossing the 180° line, which is discussed later in this chapter). Some directors say that for a good continuity edit, both shot size and camera angle should change. Others say that one or the other is sufficient. The bottom line is that new information needs

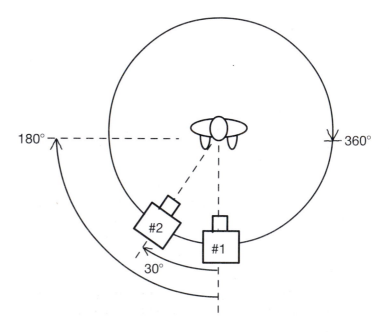

Figure 8.4 If you imagine a circle of 360 degrees around the subject, the camera angle should change at least 30 degrees but not cross the 180-degree line (illustrated later in Figure 8.9).

to be given to the viewer to justify the edit. That can be a different perspective on the same subject, through shot size or angle.

Shot Size Sequencing

Proper use of continuity avoids confusing the audience and gives them the information they need to know. The human brain processes objects and events in the world around it in many different ways. One way is through deductive reasoning. In **deductive reasoning**, we take in the big picture, clarifying the overall environment and relationships between people and things within it. Then gradually, we focus on specifics within the environment, being drawn for various reasons to particular subjects. It may be color, movement, sound, or nonverbal expression that draws our attention. Once we focus on and absorb the information from that primary subject, we then tend to turn our attention to the people or things that are affecting our main subject or being referenced by it. Picture it this way:

Wide shot (WS)—A city street with people walking down the sidewalk; heavy traffic moves along slowly, and a small cluster of people stops in the middle of the sidewalk.
Medium shot (MS)—An older couple watches in confused silence as a young woman speaks loudly with desperation and motions wildly.
Close-up (CU)—The young woman suddenly looks to her right and appears fearful.
Cutaway—A MS of a man approaching her, looking angry.

First we saw the setting for the action. The people who are stopped in an otherwise busy scene draw our attention. We needed to see what was happening within that small group of people. The voice and wild movements of the young woman establish her as the main subject that we want to know more about, so we are introduced to her in a close-up. When she looks out of the frame, we want to know what she is looking at that is causing her fear. We are shown the cause of her reaction. This is a classic WS-MS-CU-cutaway sequence of shots that is part of continuity style. Not all scenes will or should follow this sequence, but the way this pattern gives the audience what they need to know when they want to know it is key to continuity sequencing. In this way, each cut is motivated—there is a reason, related to the story, to make the change.

Another approach would be **inductive reasoning**. Instead of starting with the big picture and bringing us closer to the important details, an inductive sequence would start with the details:

CU—A woman's feet in sandals, standing on pavement with patches of snow and ice.
CU—A taxi rushes by. We hear a woman's plaintive ramblings while we see the faces of commuters walking down a city sidewalk, staring straight ahead.
CU—A woman's face is desperate as she rants and waves her arms.
MS—An older couple looks frightened as they stop, look at the woman, and look helplessly at each other.
CU—An angry man quickly approaches.
WS—The angry man grabs the woman's arm and pulls her down the sidewalk as the old couple moves away and the other pedestrians ignore the situation.

Ultimately we know what has happened, but each close-up, leading up to the final shot, gives just a hint of what's going on. Presenting intriguing bits of information (which we hope are intriguing enough to keep the audience engaged until the larger situation is revealed) creates suspense. The story is told in a clear, logical way in which each cut is motivated, giving the audience the next piece of information needed to understand the situation and, therefore, keeping the audience's minds on the story, not on the editing. That's continuity.

Eyeline Match

Another rule for continuity that relates to how shots are sequenced concerns a subject's **eyeline**. If in the first shot a subject looks off screen, the following shot should show what the subject sees. This will satisfy the need for information that you have set up with the first shot, enforcing the cause-and-effect relationships expected in continuity editing. Also, the angle of the subject's eyeline should match the position of the object or person at which they are looking. If you wish to imply that a man and woman are looking at each other, and the woman is looking down in the first shot, the man should be looking up at her in the subsequent shot (Figure 8.5).

Props, Costumes, Hair, and Makeup

There are many well-known examples of continuity errors involving props, costumes, hair, and makeup, even in large-budget Hollywood films. There's a shot of the leading man holding a glass of amber-colored liquid. Cut to a shot of the leading lady. Cut back to a shot of the leading man now holding a glass of clear liquid. You might notice it; you might not. If you do, it calls attention to the fact that this scene is not taking place in continuous time; it is a series of pieces of multiple takes of different shots, captured out of sequence, and reassembled in the editing room. In one take, a glass of amber-colored liquid was prepared as a prop. In another take, shot perhaps after a lunch break or the next day, a different production assistant filled the glass with a clear liquid. The editor decided the line of dialogue was better delivered in the first take and the next line was better in a subsequent take. The editor was more focused on performance or other technical issues, and the error was missed (or caught and the decision was made that few would notice it). Many viewers will not notice the error, but ones who do, even on an unconscious level, will feel uncomfortable. Their sense of time and place is disrupted. That's one kind of jump cut.

Lighting and Sound

Similarly, changes in light quantity, quality, color, or direction, not explained by any on-screen motivation, can disrupt continuity. This is particularly a possibility when relying on natural light that changes throughout the day or when the sun goes behind a cloud. If you're cutting back and forth between two actors and one actor's lines were shot in direct noonday sun and the other at blue dusk, the two won't seem

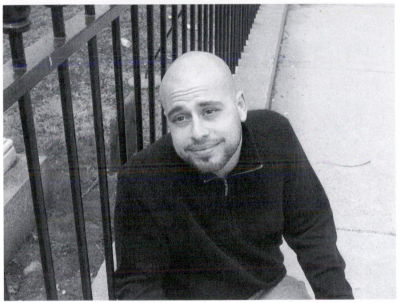

Figure 8.5 To maintain continuity, match the eyeline of your subjects. If one shot shows a woman looking down, seemingly toward a man in the scene, then the shot of the man should show him looking up at her.

to be speaking to each other in the same time and location when edited together. This is a disruption of continuity or a jump cut.

Likewise, sound quantity, quality, presence, and direction should be consistent. If the same two actors just discussed are speaking to each other and one's lines were recorded with a different type of microphone or a different distance from the mike (even though the shots are the same size), or a train was passing in the distance in one shot but not in the other, continuity is broken. Even just the change in the direction to which the mike is pointed—first toward the interior of the house, then out a window—can substantially change the sound of the background. Though some of this can be compensated for during audio mixing, not even close to everything can be "fixed in post."

Screen Direction

Continuity of screen direction is often called "adhering to the 180-degree rule." For example, we see a close-up of a woman looking toward the right side of the screen. Then we see a close-up of a man, looking screen left. Assuming the backgrounds look similar and other rules of continuity are followed, we accept that they are in the same location looking at each other, even if we have not seen them together in the same shot (Figure 8.6). Now imagine the same scenario, with the exception of the direction in which the woman is facing. Both actors are looking screen left. They no longer appear to be looking at each other (Figure 8.7).

Figure 8.6   One shot with the first subject looking screen right is followed by a shot of a second subject looking screen left. It appears as though the two are looking at each other, as long as other rules of continuity are followed.

Figure 8.7   If two shots are edited together so that the subjects are facing the same direction, they do not appear to be looking at each other. This will happen if you cross the 180° line.

Here is another example. We see a car driving up a hill, moving from the left side of the screen to the right. We see a second shot of that car on a country road, still moving left to right. We get a sense that a journey is under way. Now cut to a suburban street, where the car is now moving right to left. Our sense of journey is interrupted. We get a sense that perhaps the car has turned around and headed back to where it started (Figure 8.8).

The way to maintain continuity of screen direction as you go from shot to shot is to control the placement of camera positions. You want to position the camera wherever you need to be to cover your subject best, but continuity of screen direction dictates that you cannot move the camera without giving thought to what that new position will mean to the viewer's sense of spatial orientation. An imagined line or axis, which helps maintain continuity, connects the two subjects in the first example or defines the path of movement in the second. Once that axis, called the **180-degree line**, is established and a first camera position is chosen, subsequent camera positions must remain on the same side of the line in order to maintain continuity of screen direction. In Figure 8.9, the shot from camera position #1 would result in the woman facing screen right. Camera position #2, from the same side of the line, would give a **reverse angle** shot of the second woman facing screen left. As you cut between the two angles, the two would appear to be facing each other (see Figure 8.6). In Figure 8.10, camera position #2 crosses the 180-degree line. This will cause both subjects to face left (see Figure 8.7). The two would not appear to be looking at each other, creating disorientation for the viewer. Figure 8.11 shows approximate camera positions for the traveling car in Figure 8.8.

Figure 8.8 Continuity of screen direction helps the audience perceive the car as continuing its journey. Reversing the screen direction makes it seem that the car has turned around.

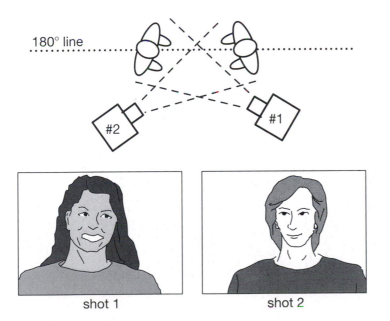

180° line

#2   #1

shot 1   shot 2

Figure 8.9 A 180-degree line is created by the gaze of the subjects. Staying on one side of the line or the other maintains consistent continuity of screen direction.

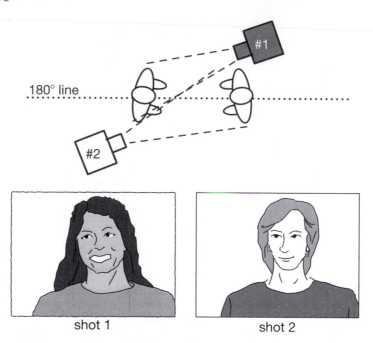

Figure 8.10 If the second camera position is on the opposite side of the 180-degree line, continuity is broken.

shot 1

shot 2

Figure 8.11 The 180-degree line here is created by the movement of the car. Camera position #1 establishes a left-to-right screen direction. Camera position #2 maintains continuity of screen direction. Camera position #3, however, crosses the 180-degree line and therefore reverses screen direction, making the car move right to left across the screen.

Does establishing a particular spatial orientation for the viewer mean that you can never change it? No, of course not—that would mean that once you shot from one side of the room, you could never shoot from the other or once you showed the car moving left to right, you could never show it moving right to left. What's important is that you realize that by establishing a camera position on one side of the

180-degree line, crossing it requires either reorienting the viewer's sense of space or risking disorientation in the viewer. Sometimes disorientation is what you want. For example, a lost child runs right to left down one city street, left to right down the next, toward the camera then away from the camera. We get a sense of the child's confusion. A chase scene where screen direction reverses itself gives a sense of chaos, danger, and loss of control.

However, if you want to cross the 180-degree line and maintain continuity, you must somehow reorient the viewer. This can be done is several ways. A tracking shot can move the camera position across the 180-degree line to the other side, gradually reorienting the audience's sense of their point of view relative to the subjects. You can shoot a wide shot from overhead, making it clear where the subjects are, relative to each other, or you can shoot directly down the line, then move to the other side, which moves the viewer in increments (Figure 8.12).

Figure 8.12 Shooting straight down the 180-degree line. It helps to reorient the viewer and make it appear as though the subject has not changed directions.

Maintaining Continuity in Production

In the production stage, visualization of the sequencing process drives decisions about what and how material is captured. If you know that your piece is going to be edited in a continuity style, then all the issues of continuity need to be carefully monitored. In narrative fiction productions, an assigned person often tracks issues of continuity, such as costumes, hairstyles, props, screen direction, lighting conditions, and background audio, with written notes, still photos, and videotape. Continuity gets tricky because narrative fiction is most often shot out of sequence with a single camera. Shooting schedules are based on efficiency, not the order in which shots will be in the final film or video. So shots that follow each other in the edited piece can be produced hours, days, or weeks apart. Interiors might be shot in Hollywood but exteriors in Istanbul. But if an actor walks out of an office wearing a jacket and carrying a briefcase and is seen in the next shot on the street outside the office building "jacketless" and with a backpack, the sense of seamless continuity has been broken.

When producing narrative fiction, the decisions about composition and shot sequencing have usually been made during preproduction, through the creation of storyboards. When shooting a nonscripted nonfiction piece or one that will be scripted later, those decisions are made in the field. A good cameraperson will be thinking in terms of the editing room and of how shots will fit together. She or he will shoot sequences of shots, sequences that we hope match the vision of the maker. If following the conventional pattern of WS-MS-CU-cutaway, the camera operator will make sure she or he captures those shots in such a way that they can be logically assembled later.

MONTAGE

Continuity style is only one approach to sequencing material, though a very pervasive and common one. However, some makers feel that the invisible, seamless editing of the continuity approach or the

Sergei Eisenstein (1898–1948) was born in Latvia and became a Bolshevik with the advent of the Soviet Revolution in 1917. For the rest of his life, he promoted the ideals of the Revolution through his films. He made only seven films, including his first feature, *Strike,* in 1924, *Battleship Potemkin* in 1926, and the first two parts of his unfinished trilogy, *Ivan the Terrible,* in 1945 and posthumously in 1958. In his writings, Eisenstein supported the idea of creating meaning through juxtaposition, freely manipulating time and space. In his films, he applied that theory. He published collections of his theoretical essays, *Film Sense* (1942, U.S. publication) and *Film Form* (1949). Eisenstein is the best known of the Russian school of filmmakers, which also included Vsevolod Pudovkin.

unbroken time relationship of the long take misses the essence of media. The recording and assembly of sound and image allow freedom of movement through time and space, defiance of chronology, and the creation of meaning through juxtaposition. This describes the approach to sequencing called **montage**. Montage is an important term that is used in many ways. To some, it implies any fast-paced assembly of sound and image. In French, it is the translation of "editing" in general. To Sergei Eisenstein and other followers of the Russian school of film theory in the early 20th century, it meant the essence of film art (Go to the Source—Sergei Eisenstein). Meaning was not created within a shot but as a result of the viewer contrasting and comparing the content of adjacent shots or the relationship between the sound and the picture.

Whereas the continuity style creates logical, chronological storytelling, montage elicits an emotional response from the viewer. Overall meaning is a result of a **gestalt** process in which meanings logically might not seem connected but make a connection in the viewer's mind on a subconscious level. (Gestalt theory is discussed in Chapter 2.) For example, you're trying to create a sense of loneliness or isolation in the mind of the viewer. A montage approach would create that sense by having a shot of an elderly woman rocking in a rocking chair followed by a shot of a young man standing still on a busy city sidewalk, while many people hurry by, not seeming to notice him. This is followed by a shot of nearly bare tree branches with just a single dry leaf left hanging on a branch. The shots have no relationship in terms of time, place, or logical narrative flow. Shown together, though, they have the potential to elicit an emotional reaction in the viewer. Unlike continuity editing in which the viewer is asked to accept certain conventions to help make logical, linear sense out of a series of shots, the montage approach requires a different kind of mental activity on the part of the viewer. With continuity, the viewer uses logic to understand the story—"First, I see a shot of the woman looking off screen. Then I see a shot of the car driving away. She must be watching the car." With montage, the viewer is asked to respond viscerally to the material—to feel first and think later about the meaning or story of the piece.

It's important to realize with montage that it is the sum of the shots—the association made in response to the juxtaposition—that creates the meaning, not the individual shots themselves, and the sum is greater than the parts. In the earlier example, if the same shot of the old woman was followed by one of apple pie coming out of the oven and gingham curtains blowing in the sunshine, a sense of fond nostalgia might be the result.

VERBALLY DRIVEN STRUCTURE

Another approach to linear structuring is less recognized by textbooks, but it is common to viewers. Sometimes called a *compilation* approach, the term **verbally driven structure** is more descriptive. This describes media pieces that deliver information, make an argument, or tell a story through the words of a narrator, the voices of interview subjects, or a combination of the two. The approach of this type of piece is logical, not visceral, but few attempts are made to maintain continuity of time and place. Images jump through time and space as they illustrate the words of the narrator. A narrator speaks of advancements in medical technology while access to quality medical care for many people in the world decreases. We see images of gleaming, high-tech laboratories, operating rooms with bustling medical personnel, a healthy looking man walking on the beach (described as the recipient of a transplant), a line of young children in school uniforms waiting to receive inoculations, a young mother holding a listless infant, barely dressed children playing near stagnant water, and an emaciated old man, lying in bed and staring into the camera. If viewed without the accompanying audio, these pictures might be perceived as being related in some way, but the relationship would be difficult to discern. They might even appear to be a visual montage, eliciting a sense of the world's inequities. Clearly, though, there is no sense of continuous time or place as we jump from current time to the past, from one side of the globe to another. The intended message becomes clear only when we hear the sound track. The voice of the narrator fills in facts and provides context. The narration connects one image to the next, resulting in a sense of cohesion. A thesis is logically presented and defended.

The same type of structure can be made out of interview material. Pieces of interview, or **sound bites**, are structured to tell the story and present the information. There may or may not be sections of narration that introduce the topic, add information, or create smooth transitions. There may be visuals that illustrate or complement the verbal soundtrack, or we may be looking at the subject or narrator who is speaking. This visual material that supports the dominant interview footage is called **b-roll** footage. This term derives from the process of cutting film, which we will discuss in the next chapter.

If the piece makes more sense as you are hearing it but not seeing it (rather than the other way around), that is a good indicator of verbal -driven structure.

BREAKING THE RULES

"Rules are made to be broken." "You've got to know the rules to break the rules." Like many clichés, these hold some truth. Many of the conventions of the media, particularly of structuring material, are just that, conventions. They may be based on observations of human perception, but that certainly doesn't mean that it's the only way to do things. Following the rules usually means that your technique will not be in the forefront, your work will be in a form that is familiar to most people, and therefore it will be largely invisible. This can be a good thing. Invisible form means that the content dominates. The audience focuses on the story or information or emotion evoked.

Sometimes, though, you want to use the form to enhance the content. By using the medium in unconventional ways, you can create a sense of discomfort that may reinforce your content or provoke your audience to think about familiar content from a new perspective.

APPLICATIONS OF STRUCTURE

Let's take a look now at continuity across the media. Continuity style editing is most often associated with the medium of film and the genre of fiction narrative. As previously mentioned, however, continuity style appears in other media and genres as well.

MULTICAMERA VIDEO

In multicamera television, such as news, talk, and game shows, continuity is readily apparent. It is not talked about much because some aspects of continuity are inherent. The director calls for the live transition from one camera to another. Imagine a cooking show where the chef is covered by a centered camera, framing a medium long shot, a close-up camera of the chef, and an overhead camera for close-ups of the food preparation. As the chef explains how to filet a fish, the director calls for a close-up of the knife and cutting board. When the chef turns to the camera and asks, "Now isn't that easy?" the director calls for the close-up camera. You don't need to worry about continuity of action, props, or makeup because the change of shot is happening in real time. You do need to worry about shot sequencing and continuity of screen direction. If two cameras are positioned on opposite sides of the 180-degree line, you will have the same problem as if shooting with a single camera (Figure 8.13). Also, continuity of light and color can be disrupted in a multicamera shoot if the cameras are not adjusted to match each other.

Many multicamera sitcoms are shot on film, so they cannot be edited live. Because film requires processing, it has to be structured in post-production. In this case, several cameras film from different angles, then the shots from the best angle at any given time are edited together. As long as the match point is found and continuity of screen direction adhered to, continuity should be maintained.

Multicamera programs shot on video, especially drama or comedy shows (as opposed to news, talk, or game shows), will often record the output of the individual cameras while simultaneously doing live

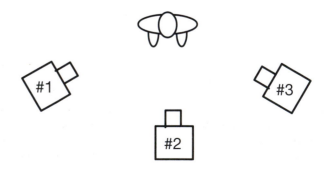

Figure 8.13 Cameras in a multicamera shoot rarely cross the 180-degree line because of the possibility of cameras appearing in each other's shots. Here is a typical three-camera setup.

editing. This allows them the efficiency of editing live and also the safety of having the whole show recorded from each camera's point of view. If there is an error in the live editing, it can be fixed in post-production.

OBSERVATIONAL DOCUMENTARIES

Single-camera documentaries also use continuity editing. However, the approach is a bit different. Unlike shooting with actors in which scenes are broken down into shots that can be done several times, documentary filming does not allow that kind of control over the situation. Yet generally a documentary maker wants to avoid jump cuts and awkward camera movements as the camera operator moves from one position to another and then reframes and refocuses. If you are shooting footage of prison guards overseeing a work detail, you can't ask them to stop in the middle of what they're doing and repeat it so you can reset at a different camera angle and overlap the action. It might be possible to shoot the footage so you can "fake" a matched cut by cutting to a repeated action (like a prisoner digging a hole). The downward motion of one digging action from in front of the prisoner can be matched to the downward movement of the same prisoner still digging a minute later from the side. This would not be indicative of real time, but it would maintain a smooth visual continuity of motion. Another approach would be to cut from the prisoner digging to a shot of the guard watching to another shot of a different prisoner resting on his shovel, back to the first prisoner, still digging from a different angle. Such a transition to another related subject or object that seems to be a logical part of the story is called a **cutaway**. You may or may not have maintained accurate continuity of time, but you have built a continuity sequence that smoothly transitions from one camera angle to another. You could have also just shot the whole action as a long take, using camera movement to move the viewer's point of view from the front of the prisoner to the side. While this last option may seem the most "real" because it does maintain a real time relationship between the activity and its representation on screen, all are techniques commonly used in nonfiction films and videos to maintain continuity.

Some makers prefer to reject conventional rules of continuity in nonfiction shooting, feeling that including the jump cuts and evidence of reframing shots adds an aesthetic of reality and immediacy to their work. The rejection of continuity then becomes a style in itself. In the past several years, evidence of this approach to nonfiction shooting has been embraced by some fictional programming, such as the prime-time drama series *NYPD Blue*, created by Steven Boccho and David Milch for ABC in 1993, and *Homicide*, created by Barry Levinson for NBC the same year. Although not a necessity when shooting fiction, which allows for multiple takes and smooth transitions, the aesthetic approach that uses jump cuts and handheld cameras has been used by fiction narrative makers to lend the reality and immediacy associated with documentaries to the fiction genre. We've seen it in Hollywood films, TV programs, music videos, and commercials.

A lot of skill is required in order for this "faux" documentary approach to work effectively. Although it may at first appear to have an amateur quality to it, it is a style that has evolved from a true response to uncontrolled conditions to almost a "choreography" for the camera, including quick but expert reframings, swish pans, focus shifts, and subtle camera jitter. Ultimately, though, it is still has continuity—the story unfolds in a logical, linear way. Some of the rules get broken, for effect, along the way.

AUDIO CONTINUITY

We often speak of continuity in visual terms, but even in the visual media of film and video, adhering to the conventions of continuity includes a continuity of audio. If, when cutting from one shot within a scene to another, the sound of the background noise changes noticeably, continuity is broken. This also holds true if we are experiencing audio alone. A radio drama or audio documentary requires continuity in the same way as film or video. Level, presence, signal-to-noise ratio, foreground/background relationships, and the use of sound effects must remain consistent to the sense of audiospace that the listener has established in his or her mind. It's even more important than when the visual is there.

USES OF MONTAGE

Montage has been a tool of media artists since artists first adopted film, audio, and later video as media of expression, akin to painting, performance, or the written word. Montage suggests rather than tells. It works within our subconscious minds and in the realm of emotions. It is evocative, rather than overt. All of these qualities make it an appropriate approach for complex, layered messages communicated by many media artists. Montage allows a range of interpretations. The audience filters the sound and image through their own experiences and biases. This is always the case, but the more ambiguous the delivery of the message, the more the viewer has to rely on his or her own interpretive powers. Such inexact communication might not be appropriate for a linear plot that relies on cause and effect or an instructional video, but it might be ideal for portraying a sense of disillusionment or the emotion of anger.

I made an experimental video in which I was trying to tell a story about the Soviet dictator Joseph Stalin. I wanted to ask how could such evil come from someone who started out as a newborn baby, loved by his mother? I wanted to ask, How could his daughter love a man who perpetrated such horror? I also wanted to comment on the subjectivity of history. Images I chose included close-ups of infants, tree roots in the snow, an antique wash basin filled with bloody water, a statue of a cherub, and archival film footage of early 20th-century Russia. The images are paired with two performed monologues that reflect on these questions. Did I succeed in communicating the message I intended? That is for the viewer to say. Will every viewer come away with the same meaning I started with? I'm sure they won't, nor would I want that. In this kind of work, ambiguity is positive (Figure 8.14).

Figure 8.14 Stills from the experimental video *The Day Stalin's Mother Brought Him Home from the Hospital*, produced by the author (1993).

MONTAGE WITHIN NARRATIVE AND DOCUMENTARY

Another more conventional use of montage can be seen within many fiction and nonfiction pieces. One convention of fiction narrative films and television programs is a visual montage with music that suggests a passage of time and progression of events that can be easily understood by the viewer. Images of a couple frolicking in the park, sharing a romantic dinner, taking a horse-drawn buggy ride, and talking long into the night suggest, without any dialog, a deepening romantic relationship. While adhering to the chronology of the film, the rest of which is shot in continuity style, the images are not smoothly connected by cause and effect, such as in continuity. There is more latitude in jumping through time and space, and the viewer is left to infer the meaning of the events.

Montage can also be used within a documentary as a means of introducing or summarizing the topic. A film or video documentary on skiing might begin with several quick shots of different skiers in different locations, cut together to music to give a sense of the action and excitement that skiing offers before settling into a more informational presentation of the sport. Presented as a "tease," the montage gets the audience members' attention and gives them a reason to keep watching.

An audio drama or documentary could use a montage of environmental sounds, such as traffic noise, sirens, construction sounds, and a street vendor hawking his wares, as a means of setting the location of the story.

Depending on how broadly you wish to define montage, its application ranges from common to ubiquitous. Some might claim that the entire broadcast television schedule is a montage of sound and image with the underlying message of capitalist consumption. Others would reject that claim but certainly acknowledge the use of montage in advertising to suggest associations that induce the viewer or listener to buy the sponsor's product. Montages of suggestive and evocative images with the soundtrack of a popular song are the mainstay of cable networks like MTV. What began as an expressive tool of the media artist has become mainstream. This is a common occurrence.

VERBALLY DRIVEN STRUCTURE: A STAPLE OF DOCUMENTARY

Narration in an audio program can stand on its own or be supported by sound effects, background sound, or music. In film or video, the narration is usually accompanied by the image of the speaker or an image that illustrates or complements the content of the narration.

Narration can take many forms. It can be delivered by an on-screen host or interview subject, or it can be delivered by an unseen voiceover narrator. The narration can be delivered in the third person ("Skiing is a sport enjoyed by millions") or in the first ("Sometimes I feel like I was born on skis"). First-person narration can be the voice of the maker, an interview subject, or even the voice of a fictional or re-created character that is performed by an actor.

Commonly, the narration can be performed by a combination of off- and on-screen narrators. A third-person voiceover narration explains the impact of rock 'n' roll music on American culture while we look at images of rock bands and fans from the 1950s and 1960s and excerpts from music videos. We then cut to an on-screen interview with a music historian who discusses the origins of rock music. While the critic is still speaking, we cut to an image of blues musicians. Then we cut back again to the voiceover narrator with images of early rock 'n' roll bands. Ultimately, the voices of many make up the narration, and the images provide us with a rich sense of the subject matter. The structure of the narration—voiceover and sound bites—is constructed by the maker and tells the story of the piece. The images are an important component, but the piece is driven by the words of the narration.

Certainly, a fiction piece could use a verbally driven structure. A third-person or first-person narrator could tell the story. There are many examples of independently produced films and videos, usually shorts, that use this technique. Many feature-length fiction films use narration to set the scene, create a transition, or describe a flashback. In these cases, the narration becomes a component of the film, but the overall structure remains rooted in the continuity style.

CONCLUSION

All of the approaches to linear structuring discussed in this chapter are used in all possible combinations—fiction feature films use montage sequences and voiceover narration, documentaries use matched action continuity, and radio dramas use sound montage. In most cases, you can identify the approach that dominates and provides the underlying structure to the piece. This is the structure the maker has chosen for telling the story.

PUTTING IT INTO PRACTICE
OBSERVING

As you consume your normal media diet of movies, TV, and radio, be aware of how pieces are structured. Watch and listen for examples of continuity, montage, and verbally driven structure. Be aware of how often the approaches are combined, and determine which approach is the dominant structuring device.

WRITING AND DOING

1. Choose an activity that you do every day. Now imagine that there is a camera recording it. Break it down into at least 10 different shots and storyboard them. Be sure there is a reason to transition from one shot to another and make sure your cuts are motivated—movement of the subject, close-ups for emphasis, or new information presented.
2. Choose a location. Really listen to it. Identify eight distinct sounds that could be recorded and built into a sound montage that would communicate a sense of that place. List them in your journal.

3. Choose an emotion. List and storyboard 10 different visual images that would be likely to communicate the emotion you have chosen to others.

KEY CONCEPTS

180-degree line	jump cut
B-roll	matched cut
continuity	montage
cutaway	motivated edit
deductive reasoning	reverse angle
gestalt	sound bite
inductive reasoning	verbally driven structure

CHAPTER 9

The Practice of Linear Structure

Now that you understand the theory behind the decisions you make about linear media structure, it's time to look at the techniques of editing used in media production. There are many editing methods. Some are medium specific; some are older techniques that are being replaced by new ones. However, some basic concepts apply to all methods.

SOUND AND IMAGE TRANSITIONS

One definition of editing might be the structuring of various pieces of media. If so, then it is important to look at the different ways in which these pieces can be joined—the **transitions**. The concepts are similar whether you're talking about sound or image, but the terminology differs.

The most common transition is an instantaneous and complete transition from one source to another. Visually, this is called a **cut**. For sound, it's called a **segue**. A segue is a rapid drop of the level of one source (**fade** out) and a fade in of the next. You can do a cut in audio, but it's often an unpleasant transition that is too abrupt for our ears. A visual cut and a sound segue call the least attention to themselves and keep the pace of the program moving along.

A second transition is one in which one source gradually disappears or becomes softer while another appears or becomes louder. Visually this is a **dissolve**; in sound, it is a **crossfade**. A dissolve or crossfade can soften an abrupt change or signal a change in time or place. It can be very quick, almost imperceptible from a cut, or slow and very noticeable. If you stop a dissolve in progress, you have ghosted images of two different sources, both filling the whole screen. This is called a **superimposition** (Figure 9.1). If you stop a crossfade, you're listening to a mix of two audio sources.

A *fade in* is a dissolve from black (or other solid color) to picture. The same term is used for audio as the volume increases from silence. A *fade out* gradually takes us to black or silence. Fades are used generally at the beginning and end of programs or to signal a major change in topic, time, or place.

Figure 9.1 A superimposition is a partially completed dissolve.

A less common type of visual transition is called a **wipe**. Like a dissolve, it is a gradual replacement of one visual source by another. But whereas a dissolve is a full-screen change in opacity, a wipe starts in one part of the screen and moves across the screen in a pattern. The movement can be vertical, horizontal, diagonal, or start as a shape (e.g., box or circle) and expand. A partially completed wipe is a **split screen** and can be used to obtain a particular effect, such as dividing the screen into two sections, each showing a different location (Figure 9.2). The cliché split-screen shot uses the divided screen to show both ends of a telephone conversation.

Figure 9.2 A split screen is a partially completed wipe.

LIVE EDITING

We tend to think of editing as a function of postproduction that is done after material is gathered to prepare it for distribution. If we expand the concept of editing to mean structuring, we can see that editing decisions, such as what material to use, and the duration and order of that material, can be made at different points in the production process.

A long take, as discussed in Chapter 3, requires no editing. The decisions about structuring are made as the production occurs, through blocking, subject movement, and camera movement. However, we know that media pieces that are solely a long take are rare. Other common types of production, however, do use live or instantaneous editing and require structuring during production.

Many audio productions, especially music performances, are produced by **live mixing**, and much of what we see on television is produced by **live switching**. As in postproduction, these structural approaches take the available options and make decisions about which sources will appear in what order and for what duration. The difference is that the decisions are made instantly and, if the program is being broadcast live, without a chance to change your mind or correct mistakes. Film, given its very nature and its need to be processed, cannot be edited live. The instantaneous electronic signal created by recording audio and video, however, makes live editing possible.

To understand live mixing or switching, the concept of signal flow must be understood. **Signal flow** refers simply to what information is going where, or the sequence and direction of the signals.

When mixing audio live, you have several audio sources—primarily microphones and perhaps some line sources—feeding into a mixing board. Those sources become the possible choices to listen to or combine at any given moment. The mixing board allows you to control the volume, equalization, perspective, and other audio qualities of one or more sources (Figure 9.3). Live sound mixing can be done for a live broadcast, such as a simulcast concert, or recorded live-on-tape, in which the **output** is recorded without stopping, as if it were live, and played back later. What remains common to these approaches is

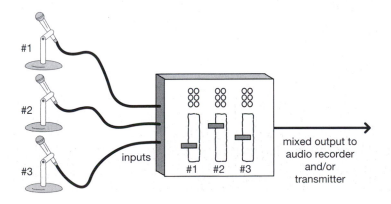

Figure 9.3 Any number of inputs can be fed into the mixer, up to the number of available channels. Mixers allow control of volume, equalization, noise reduction, and special effects. The combination of all the inputs is mixed to create the output signal. It is possible to split that output signal and send it to several locations simultaneously.

the ability to choose and combine sources and control the qualities in real time while the sound is being created. It allows musicians to play together, without interruption, with the energy inherent to a live performance. It also allows the broadcast of a live panel discussion, balancing the **inputs** of several participants and questions from the audience in a seamless auditory experience. Recording the different sources separately and editing them in postproduction into the final product could produce both of these audio works. The advantages and disadvantages of these approaches will be discussed in Chapter 11.

Video, too, can be "mixed" live with the use of a video switcher. A switcher allows inputs from multiple video sources, such as cameras, a character generator (which produces text for use on screen), a solid black signal (TV black), color bars, or a satellite feed for a news show. Like the audio mixing board, the switcher allows the technical director (TD) to choose which signal (or signals) will be seen at any given time. Each source is available by pressing one of a row of buttons (called a **bus**). A switcher often has several buses. The program bus determines what source is to be output. A preview bus sends the signal to a preview monitor so the director can see upcoming shots or effects. Cuts can be accomplished by pushing a button on the program bus. A fader bar between the program and preview bus creates dissolves and gradually transitions from one source to another and flip-flops the sources when the dissolve is completed (Figure 9.4).

Another button on the program bus combines the signals from another set of buses. A pair of buses is called an **effects bank** (Figure 9.5). A fader bar, which is positioned between the two buses of the effects bank, pulls the signal from both and combines it. This allows the switcher to do transitions, such as dissolves and wipes, and special effects, such as *keys*.

A key electronically cuts a hole in one image and replaces it with another. Some keys work on the basis of brightness or luminance.

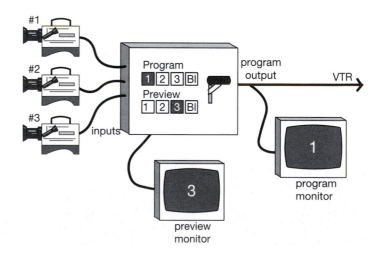

Figure 9.4 Sources that are input to the switcher correspond to buttons on the buses. The source selected on the program bus can be viewed on the program monitor and is output to the videotape recorder (VTR) or transmitter. The source selected on the preview bus is only seen on the preview monitor. A fader bar can dissolve between the program source and the source being previewed.

Figure 9.5 Effects banks make possible a cascade of effects. An effect can be created using two sources on one bank; then that combined signal can flow into another bus. Effects can be set up in advance and placed on air by selecting the button on the program bus that is receiving the output of the effects bank. In this illustration, a split screen between cameras 1 and 3 is created, using effects bus A and effects bus B. When the TD is ready to put the split screen on the air, the effects bank button is chosen on the program bus. When the "effects bank" button is activated, the output of the effects bank is put on the air.

A **luminance key** (also called an *internal key*) cuts out any part of an image that falls below a certain brightness level and fills it with another picture. This works best with high-contrast images and is often used to key another image behind text (Figure 9.6).

Some keys work on the basis of color or chroma. **Chromakeys** drop out all parts of an image of a certain color (usually blue or green) and replace the parts with another image. A chromakey is commonly used to display a weather map behind a meteorologist. The weathercaster is actual standing in the studio in front of a green screen. The operator (also called the switcher or TD) keys a map or graphic behind the weathercaster. The switcher sits in the control room with the director and other crew members, usually separated from the studio floor where the production is taking place. The TD executes the director's choice of which source is output to the transmitter or VTR. This approach allows live or live-on-tape programming with considerable shot variety. The visual output of the switcher and the audio output of a mixing board are both fed to a transmitter or VTR for live broadcast or replay without postproduction. The output of the audio mixing board is the combination of live mike sources and prerecorded line sources, such as music, narration, sound effects, or the audio track from a videotape. Much television programming is done this way because of immediacy and cost efficiency. News programs, talk shows, game shows, sports, and concerts are almost always produced live or live-on-tape. Soap operas and some situation comedies are structured through a combination of live switching and postproduction editing. Using a green screen in a studio is becoming a common practice for combining live action with animation or using motion capture to create computer animation, as discussed in Chapter 3.

Figure 9.6 The luminance key works on the basis of contrast. The dark areas of the first image are replaced by the second.

POSTPRODUCTION EDITING

Structuring a piece of linear media after production has taken place allows maximum control and flexibility. Different options can be tried and the best one chosen. It is important, though, not to rush from production into the editing room.

PREPARATION IS KEY

A plan for how material is going to be edited should be made before you even approach a piece of editing equipment. You can start editing without a plan, but your editing process will take much longer than if you do have a plan, which means missed deadlines and higher budgets. The exact process of planning may differ in some ways, depending on the type of project and personal preference, but its purpose remains consistent.

The materials to be edited should be organized and easy to locate. Whether it's an audio recording, videotape, or film, *logging* is the process of writing down the content and order of the material on a tape or reel. Material needs to be identified either by shot and take numbers that can be cross-referenced with a script or by brief descriptions of the content—sound, image, or both. Figure 9.7 shows an example of a video footage **log**. It's also common to make notes as to whether or not it was a good take, if there was a technical or performance problem, and any other information that will help you remember your material.

If you have spoken words that were not prescribed—for instance, interviews conducted for a documentary—word-for-word **transcriptions** are very helpful. These can be used to identify which pieces of interview (or sound bites) you may want to use. Transcriptions can be done on logging sheets, but it's more efficient to type them out full page (Figure 9.8).

Logs and transcriptions include a numerical indication of the exact location of each shot or section of material so it can be readily found and you know the length of each take or segment. The type of numerical indicator varies by medium and type of machine on which the material is

Figure 9.7 Logs come in various formats; this is a video footage log. They can be done by hand, or you can use the logging software that is part of your editing system. The information included can vary but generally will include in- and out-points and descriptions or shot and take numbers. Columns for comments and shot duration are also common.

Footage Log

Tape #	Shot #	Take #	In Point	Out Point	Duration	Comments
001	12	1	00:01:12:17	00:01:18:03	5:16	bad audio
001	12	2	00:01:28:17	00:01:34:25	6:08	good beginning
001	12	3	00:01:45:03	00:01:51:19	6:16	OK
001	7	1	00:02:02:23	00:02:23:06	20:13	rough pan
001	7	2	00:02:33:01	00:02:54:10	21:09	good

Tape 3
Interview with Maura Kierney

03:01:00
Interviewer: Would you tell me a little about yourself?

Maura: I'm Maura Kierney. I'm nineteen and a ranked amateur boxer. I train six days a week and when I'm not training, I hang out with my friends...my boyfriend. I'm really into music. I like rock-climbing, but boxing is my passion.

03:01:11
Interviewer: How do people react when they first find out that you box?

Maura: The reaction's not always the same, of course, but generally, they seem pretty surprised. I'm strong, but not muscle-bound. I guess I'm not what they expect as a female fighter. What does a female boxer look like anyway? Mean?...Tough as nails?...When I dress up I look pretty hot, I think. In the ring, it's different, though. I am tough and I want to win. I usually do win too.

Figure 9.8 Transcriptions are logs of material that have a lot of verbal content and little visual change. Transcriptions are commonly done for interviews.

being played back. The numerical indicator can be a **counter** or **running time** indicator (on a playback machine), an **edge number** (on film), or **timecode** (on videotape). Counters are used by film editing machines, audiotape recorders, and older, consumer-quality videotape recorders. They measure the mechanical workings of the machine playing back tape or film, such as the revolutions of the take-up reel. They give you no indication of actual time and are not necessarily consistent from machine to machine. However, if you always start at the beginning of the tape or reel and zero the counter, you can achieve a fairly accurate location. Running time, indicated on some professional audio and video tape recorders, measures the recorded material on the tape and displays the amount of time it takes to play back the tape. Although more accurate and helpful than counters, running time indicators only work if you rewind the tape completely and zero the counter every time you put the tape in.

A more accurate type of logging can be done if you assign a unique number to every frame of film or video. On film, *edge numbers* give information about the roll of film and indicate frame location. They are actually printed on the edge of the film so that they become visible when the film is processed. On still photography film, the frames are counted numerically up to the number of exposures on the roll. For motion picture film, frame numbers are printed

Figure 9.9 Edge numbers on still photography film are used to label each frame. This figure shows motion picture film, which has edge numbers at regular intervals.

in regular intervals; the exact interval varies according to the format of the film. In still photography, they are used to find the frame to be printed. In motion pictures, they are used to indicate where the film should be cut (Figure 9.9).

On videotape, *timecode* is an electronic signal, recorded as part of the video signal (or added to it later on) that assigns each frame a discrete number, listing frame number (30 to a second with NTSC, 25 with PAL), second, minute, and hour (Figure 9.10). A VTR with a timecode reader can find the exact frame you want every time. This becomes very important in certain editing processes, as we will see later. Some audio recorders can also record and playback timecode so that audio recorded with that machine could be synchronized to a video signal.

The next part of the planning process is making the decisions of what material to use and in what order. This is the process of creating an **edit plan**. Creating an edit plan or paper edit is crucial to accomplish time- and cost-efficient editing. It can be difficult to convince inexperienced media makers of the necessity of an edit plan, but experience proves it over and over again. Even if the plan changes during the editing process (and it almost invariably will), an organized plan of approach moves things along. It is also invaluable if you are working collaboratively, helping to make sure that the whole production team is seeing things in the same way and allowing more than one person to work on the editing.

The actual format of the edit plan can vary dramatically. All edit plans must include clear indications of the shots or pieces of media to be used, an indication of the order in which the material is sequenced, and numerical indications of where the footage can be found, ideally timecode or edge numbers. With a piece that has been pre-scripted, the edit plan process might just be a matter of choosing the best takes of each shot and marking them on your logging sheets. If the marked log clearly cross-references with the shooting script, it will work (Figure 9.11).

If a script has not yet been written, this is the time to do so. It only makes sense to postpone the scripting process when you don't know exactly what materials you are going to gather, such as in a documentary. If you are conducting interviews, you don't know what people are going to say until you ask them the questions. This does not excuse you from preproduction planning—quite the opposite. The planning is just different than that done for a pre-scripted piece. You still need to research your topic, identify the best interview subjects, write the questions, and sometimes pre-interview without recording to learn more about the subject

hr : min : sec : frame

| 01 : 17 : 34 : 29 |

+1 frame =

| 01 : 17 : 35 : 00 |

Figure 9.10 Timecode itself is an invisible electronic signal. The graphic representation of timecode is listed starting with the hour, then the minute, the second, and the frame. With 30 frames in an NTSC-second, the frame counter will go up to 29 then start over at 0, as the seconds increase by one. Seconds and minutes will count to 59, then zero out.

Footage Log as Edit Plan

Tape #	Shot #	Take #	In Point	Out Point	Duration	Comments
001	12	1	00:01:12:17	00:01:18:03	5:16	bad audio
001	12	2	00:01:28:17	00:01:34:25	6:08	good beginning
001	12	3	00:01:45:03	00:01:51:19	6:16	OK
001	7	1	00:02:02:23	00:02:23:06	20:13	rough pan
001	7	2	00:02:33:01	00:02:54:10	21:09	good

and form a relationship in which the subject feels trust. Often you go into shooting such a piece with an outline of the finished structure; sometimes that structure becomes clear during or after the production process. In a piece that is not pre-scripted, this stage between logging and transcribing the footage and editing is often the most challenging part of the process. This is where the story is written.

If your script is going to function as an edit plan, it must include the timecode or frame numbers for the material included (Figure 9.12).

Figure 9.11   If a production was pre-scripted, your edit plan might be your marked-up logs, indicating which takes of the numbered shots will be used.

LINEAR AND NONLINEAR DISTINCTIONS

An important distinction needs to be made between whether a piece of media is linear or nonlinear in its presentation and whether the method used to structure it is linear or nonlinear. In Chapter 7, we discussed the linear nature of movies, radio, and television. They have a discrete running time and a defined beginning, middle, and end. Nonlinear media, such as websites, video games, and interactive programming, jump through time and can be experienced in many different sequences and time frames. Linear media can be produced through both linear and nonlinear editing methods, however. In fact, at this point virtually all films and television programs and edited audio programs—although they may be linear presentations—are now postproduced using nonlinear technology.

The overused, but still helpful, analogy to explain the difference between a linear and a nonlinear process is the difference between using a typewriter and doing word processing on a computer. As you word process, you can easily insert characters or words or delete them. The software compensates for the additions or deletions by automatically moving the rest of the text to make room for added text or to delete the space created by removing text. The overall length of the piece is easily and cleanly adjusted as changes are made. Typing on a typewriter is quite different. Once you type something, it's not easy to make changes. You can use correction fluid to cover an error, but the

VIDEO	AUDIO
CU BOXING GLOVES HITTING A BAG (02:14:22)	NAT SOUND WITH RADIO MUSIC IN BACKGROUND
CU FEET JUMPING ROPE (02:17:17)	VO (03:01:18)
CU BODIES SPARRING (01:44:03) SLOW ZOOM OUT TO REVEAL TWO WOMEN BOXING	MAURA: What does a female boxer look like anyway? Mean...tough as nails...when I dress up I look pretty hot, I think. In the ring, it's different. I am tough and I want to win. I usually do win, too.
MCU MAURA (03:02:19)	SOT MAURA: I started boxing when I was twelve. My brother, Eddie, used to box and I'd tag along to the gym. For the guys mostly.
SPARRING INTENSIFIES (01:51:11) MAURA LANDS A HARD PUNCH (01:53:24) TITLE OVER BLACK	NAT SOUND MUSIC FADES IN

Figure 9.12 A script with timecode notations of where the material can be found can function as an edit plan.

white space still remains. It can be filled with something else but not taken away. Similarly, more space cannot be added or inserted.

Another important distinction needs to be made between analog/digital and linear/nonlinear. We tend to lump the concepts of digital and nonlinear together. Although most digital technologies have nonlinear capabilities, that categorization cannot be assumed. Some digital technologies are linear; some analog technologies are nonlinear. Digital video cameras process the video signal digitally, but the information is laid on videotape in a linear fashion. You have to play or fast forward through the beginning to get to the middle or end. You cannot insert or delete time into the tape. Analog film editing, as we will see, is a nonlinear process.

STAGES OF EDITING

Once preparation is complete and all possible planning has been done on paper, the actual editing process begins. It's important to stress again that the exact process varies tremendously depending on medium, budget, style or purpose of production, and personal preference. Unless the schedule is very tight and timeliness paramount (such as in broadcast news on radio and TV), there are usually two stages of editing. The terms vary, but the reasons don't. It has to do with time and money.

The part of editing that takes the most time is the creative part of deciding what should go where. It involves choosing which sound goes with which image, what shot transitions well into the next, and which edit point makes the most seamless continuity edit. Even if you've done your preparation—logged, transcribed, made an edit plan—many creative decisions remain to be made. The creative, time-consuming part of editing does not need to be done at the highest technical quality. For example, it can be done on a low-end video format, with a print of your film that has not been color corrected, and with digital media that is highly compressed and therefore of low image quality. All of those examples allow the first stage of editing to be done in a less expensive way. In some editing approaches, the first stage of editing also protects the original material from the damage that can occur during the postproduction process and maintains its pristine state for the final edited version. In film we talk about a **rough cut** and a **fine cut**. In video we talk about **off-line** and **on-line edits**. The distinctions are discussed in the following sections, but the similarity in reasoning holds.

ANALOG NONLINEAR EDITING

All analog editing methods, both nonlinear and linear (as described later), are disappearing. Some are still in use—in schools and by some professionals. For that reason, they are worth understanding, but even more importantly, the processes that have been done for many years are the conceptual models used for designing current digital nonlinear editing software. Understanding the older processes makes the current software more comprehensible.

The continuous wave of an audio or video signal recorded magnetically on tape and the chemical processing of silver halide particles on a roll of film are examples of analog signal processing. Editing in a way such that time can be easily manipulated through insertions and deletions of material (similar to the word processor, not the typewriter) characterizes a nonlinear process. Editing through physical manipulation of film stock or magnetic tape is analog but can be nonlinear. Actually, the technique of physically cutting the tape or film with a blade and reattaching the pieces in the order you want them may sound a bit primitive, but it works. Great radio programs and movies were (and occasionally still are) exquisitely edited in this way, and when you're struggling through a software manual or recreating work after a computer crash, you may wonder why we still don't do it this way.

Audio

For analog audio to be edited in a nonlinear way, it must be recorded on a reel-to-reel machine (not a cassette). Open-reel tape, however, can be edited in any of the ways included in this chapter. An open-reel recorder has a supply reel and a take-up reel with the tape traveling through a series of mechanisms including an erase head, a record head, and a playback head. The record head realigns the magnetic particles on the tape to be compatible with the recorder's input signal from a microphone, mixer, or another line audio source (Figure 9.13). Tape for

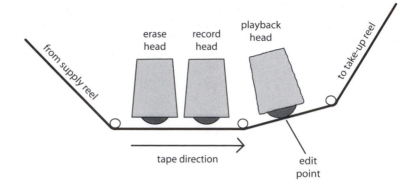

Figure 9.13 As the audiotape passes the playback head, it can be heard. That allows you to gauge where the tape should be cut.

this kind of recorder comes in 1/4-inch, 1/2-inch, 1-inch, and 2-inch widths. Wider tape allows for more tracks of audio.

Once the audio is recorded and logged, and the edit plan has determined the editing approach, the tape is slowly and carefully run over the playback head to determine the exact edit point, and a grease pencil is used to mark the cut points on the tape. Then, a one-edged razor blade or similar cutting device is used to slice the tape diagonally, using a guide so the angle of cutting is consistent from one edit to the next. A specially made adhesive tape attaches the segments of audiotape together in the proper order. The tape is applied to the base (shiny) side of the audiotape, not the dull magnetic side where the signal is recorded, and the pieces are joined without overlap. Changes can be made by removing the tape, trimming a segment or adding some in, and taping again. Time can be easily expanded or compressed. Careful marking, cutting, and taping will result in clean edits with no unwanted noise and the stability to be played many times without breaking.

Film

The process with film is similar but has a few more steps. Remember the mention of rough cuts and fine cuts on the previous page. Rough cuts are made from a print (with negative film) or a copy (with reversal film) of the film that went through the camera. In the case of negative film, it's necessary to make a print of the camera negative to see what you've shot. Sometimes a print is made quickly and rushed back to the filmmaker to be viewed the next day. This allows the filmmaker to ensure that the film is acceptable, both technically and in terms of content and performance. These prints are called *dailies*. The term for any rough print of a camera negative is a **workprint**. A workprint is normally made without any exposure or color corrections, so it is also called a *one-light workprint*. It's cheaper to make a one-light print, and the lower quality doesn't matter at the rough-cut stage. A workprint is used for editing. If the budget allows, a corrected or *timed workprint* can certainly be made, particularly if there is some question as to whether the film can ultimately be printed to look the way the filmmaker wants. In printing a timed workprint, each shot is analyzed then corrected for exposure and/or color balance.

If shooting reversal film, it's possible to edit the camera original, but there is obviously the danger of damaging film that cannot be replaced. Workprints can also be made from reversal film and are recommended because the editing process can cause scratches and broken sprocket holes in the film.

Next, if working with sound, the workprint needs to be synchronized with the recorded sound. This is called *synching your rushes*. Regardless of what format the audio was originally recorded on, it needs to be transferred or dubbed onto **mag stock**. This is a 16mm or 35mm audiotape with sprocket holes that match the film. The film and sound need to be synched for each shot or each time the camera starts and stops. The dailies or workprints need to be logged, so you know the edge code numbers for each shot.

The mag stock needs to be marked with the edge code. If you slated each shot as you should, you line up the visual frame where the slate first closes to the first frame of the mag stock in which you hear the sound. This works because of the synchronization of timing between your film camera and tape recorder provided by the crystals in each (see Chapter 6). You need to do this for each shot. After synching the rushes, each shot or *clip* (with or without accompanying sound) needs to be neatly filed. Clips are usually labeled and hung in clean bins on wheels that look like big laundry bins, with rows of hooks suspended above them. Many types of digital editing software use this organizational model and the terminology of **clips and bins**.

Creating the Rough Cut

Once the organizational work has taken place, assembly begins. You start with some white *leader* (solid white film stock) and a universal visual countdown, which synchs up with a beep on the mag stock (Figure 9.14). There are different approaches to editing a film. Some editors roughly string scenes together (forming an *assemblage*), then go back and fine-tune. Some editors work more precisely from the beginning. Strong organization is important so nothing gets lost.

Analog film editing can be done with a supply reel, a take-up reel, and a viewer, which is operated by hand. However, it is generally done on a motorized flatbed (see Figure 6.4 in Chapter 6) or upright film editor that allows the synchronized playback of picture and synchronized

Figure 9.14 Universal countdown leader is placed before the actual start of the film. At the frame of the leader that is marked as #2 in the countdown, a hole is punched. The frame of mag stock that corresponds to the #2 film frame is also marked. This lets you sync up the sound and image each time you play back the film.

sound. When the desired edit point is found, a splicer is used to cut the film on the frame line and the mag stock on an angle. Film splices can be either taped or cemented together, but at the rough-cut stage, tape is usually used. It's easier to do and easier to change without losing frames. The special tape is applied to the base (shiny) side of both film and mag stock. *Trims* (the pieces of film and mag stock not used) are labeled and filed in the bins, because you might decide later that you need them. The film and sound grow correspondingly on separate reels or *cores* (a small plastic center that the film and mag stock wrap around).

As with analog nonlinear audio editing, time can be manipulated by removing or adding frames and the corresponding mag. Shots can be moved by physically reattaching them to a different point in the film. Additional sound tracks are often added. Some might contain dialogue, sound effects, music, or narration, but they all need to be the same length. This is accomplished by placing *slugs* or solid *leader* where there is no sound on that track to maintain synch between sound and picture (Figure 9.15).

Once the rough cut has been completed and approved, it is time to create the fine cut. With its separate reels of picture and sound, the rough cut can only be viewed on an editing machine or with the use of a special double-system projector. The film is uncorrected; the sound is a straight transfer from the original sources, unmixed. The only transitions are straight cuts. The film is far from finished.

A/B-ROLL EDITING

For the final cut, the picture is dealt with first. The rough cut is used to determine how the camera original film (negative or reversal) will be cut. When working with 16 mm, if the film is going to have any visual transition other than a straight cut, including titles over picture, an A roll and a B roll of film need to be created. As previously explained, a dissolve, fade, and wipe contain two separate visual sources. In film, a dissolve or wipe is created as a double exposure of two negatives (or pieces of reversal) onto the positive film print. The negative is cut to match the rough cut, so the rough cut needs to be constructed in such a way as to allow the exposure of both pieces of negative. By separating the rough cut into two reels, they can overlap as needed

Figure 9.15 Different types of sound are generally assigned to separate audio tracks to keep the sound in sync; slugs need to be added where there is no sound on that track.

Figure 9.16 A and B rolls are created by alternating or checkerboarding the film shots. This allows the addition of extra footage to overlap the other shot and create a dissolve.

(Figure 9.16). More complex effects might require more reels (e.g., C, D). With A and B rolls, a checkerboard pattern is created, alternating shots throughout the film. Once A and B rolls are created out of the rough cut, the negative can be cut accordingly.

The negative must be handled very carefully because any dirt or scratches will end up on the final print. This process of cutting and splicing the negative is called **conforming** the negative. At this stage, cement splices are needed, a precise skill of scraping emulsion off one frame and overlapping it with another, using an adhesive to make a strong bond. Another advantage of A/B-roll editing is that a frame of the alternating black leader can be scraped and cemented, resulting in invisible edits.

SOUND MIX

The sound, too needs to be prepared before making a print. At this point you might have 2 tracks of mag stock, or you might have 50. *Cue sheets* describe how all the tracks should fit together (Figure 9.17). If there were several tracks, *premixing* would occur. Music tracks, sound effects, and various dialogue tracks can all be mixed down to a single track. Finally, a *rerecording mix,* which creates the final soundtrack, is created. This could be a simple mono mix or one created in stereo or even surround sound. Levels need to be balanced and equalized if needed, and the sound should be otherwise improved or *sweetened.*

Answer Print

The prepared negative (or reversal) and the mixed soundtrack are then sent, with sync points, to the lab to be combined into a composite **answer print**. Exact preparation of the film, mag, and cue sheets should always be discussed with the lab early in the process because preferred methods vary by lab. The first answer print is rarely the last; adjustments to exposure, color, and sound are common. Ultimately, a release print is approved and ready for distribution. All this assumes a "pure" film process from shoot to distribution, a model that is increasingly rare.

ANALOG LINEAR EDITING

Analog linear editing methods are used to edit both audio and video electronically. Audiotape and mag stock can be cut like film, but for

	A Narration	B Dialogue	C Dialogue	D Dialogue	E Music	F Music	G SFX	H SFX
	0 ← — — — — — — — — PIX START — — — — — — — — → 0							
	3' 24" ← — — — — — — — BEEP — — — — — — — →							
5'					4'			
10'								
15'	15' 5" "The first time..."				UNDER			
20'								
25'								
	29' 4"							
30'		"Hey Harry..."						33' 21"
35'		"...home" 37' 2"	"Your mother..."		35'		36' 27" train	
40'							42' 2"	birds
45'			"...trouble" 48' 33"	"We'd better go..."				
50'						53' 6"		54' 11"
55'				"...tomorrow" 57' 8"				

Figure 9.17 A cue sheet prepares you to do your sound mix. Tracks, transitions, in and out cues, and footage length are marked.

video, this is a problem. In the 1950s, when video technology was new, video was cut this way, but lack of a clear frame line and the complex nature of the video signal caused the edits to be quite rough. This method was used only for assemblages of program sections, not for shot-to-shot editing. The development of audiocassettes made audio-tape splicing impractical.

Electronic editing works for both the audio and video signal. In its simplest form, it is quite simply dubbing or copying the pieces of sound or image from one tape deck to another in the order that you want them.

The recorded material is played on a **source deck**; the edited material is recorded on a **record deck**. A *controller* may connect the source and record deck to automate the process. A controller allows accurate

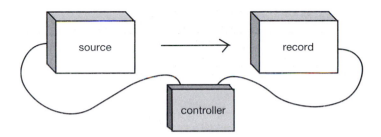

Figure 9.18 The source machine plays back the material. The record machine records the pieces you want in the order you want them. A controller allows for more accurate in-points and greater efficiency.

cueing of the two tapes and *pre-roll*, or backing up of the tapes, before the edit points to ensure that the machines are running up to speed when the edit takes place (Figure 9.18).

Drawbacks

Electronic editing is a simple and reliable way to structure audio and video material, but it has two major drawbacks. One such issue is the generational loss that is inherent in analog recording. Each time an analog electronic signal is copied, both image and sound quality are degraded. Generational loss is more severe when using lower quality tape formats (like VHS) and connections (like unbalanced audio connections and composite video connections), but it exists in any analog dub (Go to the Source—Analog Connections). Analog video editing often results in a release copy that is several generations (copies) away from the original video—and it shows.

The second drawback is the inherent linearity of the process. (Remember our typewriter and word processor analogy?) When laying down pieces of audio or video, you need to lay them down in order, and in doing so, you are strictly defining the time frame. You can't trim a few frames and pull the two ends together. You can erase a few frames, but you will be left with a blank spot in your program. To fix it, you must reedit everything that follows that point (Figure 9.19). The other solution is to edit the program before the change onto another tape and then edit the rest of the program after the change onto the new tape, but then you've lost another generation.

Audio

Sometimes audio is edited by assembling single sources, one piece of audio after another, but most audio editing is the combination of many sources mixed together. In this case, editing takes place much like live audio mixing but with the capability of going back and making changes. Instead of live inputs, as discussed at the beginning of the chapter, taped sources are fed into a mixer, combined together at the desired levels and sound quality, and output to a record deck. This, too, is a linear process and much like the linear on-line video editing described later.

Video

Like the rough-cut and fine-cut stages of analog film editing, linear video editing has its stages as well. After logging, transcribing, and

---

Go to the Source— Analog Connections

There is a variety of ways to transfer analog video and audio signals:

Composite, the National Television System Committee (NTSC) standard, carries the full video signal (color and brightness) through one wire, using a BNC or RCA connector, but it has the lowest quality. Audio is carried in one (mono) or two (stereo) RCA connectors.

S-Video (or Y/C) is a consumer format that is of higher quality than composite. The color and brightness information is separated, resulting in cleaner video. It requires two wires.

Component is a professional video signal that breaks the signal into three parts. This provides the highest quality analog video transfer. Component YUV separates the signal into a luminance and two chrominance channels (from which the third primary color can be determined). RGB component separates the signal into the red, green, and blue primaries.

Balanced audio includes two conductors and a shield. It uses an XLR connection.

Unbalanced audio has one conductor and a second wire that functions as both a conductor and shield and is more susceptible to interference. It generally uses an RCA connection.

Figure 9.19 The addition or deletion of material during a linear edit requires you to reedit everything that follows. **A**, Removing a shot leaves blank tape. Everything after shot 1 needs to be laid down again. **B**, The addition of shot 2A requires everything after shot 2A to be reedited in order to compensate for the change in running time. Remember the tape is not being cut, just copied from one tape to another.

creating the edit plan, video assemblage begins. Generally an **off-line** *edit* comes first. As with the rough cut constructed from the one-light workprint, the emphasis during the off-line process is on structure and content, not image quality. For that reason, work dubs or copies of the camera original tapes are used as source tapes to protect the originals. The generational loss does not matter at this point. Some video editors like to burn in timecode on their work dubs. A burn-in is a graphic representation of the timecode signal on the videotape (Figure 9.20). These burned-in tapes, or *window dubs,* can be used for logging and off-line source tapes. Often off-line editing is done at a lower quality and less expensive format than the originals were recorded on. VHS or S-VHS formats are fine for off-line editing. The off-line stage is the time-consuming one. There is no use paying for equipment that you don't need at this point.

Your record tape needs to be prepared as well. If you are **assemble editing**, you can edit directly onto a blank tape. Assemble editing restricts you to editing the full video signal, including video and audio together, onto the record tape. This does not allow separation of audio and video signals or the use of multiple audio tracks for voiceovers or music. More commonly **insert editing** is done, which allows for just an audio track or the video portion of the signal to be edited. In order for this to work, however, an unbroken video signal (usually TV black) with timecode needs to be laid down on the record tape before editing. This provides the *control track* to keep the signal stable. A control track is an electronic signal that provides regular timing pulses for the video signal. It is analogous to the sprocket holes in film that allow it to move through the projector at a consistent rate.

Generally, an off-line setup has just one source deck, a controller, and a record deck, which means only straight cuts are possible. Effects, other transitions, audio sweetening, and titles are left for later. The order and length of shots are determined off-line.

Figure 9.20 A graphic representation of the electronic timecode can
be keyed into the image, showing the
specific identification for each frame of
video. These window dubs can be used
for logging or off-line editing. Once on
the tape, the burned-in timecode cannot
be removed.

Edit Decision List

After the off-line edit (sometimes also called a rough cut) is complete,
preparation for the final editing stage or **on-line edit** takes place. An
edit decision list (**EDL**) is prepared from the off-line edit. The EDL is a
list of every shot or piece of audio, described by timecode in-points and
out-points. The timecode of the record tape, created when the control
track was laid down, is listed too. If a transition other than a cut is
wanted, extra frames need to be included. When done by hand, this is
an exacting, time-consuming, and important step. It ensures that your
final on-line version will match your off-line plan. Some higher end
linear editing systems are computerized to keep track of your in-points
and out-points and compile the list for you (Figure 9.21). (All digital
nonlinear systems compile EDL data.)

On-Line Edit

An on-line editing suite has all the bells and whistles. You should produce your on-line edit using the highest quality format you can afford.
An on-line suite has an audio mixing board, though you may have
premixed your audio at a sound studio. It has a character generator,
special effects generator, and at least two source decks and a switcher.
This is analogous to the A/B rolls in film editing. To create a dissolve,
fade, or wipe, you have two sources on-line at a time. A switcher
will electronically combine those two sources, but the sources themselves need to be fed to the switcher by two video sources (VTRs in
this case).

The original tapes are now used as sources (to minimize generational
loss), and the program is compiled according to the EDL. Although
changes can certainly be made at this point, it is best to have your
decisions nailed down because a good on-line suite rents for several hundred dollars an hour. At this stage, the emphasis is on image and sound

```
TITLE: EVVY Promo 10 56 41 PM
FCM: NON-DROP FRAME
FCM: DROP FRAME
001  001      NONE C      02:24:33:19 02: 24:35:09 00:00:06:05 00:00:07:25
AUD   3
CLIP: 1-02.18.50.10-V80
AUDIO GAIN IS 6 DB AT 00:00:06:05
AUDIO GAIN IS 6 DB AT 00:00:06:07
AUDIO GAIN IS 6 DB AT 00:00:07:25


FCM: NON-DROP FRAME
002  002      A    C      00:00:00:00 00:00:30:22 00:00:07:16 00:00:38:08
CLIP: Are ya gonna go my way
AUDIO GAIN IS -6 DB AT 00:00:07:16
AUDIO GAIN IS -6 DB AT 00:00:37:00
AUDIO GAIN IS -11 DB AT 00:00:37:18
AUDIO GAIN IS -59 DB AT 00:00:38:03
AUDIO GAIN IS -59 DB AT 00:00:38:08


003  003      A2   C      00:00:00:00 00:00:30:22 00:00:07:16 00:00:38:08
CLIP: Are ya gonna go my way
AUDIO GAIN IS -6 DB AT 00:00:07:16
AUDIO GAIN IS -6 DB AT 00:00:37:00
AUDIO GAIN IS -11 DB AT 00:00:37:18
AUDIO GAIN IS -59 DB AT 00:00:38:03
AUDIO GAIN IS -59 DB AT 00:00:38:08


004  004      V    C      00:09:41:08 00:09:41:22 00:00:08:03 00:00:08:17
CLIP: Graphics


005  005      V    C      04:37:25:03 04:37:25:15 00:00:08:19 00:00:09:01
CLIP: Open Dance


006  006      V    C      01:24:14:03 01:24:14:16 00:00:09:03 00:00:09:16
CLIP: Lizardman


007  005      V    C      05:08:51:20 05:08:52:04 00:00:09:17 00:00:10:01
CLIP: Hosts2


008  007      V    C      02:12:56:04 02:12:56:17 00:00:10:02 00:00:10:15
CLIP: Guest1


009  004      V    C      00:15:49:06 00:15:49:19 00:00:10:16 00:00:10:29
CLIP: Graphics


010  005      V    C      05:58:37:09 05:58:37:23 00:00:11:00 00:00:11:14
CLIP: Winner1
```

Figure 9.21 An EDL includes all the shots and pieces of audio that will be in the final video. Here is a computerized EDL that shows shot numbers, whether a source is audio or video, audio levels, and in- and out-points of both the source and record machines. (Courtesy EVVY Awards, Emerson College.)

quality, effects, and transitions. You create your **edited master**, dub a *protection master* for backup, then take the master tape to a duplication house where copies can be made on the format that fits your needs.

DIGITAL NONLINEAR EDITING

The last several years have brought much innovation to the media production process. Of all the changes, the most dramatic one is arguably in the area of audio, film, and video postproduction. The inherent advantages of combining digital technology and nonlinear processing not only have made the editing process more flexible, but the creation of a common postproduction playing field has opened up new possibilities for media convergence.

Digital, nonlinear editing has made high-quality, low-cost, portable postproduction a reality. The high-end digital nonlinear systems still run in the six figures, but a $1000 laptop, less than $1000 of software, and a digital video camcorder can give you image quality, editing functionality, and effects that were only possible for a hundred times that amount not long ago. Plus it can go anywhere. Footage can be edited in the field or on the way back.

Many pieces of software are on the market for editing images and sound. It is well beyond the scope of this book to describe them all or to instruct you in their use. New offerings are constantly being introduced, as well as new versions of current offerings. Avid from Avid Technology, Final Cut Pro from Apple Inc., and Premiere by Adobe Systems, Inc. are three that are widely used for video and film editing. Some applications are extremely inexpensive, and some are bundled with software that comes with a personal computer purchase. Some systems cost a quarter of a million dollars and, in addition to editing, perform complex digital effects.

Obviously, video editing software also edits audio, but there are programs that work exclusively with audio, such as Pro Tools by Digidesign (a division of Avid) and Adobe Audition (formerly Cool Edit Pro by Syntrillium Software). Pro Tools is the industry standard hardware and software combination. With audio editing software you can edit audio but also much more. You can process, sweeten, and mix up to 128 tracks of simultaneous audio recording and playback. Pro Tools and other audio programs can be used for audio-only productions, but they are also used to mix audio for film and video. Although video editing applications include varying capabilities to sweeten and mix audio, some makers demand the more enhanced audio capabilities of specialized applications.

No matter what system you're using, some common characteristics and issues will help you use whichever system you choose or have access to.

THE DIGITAL ADVANTAGE

The digital aspect of digital media technology is generally considered an advantage. Some prefer the sound or look of an analog reproduction, but the practical advantages of digital advancements cannot be disputed. The machines used for digital technology are smaller and lighter. Though any new technology is more expensive until development costs are recouped and enough consumer acceptance allows mass production, digital technologies ultimately allow higher quality for less money. An example of this is that a consumer-grade high-definition video (HDV) camcorder for under $1000 can record resolutions of 1080i and CD-quality sound. The earliest VHS camcorders, which had vastly inferior image and audio quality, cost almost twice that much.

Digital technology also produces cleaner reproduction of sound and image and is not susceptible to the same kind of generational loss that is inherent with analog processes. Because a digital signal is sampled and quantized and not reproduced in its entirety, as in analog signal reproduction, much of the extraneous noise (be that aural or visual) can be avoided. Furthermore, the dubbing or copying of a sampled signal is not susceptible to the increased interference and subsequent signal degradation that occurs when analog signals are copied. The lack of generational loss only holds, however, when digital connections are maintained from one copy to the next. A digital signal dubbed by means of an analog audio out or video out connection becomes analog and is subject to analog's degradation of quality. Compressing and decompressing a digital file can also cause some degradation of quality.

To use a digital, **nonlinear editing** (**NLE**), system, the sounds and images to be edited need to be in digital format. Some material might already be digital, such as a cut from a music CD or a digital still image. Other sources, like video and recorded audio, might start as purely analog, such as wild sound recorded on an audiocassette recorder or a VHS videotape. Other audio and video sources may have been recorded on a "digital" tape format, such as DV (digital video), HDV, or DAT (digital audiotape), but those formats are not completely digital. They are digitally processed—the audio and video signals were sampled, quantized, and converted into ones and zeros—but then the subsequent digital information was laid in a linear fashion on a tape. These signals have the digital advantages of being cleaner and not being susceptible to generational loss, but you still need to play through the beginning to get to the end and you cannot insert or delete, just like other linear formats. Therefore, they need to be played back in real time and saved in a digital format that can be recognized by the computer.

Increasingly, audio and video are being recorded on a tapeless device, such as an audio flash recorder (discussed in Chapter 5) or video camcorders that record a digital video directly to a removable hard drive or a PC's internal hard drive.

NONLINEARITY AND RANDOM ACCESS

The nonlinearity of digital NLE systems takes its flexibility of use well beyond that of analog nonlinear audiotape or film editing. Although sometimes used interchangeably, nonlinearity and random access are separate but related concepts. Random access refers to the ability to jump instantaneously from one point of information to another. Instead of needing to play through the beginning and middle to get to the end as you do with a movie on videotape, random access allows you to jump to the end, to the middle, and back to the end, as you could with that same movie on a DVD.

Nonlinearity refers to the flexibility of the time frame (the old typewriter/word processor analogy) and the sense that there is no prescribed beginning, middle, and end and that the meaning can be explored through various sequencing.

When we talk about editing films and videos, we're talking about editing linear forms of media using a nonlinear technology. This means that the final product will have a beginning, middle, and end, but it's possible to edit the end first, go back to the beginning, then change the ending, and then insert something between them. You can do this with analog nonlinear film editing too, but you'll spend a lot of time fast forwarding and rewinding the reels of film because analog editing technologies do not have random access. Digital technology enables the random access *and* the nonlinearity.

THE PROCESS

Although software differences, project demands, and the editor's personal preferences can all vary, in basic terms, the digital, nonlinear edit works like this:

1. *Logging*—Footage is logged, and decisions are made about what material will be used. Sometimes logging is done in the field, sometimes after the production process.
2. *Capturing*—Video and audio files that are analog or were recorded on digital tape are transferred in real time into digital files. They might or might not be compressed during this process. If recorded directly to a form of digital storage media (i.e., CompactFlash card, external hard drive, Panasonic P2 card), the files simply need to be imported.
3. *File management*—Small text files that describe the shots (clips) are created and stored in folders (bins) in an organized manner. The actual video files and the audio files are stored as much larger media files.
4. *Sequencing*—The pieces are assembled into a sequence or program file, displayed on a *timeline*. Transitions, titles and credits, and graphics are added. Often files are exported to other applications for compositing or other effects and then imported back in.
5. *Mixdown*—The separate audio tracks are mixed to a single track with balanced levels.
6. *Output*—The desired product is output to a DVD, videotape, web application or server, or a digital edit decision list that is used to do an on-line edit elsewhere.

Logging

Whether editing through analog or digital means, all of the steps of logging, transcribing, and preparing edit plans are important for organized and efficient editing. Logs can be done manually, as with analog editing, or by means of logging software included with your editing application. You still need to review your footage and make a decision about what material is usable and what isn't. If you store the in-points and out-points of the usable footage in your editing program, it can automatically carry out the next stage in the process.

Capturing

Capturing is the process of bringing audio and video files into your editing software program. To edit audio or video that is recorded as analog or as digital tape through digital, nonlinear means, you must first **digitize** it. This is the process by which the audio and video signals are converted to a digital format and stored so the editing software will have access to it. To do this, a playback machine has to be input into a computer and the media played in real time, while the software samples the signal and stores it. Exactly how the playback machine interfaces with the computer can vary from a FireWire connection that maintains digital quality to a *converter* box that converts analog signals to digital (Figure 9.22). Your recording format, playback VTR, editing computer, and software all affect the choices you have in terms of inputting video and audio. Sometimes digital quality is maintained throughout.

Sometimes analog is converted to digital. Sometimes digital is converted to analog and back to digital. Preserving a digital signal throughout the process ensures the highest quality. Professional digital formats like Digital Betacam use a Serial Digital Interface (SDI) connection. For DV formats, FireWire or USB 2.0 is generally used (Go to the Source—USB/FireWire). Analog formats can provide many options, as previously discussed.

It used to be that for film to be digitized, it first had to be transferred to video. A film-to-tape transfer is done with a piece of equipment called a *telecine*, which is basically a combination of a film projector and video camera. The film sound and image are recorded onto videotape, adding timecode in the process. This process is still used, especially if the footage was shot for television or for video distribution. This process is being replaced, however, by the used of digital film scanners, which can scan each frame of film, creating digital files directly from the film, bypassing the videotape stage.

The real-time digitizing process, although time consuming, is necessary, at least as far as tape-based material is concerned. As the video process becomes tapeless (discussed later in this chapter) the digitization step can be skipped. If you have used logging software to log your footage, it is possible to *batch digitize* your footage. The software will read your log and ask you to insert the appropriate videotape into your digitizing deck. Then the software will search the tape, according to timecode, for all the logged shots that you have chosen to digitize, digitize them, and then ask for the next tape.

Audio or video material that already exists in a digital nonlinear form does not need to be digitized. Nonlinear video or audio material obviously cuts time from the editing process. This includes material recorded directly on CD, DVD, mini disc, or a flash memory or hard drive.

File Management

File management is an important part of digital nonlinear editing. As you capture a piece of media (sound and/or image) two types of files are created. The first type of file has information describing a piece of media—timecode in-point and out-point, tape number, and so on. It is stored as a small text file, usually called a *clip*. Clips can then be organized into named *bins*, or folders, as the editor sees fit. (Remember the discussion of analog film editing where the film was cut into shots or clips and organized in the rolling bins?) Clips and bins should both be named. Some editors group all the shots from a scene, according to the script, in a bin. Some group similar shots; for instance, all interview sound bites from the artist in one bin, shots of her paintings in another, and shots of her interacting with art students in another.

Go to the Source—
USB/FireWire

USB and FireWire are two methods for transferring digital material from one device to another. USB (Universal Serial Bus) came first, but its maximum transfer speed of 12 megabits per second (Mbps) was not fast enough to be practical for video transfer. FireWire is Apple Computer's brand name for its version of a peripheral standard that allows faster transfer of digital information—up to 400 Mbps in its initial version. The generic name, IEEE 1394, was developed with the support of the 1394 Trade Organization, a cooperative venture of the major computer manufacturing companies. In May 2002, the 1394 Trade Organization agreed to adopt the FireWire trademark, logo, and symbol for the IEEE 1394 standard, also known as i.Link, as developed by the Sony Corporation.

The original version of FireWire transferred data at a rate of up to 400 megabits per second (Mbps). The newer version transfers at 800 Mbps; thus the two standards are differentiated as FireWire 400 and FireWire 800. Both FireWire and USB are generally hot swappable, which means you don't have to turn everything off to connect or disconnect them. You can also connect several devices, sequentially, to one FireWire outlet. When used for digitizing a video signal, the FireWire cable carries both audio and video information. It became the standard for DV transfer. In 2002 a faster version of USB—USB 2.0—was introduced with speed comparable to that of FireWire 400 (up to 480 Mbps). Wireless USB was introduced in 2006. Drives are being marketed that have both FireWire 400 and 800 and USB 2.0 jacks.

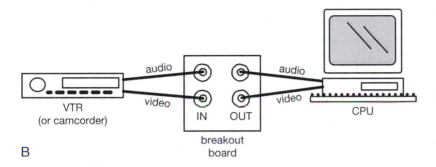

A

B

Figure 9.22 The process for inputting your video and audio into the computer for editing can vary. Newer camcorders have a FireWire jack, which permits a direct digital connection to a personal computer, also with a FireWire jack. **A,** It may be necessary though for the signal to undergo some conversion to make it compatible with your computer and software. Analog video signals can be component, S-VHS, or composite, with component being of higher quality. Audio signals can be balanced (using an XLR plug) or unbalanced (using an RCA plug), with balanced signals being of higher quality. **B,** Analog signals need to be converted to digital, using an external converter box or an internal video capture card in your computer.

Different software works differently, so it's difficult to give specific instructions for organizing your electronic files, but attention given early on to organizational issues, such as backing up your files, consistently naming tapes, noting where you are saving different files, and placing your clips into bins in a logical, easily retrievable way, will save you considerable time and aggravation in the long run.

The second kind of file created when you digitize is a *media file.* Where the media really is and how it is accessed is important to the understanding of how digital nonlinear systems work. Media files are stored on whatever large storage device you're using. They are the actual audio and video material. Once created, the editing software can then randomly access those same media files in many ways and many times. When you create a clip and put it in a bin, neither that clip file nor that bin file actually contains any media. They are simply **pointers** (indicators of what audio or video material is stored where). In terms of *bytes* (units of digital data), the pointer files are very small. You can copy a clip without discernibly increasing the size of your whole project file. You're not copying the media; you're just copying the information about how to access that media when it's called for (Figure 9.23). This signal flow issue is a somewhat abstract but important distinction. Project files other than your actual media files (e.g., clips, bins, programs, transitions, audio settings) are all very small files and can fit easily on a flash (or thumb) drive. You need both the pointer files and the media files to play back any media. The pointer files are simply saying, "Go to the media files, find the shot that starts with this timecode address, and play it until it reaches this timecode address."

Figure 9.23 When you choose a clip to view, what you're choosing is identifying information that can direct the software to the file that actually holds the digitized media file. The clip file (a very small text file) is simply a pointer to the much larger media file. Access to both the pointer and media are necessary to play back the video.

Storage As the material is captured, it needs to be stored. There are many possible places to store media. It can be stored on the hard drive of the computer that holds your editing software, but this only works if you are going to be editing on the same machine all the time. This is usually the case if you have your own editing setup at home but not if you're editing within a school or professional environment. If you do store media on a hard drive, some software manufacturers recommend that the media files be kept on a separate drive or a separate partition of your hard drive from the editing software to avoid conflicts. Media can also be stored on an external hard drive as well. If you are going to edit directly from the external drive, the connection between your PC and the external drive needs to be fast enough to enable playback of video. FireWire, discussed earlier, is the most common means of transferring and connecting media files. If video is stored on a slower drive, it may need to be digitized to the hard drive of the computer first, then transferred to the slower drive for storage. The media files can then be transferred back to the hard drive each time you edit. Media can also be stored on a *network,* which is simply a connection to large, shared storage, and is available to individual users on demand. This is an increasingly common scenario for large projects with multiple editors.

What storage medium you use and how much it can hold become very important when working with audio and especially video because the digitized signals take up a lot of digital space, or *memory*. Digital material is measured in bytes, thousands of bytes (*kilobytes*, or KB), millions of bytes (*megabytes*, MB or megs), and billions of bytes (*gigabytes*, GB or gigs). As a comparison, one page of this text in a word processing software creates a document of approximately 16,000 bytes. One minute of digitized uncompressed standard definition video takes up 1.4 gigabytes or 1,400,000,000 bytes of space. You're generally going to digitize at least two to three times more material than you actually use, so when editing a feature-length film or even a half hour short, you are using a lot of storage.

Compression For this reason, video is often compressed. Analog video is compressed when digitized and possibly when output. With digital video, compression can occur in the recording process, when capturing into editing software, or when outputting. Audio, while taking up more memory than text, takes much less than video. It is, therefore, less necessary to compress audio, but it is still common. **Compression** is a means of making a file smaller by ridding the signal of redundant information or rearranging data for more efficient storage. Think about a sequence of video frames of a woman in a blue jacket talking in medium close-up. The visual information is scanned and encoded 30 times per second, but much of the information stays the same. There are small changes as the mouth opens and closes and the head position changes slightly, but the information for a good bit of the frame (e.g., the jacket, the background) remain very similar if not identical (Figure 9.24). There is redundancy within the frame and also frame to frame when shooting film or video. Compression results in less information to be stored.

Compression is either *lossy* or *lossless*. Lossy compression reduces the amount of data by dropping repeated or redundant information. This can result in more extreme compression but can also result in loss of quality. High levels of lossy compression result in digital artifacts. Artifacts are errors in the image caused by not sampling enough information. Areas of the frame are not being sampled; similar colors and tones in adjacent areas are determined. Once determined as similar, the already sampled information is simply repeated, rather than sampled. Because the adjacent area is similar but not exactly the same, subtleties of shade and outline will not be reproduced. This results in the appearance of "blocks" of color, as opposed to a more accurate representation. The less sampling (the higher the compression), the more obvious the artifacts (Figure 9.25).

Lossless compression does not drop data but instead rearranges it so it can be stored more efficiently. No quality is lost, but the information is not compressed as much as with lossy. Some newer types of lossy compression are considered to be "visually lossless" because, while omitting some information, the difference cannot be noticed by the human eye.

A codec is necessary for compression of video to take place. A **codec**, standing for compression/decompression, is a mathematical

Figure 9.24 There is much redundancy in most video shots. If only the new information is stored for each new frame, file size can be radically reduced.

Figure 9.25 Extreme artifacts are obvious in this highly compressed image.

model that determines exactly how the compression should take place. Some codecs are hardware based, and some are a part of a software application. There are many different ones; some are better for video on the web, others for computer animation. A codec or several codecs are built in to editing software. DV has its own codec, and compression takes place in the acquisition stage. DV compresses at a rate of 5:1. This means that the recorded image takes up five times less information than uncompressed NTSC video. No further compression is generally needed, as the video is digitized by an NLE. Common video codecs for outputting video are MPEG-2 and MPEG-4, which are discussed further in Chapter 10.

Compression can also be **intraframe** or **interframe**. Intraframe (or spatial) compression accomplishes the compression process within each frame of video. It looks for redundancies on a frame-by-frame basis. It allows you to edit at any frame. The DV codec uses intraframe compression.

Interframe (or temporal) compression reads and averages several frames and then makes the adjustment. *GOPs* (group of pictures) are looked at for redundancies. As stated, film or video has substantial frame-to-frame redundancy, so interframe compression can result in more compression with less quality loss. With interframe compression, you have different kinds of frames. I-frames contain all the information. B-frames and P-frames contain the information that has changed. The GOP will be a pattern of these frames that repeats during the compression process. The number of frames in a group can vary but is typically 6 or 15 (1/2 second).

Because it allows for more compression with less quality loss, interframe compression is effective for compressing video for distribution. MPEG-2 is an interframe codec used to compress video for DVDs, digital cable, and DBS (Direct Broadcast Satellites). The HDV format uses MPEG-2 to compress video during acquisition. This allows HDV to fit on the same size cassette as the standard definition DV. It was not initially used for NLEs because either you had to edit only on an I-frame (vastly limiting your editing choices) or use a costly, time-consuming conversion (or transcoding process); however, that is changing. New versions of Avid and Final Cut for HD allow *native* (or untouched) editing of HDV. Simply put, you can edit on any frame. If you choose a P-frame or a B-frame, instead of an I-frame (the one with all the information), the software will transcode just that frame. That doesn't take long; it's virtually real time. The codec used for outputting from an NLE depends on the final delivery of the project, and many factors come into play. For DVD distribution, you would probably use an MPEG-2 codec; for the web or iPod video, the highly compressing MPEG-4 is a good choice.

In addition to compression, smaller file sizes can also be obtained by decreasing the frame rate (from 30 frames per second to 15, for instance) or by making the frame size smaller than full screen. These are approaches used more for video when used on the web or as part of an interactive application. The general principle holds:

LESS INFORMATION = SMALLER FILE SIZE

Sequencing

Once your material is digitized and organized, you're ready to actually edit. One of the advantages of digital nonlinear editing is that the technology accommodates many approaches to the editing process. Some editors like to lay the whole piece out in broad strokes, then go back and fine-tune. Others work each edit carefully before moving on. Some like to think of the project in sections, making different versions of each section and trying it with different versions of other sections. All of these approaches and many more can be accommodated. You need to discover through experimentation what works best for you.

However you go about it, you will end up structuring the digitized clips into a sequence or program. The model of a timeline is generally used. A **timeline** is a graphic representation of the sequence you are putting together. Remember, you're not actually cutting or copying any media as you edit; you're constructing a list of pointers (an EDL) that refers to the media files created when you digitized. The timeline is a graphic model of that list. When you play back the timeline, you are accessing the EDL that randomly accesses the media files and plays them back on your computer screen in the order you have indicated in your timeline (Figure 9.26).

Editing software generally allows at least two tracks of video (sometimes many more) to be edited. Remember the concept of A/B rolls. Multiple tracks of video allow dissolves, wipes, fades, keyed graphics, chromakeys, and other effects, although many editing applications allow you to do transitions within a single video track. Transitions need to be created and often *rendered* (processed) by the computer. Recent improvements in software have greatly shortened or even eliminated rendering

Figure 9.26 Here are screen captures from two popular nonlinear editing systems. **A**, Interface from Avid Xpress Pro. Source material is displayed on the left, the edited sequence on the right. The timeline shows one channel of edited video clips and two audio channels. Avid is considered by many to be the industry standard. (Courtesy of Avid Technology.) **B**, The interface from Final Cut Pro 6. A Macintosh-only product, Final Cut Pro is used extensively by professional and consumers. (Courtesy of Apple Inc.)

time, resulting in what is called real-time transitions and effects. If more complex effects are desired, it is often possible to create them in more specialized software programs and import those files into the editing application. AfterEffects, made by Adobe, is a popular choice for creating motion graphics and layering graphic sources (*compositing*).

Similarly, editing software includes capability for creating titles and credits—a character generator (CG) program. CG programs offer the capability to key text over an image, a variety of fonts and sizes, and the means to make text move, roll (vertically), and crawl (horizontally). Some CG programs are better than others, and some editors prefer to create titles in another graphics program, such as Adobe Photoshop, and import the files into the editing software.

Most audio programs include several tracks, level controls, equalization, and simple processing. For basic audio editing and mixing, the included features are fine. For high-level productions and complex sound design, you might want to explore specialized audio software, such as ProTools.

The off-line/on-line model still exists in some postproduction facilities in terms of effects. High-end editing and compositing software packages, like Smoke, made by Discreet Logic, can import a timeline created on an Avid or other NLE system and add sophisticated compositing effects. If even more complex effects are required, Flame can be used, and then you can export the files to Smoke, which can edit them into the program. Smoke is more expensive than an NLE system such as Avid Media Composer. So the bulk of the editing work can be done on the less expensive NLE and polished on the NLE/compositing system. This is changing also because lower end systems are increasingly adopting more sophisticated features.

Mixdown The audio mixdown can be done by either using the audio mixing features included in the editing software or by exporting the timeline to an audio application such as Pro Tools, You may have just 2 tracks; for example, the synch sound track and a music track. You may have 8 or 16 or more. Dialogue might be separated into several tracks. There may be one or more sound effects tracks, a voiceover track, an ADR track, etc. The mixdown is where the relative level of each track is determined and where fade ins and fade outs are fine tuned. Some of the audio may have technical flaws that require sweetening. Perhaps there was too much ambience recorded, relative to the dialogue. Or perhaps an electronic hum was recorded with the sound. If done with a separate software program, the final mixdown is imported back to the NLE and synched up wit the picture.

Output Output is the exporting of the finished program to the format needed for distribution and exhibition (discussed in Chapter 11). The output can be something as simple as a single DVD burned for your class assignment or as complex as an EDL used to conform film negative that results in thousands of film copies sent out to movie theaters all over the world. DVDs can be burned directly from your NLE system, but because DVDs are compressed, often you will want to create an uncompressed *master* tape, and ideally a *protection master*. If a video is broadcast or screened at a festival, in most cases a DVD will not be acceptable. Master tapes should be at the highest quality video format available to you. From the master tape, you can make multiple copies of whatever format you need.

If you need a large number of DVDs, they can be *duplicated* or *replicated*. Duplication is better for producing under 500 copies. Data is burned onto the DVDs directly. For large quantities the replication process creates a *glass master* on which the data is embedded in the disc's surface and then sealed to protect it. It results in more reliable DVDs but the price of this process generally makes it practical for large numbers of copies. You should also save your project files. It is less important to save your media files, if you have the camera-original tapes. You can always redigitize your timeline from the original tapes. As we transition to tapeless cameras, it will be important to save those original media files in case you ever want to re-edit.

ISSUES OF CONVERGENCE AND COMPATIBILITY
FILM TO VIDEO

Digital nonlinear editing has become the dominant method of editing for both film and video. Even before digital nonlinear editing, some makers were transferring film to video to be edited for video distribution or broadcast (Go to the Source—Film in the Early Days of Television). They were also using video editing to off-line edit before conforming film negatives. The advantages of digital nonlinear editing have led to increased overlap between the two media, but there are still differences that need to be taken into consideration.

As we know, film and video are usually exposed at different rates. Film is exposed at 24 frames per second (fps). NTSC video is exposed at 30 (actually 29.97) fps, and PAL and SECAM standards at 25 fps. HD uses variable frame rates. This difference becomes important when film is transferred to video. When working with NTSC video, during the telecine transfer, a *pulldown* is done, which means that some film frames are transferred twice to compensate for the difference in frames per second. The first frame of video is transferred as the normal two fields. The second frame is transferred as three fields. Then, the whole transfer (including audio) is slowed down one-tenth of one percent to compensate for the difference between 30 fps and the actual 29.97 fps of NTSC color video. If the footage is going to stay on video for distribution, that takes care of it. If, however, the tape is going to be transferred to a computer editing system that is made for film editing, the tape will be converted back to 24 fps and sped up one-tenth of one percent when digitized into the system. This is necessary so the footage will remain in synch with the original film negative that eventually will be conformed and printed into release film copies.

Because the 24-fps frame rate of film and the 25-fps frame rate of PAL is so slight, the difference can be handled by speeding up the film playback slightly in the transfer. The difference is not visible to the human eye.

New HDTV standards that allow recording at a variety of frame rates, including 24 fps, simplify the process in some ways. If you know you are shooting HD to be transferred to film, you would probably want to shoot at 24 fps. HD editing software allows you to edit at 24 fps, making pulldown unnecessary. But the variety of frame rates possible can create confusion itself if you are not consistent and careful about your choices.

Digital Intermediates

Digital intermediates have been around for awhile. Basically, a digital intermediate happens anytime you take a piece of media (analog or digital) and digitize or copy it into a software application where you manipulate it and then output it again. This includes taking a JPEG image from your digital camera and bringing it into iPhoto where you rotate and crop it and then print it out. It includes taking your soundtrack from Final Cut Pro, importing it into ProTools for mixing and sweetening, and exporting back into Final Cut to print to tape. In essence, postproduction has become a series of digital intermediate stages.

Video editing has become an entirely digital intermediate process—from tape to digital and back to tape. The workflow of film editing is changing, however, as the transfer from film to tape is no longer necessary. As mentioned earlier in the chapter, film scanners can now go directly from film to digital files. Once digital files are created, there are many possible workflows. Different members of the postproduction team can be working simultaneously—doing off-line editing, special effects, color correction, and so forth. The edited film can be output to several formats—film, DVD, Internet streaming. The analog conforming process of painstakingly cutting fragile negatives can be bypassed. Encryption can be added to the files to protect against piracy.

The downside (of course there's a downside) is the huge amount of digital storage necessary to digitize 35 mm film. We're talking millions of megabytes (*terabytes*) of storage. Transferring and rendering of files this large can take a very long time. Also there is the issue of the lessening but still real differences in the color and contrast quality of digital images vs. filmed ones.

Some Hollywood features that are digitally generated, through HD and/or computer animation and special effects, go to film only at the end of the workflow for distribution. As digital projection becomes more widely accepted, movies may never be on film at all.

PC VS. MAC

Another issue of compatibility is the operating system of the computer used to run the editing software. Most early systems were developed exclusively for the Macintosh platform because Mac was the dominant platform for graphic use. This has changed somewhat. Some systems use the Windows operating system. Avid, a major presence in digital nonlinear editing and once offered only on Mac systems, is now cross-platform within specific system requirements. Final Cut Pro is an Apple product and works only on Macs. Adobe's Premiere was not released for the Mac for awhile but now has been. The computer world is increasingly cross-platform, but going from one to the other can cause problems of which you need to be aware.

CONCLUSION

In a field that changes so quickly, it is hard to know if today's trends, practices, and ideas will be discarded in favor of better ideas. As few developments, although only in the early stages of acceptance, certainly seem worth mentioning.

TAPELESS CAMERAS

Tapeless cameras that were in development just a few years ago are now a part of the industry. They exist at the consumer levels with camcorders that record to a DVD or CompactFlash drive and with professional models that record to removable drives or directly into PCs. In addition to the time savings of not needing to digitize footage, tapeless cameras employing solid-state technology are less susceptible to being jostled in the field and are not affected by extremes in temperature or humidity in the way tape recorders with their moving parts are.

BROWSER-BASED EDITING

Browser-based editing has gained popularity within some segments of the market. Browser-based or network editing means that instead of storing project files and media files locally on your hard drive or removable drive, they are stored on a network server. The server is connected to individual workstations by a number of possible means, ranging from fiber optic cable to phone lines. Fiber optics allow huge amounts of information to travel quickly, therefore offering the possibility of uncompressed video moving from server to workstation to server. Phone lines allow much less information to travel at one time and therefore require heavy compression of media files, but phone lines are highly available, which means great accessibility. Servers that generally have huge storage capacities are an obvious advantage for video. The even bigger advantage, though, is the centralization of storage, versus the localization of files saved on your own computer. Teams of people involved in postproduction—picture editors, sound editors, sound designers, animators—can all be working on the same files, and a work in progress can be very quickly sent to clients and executive producers for approval. For large, collaborative projects, this approach makes a lot of sense. For it to work well, high-quality maintenance of the network and excellent organization and management of the postproduction process are crucial.

On the other end of the spectrum, in 2007, Adobe, through the personal media website Photobucket, introduced a web application that allows simple editing within your web browser, without the investment in editing software. It is not intended for professional use but by consumers who want to edit their videos before posting them to sites such as YouTube.

PUTTING IT INTO PRACTICE
DOING

Find out what editing methods are available to you. Read the manuals. Learn the specific techniques of capturing media, file management, editing, and outputting. Shoot the continuity storyboard that you created in Chapter 8. Edit it together, using at least two audio tracks. Output it to tape.

KEY CONCEPTS

answer print	conforming
assemble editing	counter
bus	crossfade
capturing	cut
chromakey	digital intermediates
clips and bins	digitize
codec	dissolve
compression	edge number

edit decision list (EDL)

edit plan

edited master

effects bank

fade

file management

fine cut

input/output

insert editing

interframe

intraframe

live mixing

live switching

log

luminance key

mag stock

nonlinear editing (NLE)

off-line edit

on-line edit

pointers

rough cut

running time

segue

signal flow

source/record deck

split screen

superimposition

timecode

timeline

transcription

transitions

wipe

workprint

CHAPTER 10

Nonlinear Structure

UNDERSTANDING NONLINEARITY

Nonlinearity is a broadly used term that can be applied to many aspects of the media-making process—the story, the production and postproduction process, and, finally, the distribution medium. A traditional narrative story (linear) might be shot on film (linear), edited digitally (nonlinear), and distributed first theatrically (linear) and then on DVD (nonlinear). The goal of a video game might be to fight off all the dragons until you can capture the magic chalice (linear), using computer-animated (nonlinear process) video sequences (linear) that can be experienced in a different order every time you play (nonlinear) and distributed on a DVD (nonlinear).

We generally consider a movie to be linear and a video game nonlinear. What makes the difference? Perhaps it comes down to the intended experience for the user or viewer. This intention must be supported by the method of delivery—a digital form with a means for the user to both receive and input information. Nonlinear, in terms of the user experience, means nonsequential or multisequential. It means that experiencing the story in an A, B, C order is no more or less meaningful than C, B, A or B, A, C. One sequence might communicate a slightly different message than another, but all are valid. You might use a nonlinear editing software program to edit a film. You might take a linear video and stream it over the Internet. What we're focusing on here, though, are works of media that are nonlinear in structure. They have a **branching structure**, as opposed to moving in a straight line. The user can control the branching as she or he either chooses from options predetermined by the maker or has the ability to make her or his own decisions to determine the narrative. The branching may be controlled mathematically in response to performance, as in a video game where you move on to the next level after capturing all the keys. Branching can also be programmed to happen randomly; for example, if you take a quiz multiple times, the questions are in a different sequence each time. Generally, a truly nonlinear media experience suggests that it will also have *random access* and be *interactive*.

RANDOM ACCESS

As discussed at several points in this text, **random access** is the ability to jump quickly and easily from one part of a piece of media to another in any direction or order. A book or magazine has manual random access. Digital technology has random access as a result of the very nature of how digital information is stored. There is no need to fast forward or rewind as there is with film or tape. Random access means that a nonlinear structure can be experienced smoothly with little or no wait while one of a number of possible paths through the material is chosen. The user of the program can drive the random access by making a choice or selection. Random access can be driven by the program itself, such as when completing a section automatically takes you back to the menu page.

INTERACTIVITY

Interactivity means that the user and the program react to each other. Interactivity provides an active rather than passive experience. The program provides choices, and the user makes selections and performs a task. Based on the user's performance of that task, the program reacts differently. For example, in an educational program, correct answers will take the user to the next level of difficulty, but incorrect answers will cause the section to repeat or move to a less rigorous level. You can have a lot of interactivity or a little; the user can have many options to choose from or a few.

Interactivity relies on a means of inputting and outputting information between the user and the program. Users can input into a program by means of keystrokes, a mouse, a touch screen, a controller, or even his or her voice. The program outputs information to a user by displaying images on a screen and playing sound through a speaker or other type of output device. With **virtual reality**, or a three-dimensional computer environment, inputting and outputting occur through goggles, earphones, and gloves (Go to the Source—Virtual Reality).

Operating your TV remote control is an example of primitive interactivity, but a media work that is truly interactive allows the user and the program to react on many levels. Developments in **artificial intelligence** are allowing interactivity to become more sophisticated and intuitive (Go to the Source—Artificial Intelligence). The computer behaves more like a human brain, interaction becomes more individual, and the program's responses more multilayered—more like our own.

Interactivity works with random access and a nonlinear structure to provide a dynamic media experience. Random access provides the means for us to experience the content nonlinearly. Interactivity drives the nonlinear progression as the program and user respond to each other's messages.

NONLINEAR DESIGN

We have all experienced nonlinear information structuring, such as a college website that gives you access to calendar listings, announcements, course listings, historical background, academic programs, and faculty. Perhaps it also provides a gallery of student work and interviews with key leaders of the institution. Progression through such a site is based primarily on the user's information needs and the design

Go to the Source—
Virtual Reality

The technological roots of virtual reality (VR) date back to the 1960s. VR applications allow a user, typically wearing goggles, a headset, gloves, or a body suit, to interact with a three-dimensional sensory environment. Three-dimensional modeling and simulation programming respond to motion sensors on the headset, gloves, or other input/output devices, changing the image, sound, or even simulated sense of touch or motion. Early VR uses were mainly military, simulating combat situations or flight training. Newer VR uses include games (typically with lots of shooting) and job training. VR allows one to train or play in dangerous situations without the risk of actual physical harm to self or others. VR is also used for envisioning future home improvements, shopping for new homes, touring faraway places, and participating more actively in interactive narratives.

of the site. Many areas of design are called on to create a nonlinear interactive piece.

Information design, which comes first, is the structuring of content. No matter how complex or diverse the content, successful information design must serve the expected needs of the user. Information design can also be thought of as the description of the story you want to tell—fiction or nonfiction. Basically, information design is the ordering, identification, and creation of content.

Navigation design is the process of determining all of the possible ways a user can move through your piece. Can they choose from six different options on a main menu page? Can they choose to go back to that menu and make another choice at any time? Can they cross from the middle of one information sequence to the middle of another or do they need to go back to the beginning of the second sequence? These are all questions a navigation designer must ask.

In a nonlinear piece, the information and navigation design result in a branching structure that is visualized by a **flowchart**. A flowchart is the nonlinear equivalent of a storyboard. It diagrams the elements of the piece and the possible paths through them (Figure 10.1). Flowcharts show not only a variety of choices at each junction but also the possible directions of movement through the material—forward, backward, or sideways.

Hierarchies are an important concept in information and navigational design. What information or story elements are most important? What does the user most need or want to experience first? Good navigation design allows the user to flow through the piece easily in the ways that he or she wants to. Information is structured into sections or categories that make sense for the specific audience. To return to the example of the college website, the categories for a website designed for use primarily by students and staff might be different than the categories for prospective students and their parents.

Interface design determines how the user will interact with the program. Will there be buttons to click? Will there be a play, rewind, and stop interface, reminiscent of a VCR? Will the hot spots, which only become visible if you move the mouse over them, give a game-like quality to the interaction? Interface design should be based on the expectation of the user or, in some cases, intentionally thwart the expectations of the user, to present a challenge.

Software design is the planning of the actual computer programming, or *coding*, that makes the piece functional. Software design is to interactivity what information design is to content. It allows a structured approach to the process of building interactivity.

The **graphic design** creates the look and feel of the interface. Composition and layout, color, text fonts, and image styles are all involved at this stage. **Sound design** needs to correspond with all of the other design components, particularly graphic design and information or content creation. Good sound design adds a strong aesthetic component to the work and aids with navigation and interaction.

Go to the Source— Artificial Intelligence

Artificial intelligence (AI) is the attempt to have computers or computer-controlled robots perform in ways we think of as "human," such as learning, reasoning, and finding meaning. The two major approaches to AI date back to early computers in the 1950s and still exist, in a somewhat different form, in current AI research. The first approach is that of the *symbolist* group, which tries to re-create the thinking process of the human brain in a digital form. Symbolist AI gives the computer a very large number of facts and rules on how to use the facts, supplied by programming code. The other approach is that of the *connectionist* group, which tries to re-create the physical structure of the brain—neural networks—by creating many connected groups of microprocessors that can program themselves. Successful examples of AI include computer programs that can play games and recognize patterns within huge amounts of data. Computer chess games were an early example of AI. The computer started without knowing how to play chess but knowing the rules and the moves each chess piece could make. As the computer played, data about the outcomes of the moves was stored. The computer "learned" over time which moves were successful in a given situation and which were not. The stored data was the "intelligence" that allowed the computer to play chess and improve its playing over time. The more games the program played, the more data there was for it to draw on—making it a "better player."

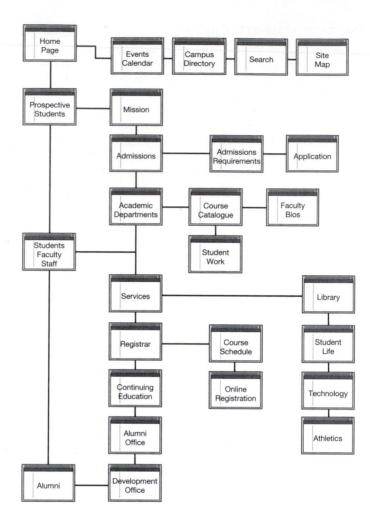

Figure 10.1 This flowchart diagrams the structure of a college website. It shows the elements and the possible paths through the material.

INTERACTIVE MEDIA

When it all comes together—the intent of nonlinear communication, the random access of digital technology, the designed and programmed interactivity—the results are hard to classify. The term *new media* is used, but it is not that new anymore. It's sometimes also called *digital media,* but as we have seen, almost all media are digital now. *Multimedia* is used but has connotations of obsolete technologies. The phrase **interactive media** is also used and is probably the best choice because almost all of the work in this genre has some degree of interactivity. Perhaps the terminology is not very important because the shifts and overlaps of the approaches and genres of media technology continue daily. The term *interactive media* includes all of the types of media we've talked about so far—still images, sound, film, video—plus text.

TYPES OF INTERACTIVE MEDIA

In the first edition of this book, new media was described as interactive, nonlinear media that was experienced on a computer screen. Now the delivery of that media content might be on your television set, PDA (personal digital assistant, such as a BlackBerry), or cell phone. The Internet was characterized as connected web pages. Now the model of the Internet as a web of connected pages does not begin to describe our Internet experience. A distinction was made between interactive media on the web and media that was distributed on CD-ROM. Now new media content on CD-ROMs is becoming rare as web functionality becomes greater. Things have changed, are changing, and will continue to change. It's difficult for an old medium (such as a printed textbook) to keep up with the ever-evolving new communication technologies. Perhaps the next edition of this text will not be on paper at all.

We're to the point where almost all media are interactive to some extent, perhaps with the exception of seeing a movie in a theater. Nonlinear and interactive media are common to your television set and your cell phone. Linear media such as movies or TV shows are increasingly common on your computer, too. Our emphasis here, though, is on works of art or communication that incorporate sound and still and moving images and where user input is key to the meaning of the work. We're talking about websites with graphics, video, and audio clips. We're talking about video games, interactive documentaries, or narratives that are most often distributed on DVD or over the Internet. Interactive media could include the release of a Hollywood film on DVD with an added interactive component, such as a director's commentary that can be turned off and on, the ability for the user to choose to stop the film and access some background information, or the choice of a variety of endings. It can be educational software that allows children to simulate the experience of flying in the space shuttle, conduct experiments, and view Earth from different locations. It can be an interactive documentary about U.S. immigration that includes video interviews with recent immigrants, archival photographs of Ellis Island, images and dramatizations of letters written by people who arrived there, and statistics of immigration patterns. It can be an art piece that makes use of cell phone technology to comment on technology and sense of place (Figure 10.2). A fictional story in which the user chooses the location of the next scene or the hero's actions or conversations can be considered interactive, as can a simulated environment such as *Second Life,* in which users control their created characters in a 3D animated world (Go to the Source— *Second Life*). What makes these experiences different from linear media experiences such as films or audio programs is the tendency to combine media forms (e.g., stills, audio, video, text, and animation) and the fact that their structure and technology allow them to be user driven and experienced in many different ways (Figure 10.3).

As an interactive media maker, your sense of storytelling is different from that used to make linear media. Traditional narrative structure of cause and effect, rhetoric, and logical building won't work—at

Go to the Source—
Second Life

Second Life is an Internet-based 3D virtual world built and owned by its residents or users. Residents create their own characters or avatars that can interact with each other. It has its own economy and currency. Residents can create businesses, stage performances, and construct environments.

Figure 10.2 Cell tagging, a web-based artwork by Brooke Knight, has viewers use their cell phones to choose a zip code. Once the zip code is chosen, the piece generates an aerial image of that area onto which viewers can draw in Flash, using the keypad of their cell phone. (Courtesy of the artist; http://transition.turbulence.org/Works/cell_tagging.)

least not in the same way. If a piece is nonlinear, its elements may be experienced in many different sequences. Progression through the piece may be based on successful completion of tasks or the uncovering of certain clues, but you can't be sure that the user will see or hear the entire piece. Characters may exhibit human-like behaviors and change their behavior in response to the user's input. The user controls the order and pacing of his or her own experience within the realm of possibilities created by the maker or as part of an ongoing, open-ended experience. It becomes an active user experience. Linear media is based on the maker satisfying or thwarting the desire of the viewer to see and hear what comes next. Nonlinear media creates many possibilities for what comes next and allows the user to make his or her own choices.

The Web

Originally the Internet was only text. Apple Computer introduced a graphic interface to computing in 1984, and as compression of sound and images became possible and bandwidths greater, sound and image became part of the web. Applications, such as Macromedia's Flash, made possible advanced graphics, animation, and video for use on websites. Flash is discussed later in the chapter.

The Internet of the 1990s is sometimes referred to as Web 1.0—the first version of the web. It can perhaps best be described as websites that, to the users, seemed like places they could visit. You could be on a site, then link to another site, bookmarking that original place to be returned to another time.

The web works on the basis of systems of hardware and software, or **web servers**, that make all documents on the servers available to those who visit the server via their web browsers. **Web browsers** (e.g., Internet Explorer, Firefox, Safari) are the computer applications that allow you to view a website on your computer. **Plug-ins** are added-on pieces of software that allow additional functionality. Uniform resource locators, or **URLs**, provide information that allows the server to find the document you wish to view through your browser. **Hyperlinks** are the programmed behaviors that allow you to go from one website or web page to another. A website presents us with a means of accessing a database that allows the user to add, change, or *mash up* content. Mashup is a term, appropriated from the music world, that refers to combining multiple assets, taken from other sources, into a website or interactive application. It is difficult to pin down all of the current developments in web delivery, so we instead focus here on some of the key developments that characterize the current status of the Internet, sometimes called Web 2.0.

Databases

Databases provide the means by which computer programs can find and select information. They have been around since the early days of the web but in the past few years have become larger and more powerful. Search engines, such as Google, rely on vast databases with complex organization. Web pages and other documents are indexed by means of key words or **tags** (or *metatags*) that describe the content.

User-Generated Content

User-generated content (**USG**), as its name implies, is the term for information (text, photos, videos, audio, games, and activities) that Internet users upload to the web or mobile device. This includes

Figure 10.3 *As American as Apple Pie* is an interactive CD-ROM. The process of baking an apple pie is used as a metaphor for telling the story of a relationship going through difficulties. As the user selects a text phrase printed over a piece of the pie, a short movie is played. The movies include dialogue and symbolic images, such as a kiss or an apple being peeled. After the movie plays, a segment of the pie recipe is revealed until all the movies have been seen and the user can see the entire recipe. The viewing order chosen by the user can affect the meaning of the story. (Courtesy of the maker, Michelle Citron.)

podcasts, blogs, video diaries, and social networking sites, such as Facebook and MySpace. YouTube is a highly successful example of a site that provides the interface and a powerful database, but lets the users provide the content through uploaded videos, comments, and rankings. Not only can content be user generated, it can also be shared and changed by other users. The online encyclopedia Wikipedia allows users to edit entries at will. Some laud such outlets as the democratization of the media; others are concerned about intellectual property rights and issues of content validation. How do you know if a contributor to a Wikipedia entry has used accurate information? Some decry the commercialization of these new forms as major movie studios begin to post film trailers on YouTube and major corporations set up business in *Second Life*.

THE PROCESS OF MAKING INTERACTIVE MEDIA

Making interactive media is similar to making linear media in many ways. In fact, you are often creating still images and linear pieces of audio and moving images that are then combined in a nonlinear branching structure. All of the issues of framing, composition, lighting, audio recording, sound design, and editing still apply, though creating sound and image for the computer screen requires certain approaches. For example, a video clip that will be distributed via the Internet may need a small image size and therefore lend itself to simple, close-up images. Bandwidth restrictions might also dictate an image with limited movement to ensure smooth playback. The need for preproduction is as acute for nonlinear media as it is for linear media, if not more so. As with linear media, the purpose and audience must be assessed. The research must be done; the story must be found. Instead of thinking about the beginning, middle, and end of your story, you need to think about all the possible ways to sequence through the many elements, or **assets**. Assets are the building blocks—still images, videos, audio clips, and animations—of your piece.

In some ways, interactive media seem to lend themselves to informational pieces like a company website or an online encyclopedia or catalog. However, interactive pieces can also contain a strong story. An interactive documentary about the history and present situation of a Native American tribe could tell many individual stories while communicating an overall understanding and appreciation of the tribe's history and culture. One section could offer videos, still images, and audio clips of tribal dance, music, and crafts. Another could contain oral histories of tribal elders describing the changes in lifestyle and living conditions that have occurred in their lifetimes. Another could have archival photos, documents, and text about life for the tribe following the arrival of European settlers. The user could take a virtual tour through a reservation. The navigation design of such a piece would most likely have a main **menu**, or a screen page with buttons allowing the user to select a certain section to explore. The navigation design would also allow the user to enter a section, explore it, and then go back to the menu to make another selection or continue from the current screen. It might also allow the user to move sideways

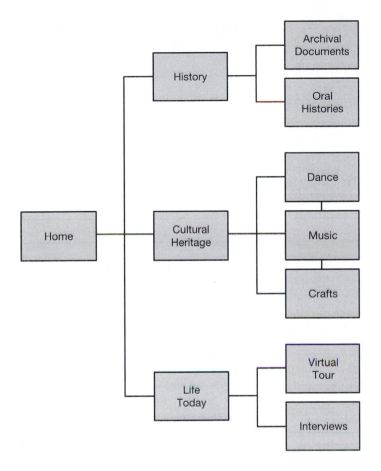

Figure 10.4 This flowchart for a hypothetical interactive documentary shows the variety of paths a user can take.

into the middle of another section or quit the application altogether (Figure 10.4). A sideways move could be the result of linked related content. Perhaps one of the tribal elders describes learning to make pottery from her grandmother. The user might prefer to go straight to the video about pottery making rather than continue with the oral history at that point. This approach allows the viewer to follow the topics or information that interest her or him most. This level of personalization increases the viewer's engagement, ultimately increasing her or his satisfaction level with the experience.

Interactive fictional narrative storytelling is still relatively rare, but it is ripe for innovation and experimentation. Media artists have been exploring how to tell stories nonlinearly and interactively for many years. The 1980s technology of the interactive laser disc was the first way to allow random access of video and audio. **Hypertext** is the computer-based telling of nonlinear interactive text-based stories. Instead of paging sequentially through a book, hypertext allows you to read a short section then choose, usually on the basis of a key word or character, to jump to another piece of the story. Depending on the sequence in which you read the material, the meaning of the story might change (Go to the Source—Eastgate). Interactive games like *Myst*, released in

Go to the Source—
Eastgate

Eastgate, a company started in 1982 and based in Massachusetts, distributes hypertext fiction, non-fiction, and poetry. Its website can give you a sense of the range of material and what reading hypertext is like (www.eastgate.com).

1994, began to explore narrative interactivity on a more mass market level. *Myst* allows the user to travel as a character through a mythic animated landscape, discovering secrets and clues, and ultimately arriving at one of a possible number of endings.

Although it may seem antithetical to our notion of narrative storytelling, which implies a distinctive beginning, middle, and end, there is no reason why a drama or a comedy can't be nonlinear and interactive. A drama could exist in which characters are presented with options for the user to choose where they go next and with whom they interact. An interactive soap opera might allow the user to control which characters will get together, break up, be abducted by aliens, or suffer amnesia. Online games, such as *The Sims* and *SimCity*, allow players to create cities and communities inhabited by residents who act in response to user input. *The Sims* lets you fall in love, have a career, raise a family, and own a home, all without leaving your chair.

TECHNICAL CONCERNS AND ACCESSIBILITY

Although the content possibilities of interactive media are endless, technology has imposed limitations, particularly in terms of **file size**, computer speed, **bandwidth**, and **access**. Advances in technology continue to reduce those limitations.

File size refers to the size of the piece of media or application. As we saw in Chapter 9, audio and particularly video files take up a lot of digital space or bytes. CD-ROMs were used to distribute early interactive media, but the limited file size (650 MB) meant that use of video was limited as well. A small video frame and highly compressed video help, but limit the aesthetic quality of your work. DVDs, at 4.7 gigabytes (GB), address this problem, allowing more than two hours of full screen, high-quality video to be stored on them. The more recent Blu-ray disc holds 25 GB on a single-sided disc and 50 GB on a double-sided disc. The competing HD DVD holds 15 GB per layer.

Personal computers have increasingly faster processing speeds, allowing smoother playback of audio and video. Widespread access to high-bandwidth Internet providers, such as cable modems and integrated services digital networks (ISDNs), and the development of streaming audio and video make it more practical to include more audio and video as part of a website.

However, access is still an issue to be considered. Today's computers are faster and more of them have DVD drives than in the past, and more people have cable modems. Nevertheless, we are only talking about a privileged sector of U.S. society and the industrialized world and a small proportion of the world's population. Compared to radio, TV, and the movies, very few people can experience audiovisual interactive media at the level that current technology allows. As makers, we are left with the dilemma of pushing the technical and aesthetic envelope or reaching a large and diverse audience. This is not a decision that anyone can make for you, but one you are making every time you choose your medium and form of distribution.

SOFTWARE APPLICATIONS

Creating an interactive piece of media often requires the use of many media-making processes and many pieces of production software. Even a fairly simple website will include text, still images, some audio elements, and, increasingly, video or animations. All of those assets need to be produced—photos taken, illustrations drawn, text written, fonts chosen, and audio and video recorded and edited. Then the assets need to be structured together for the navigation and interactive capabilities you have planned. We've already learned how to produce the basic assets; let's now discuss what needs to be done with them to end up with an interactive piece.

In the early days of interactive media, a strict distinction was made between web development and multimedia development. This was mostly because of the limitations of bandwidth (slow telephone modems) and computer speed and memory. More complex multimedia development that utilized images and sound was usually distributed on CD-ROMS and utilized software such as Macromedia's Director for authoring interactive applications for education or entertainment. As discussed, that has changed, allowing Internet delivery to be used for a broad range of advanced interactive work. Another change is that software for creating new media has become increasingly fluid—you can now work more easily with several different software programs, importing and exporting from one to another with little difficulty. Many software applications are offered as part of a bundle, such as Macromedia Studio, which groups several related applications together. At the same time, software is becoming increasingly versatile, offering broader functionality within a single application. Another increasingly common software feature is the inclusion of **templates** or prewritten pieces of code that allow users to work with the software without a lot of programming knowledge.

IMAGE CREATION

For still images to become part of a digital media piece, the images themselves must be in digital form. If a digital still camera is used, the images are stored as digital files, generally compressed to take up less memory. Most digital cameras allow a range of compression to be used. The more compression, the more images can be stored, although compression generally reduces image quality. Film-based photographs, transparencies, and illustrations drawn on paper can be digitized using a *scanner*, which reads the image and converts it into a digital file. Graphics tablets, used in conjunction with drawing and painting software, allow you to draw and paint digitally. A graphics tablet is a highly sensitive drawing surface that acts as an input device into the computer. Software converts the movement of your hand to a line on the computer screen. Using a digital pen or mouse, you can draw or paint, varying the color, texture, and line quality (Figure 10.5). Adobe Illustrator and Macromedia's Fireworks are two powerful and popular graphics creation programs.

Figure 10.5 A graphics tablet is an input device (like a mouse or keyboard) that allows you to digitally draw directly into a software application. (Courtesy Wacom Technology Corp.)

Images must be saved in a file format that is appropriate for the way in which the images will be delivered to the user. Common file formats for still images are shown in Figure 10.6. All have their strengths and best applications. GIFs are better for web graphics as opposed to photographs because they are limited to only 256 colors and support animation. JPEGs are highly compressible but use lossy compression and lose some detail.

IMAGE MANIPULATION

If images are to be manipulated or combined, an application such as Adobe Photoshop, is used. The industry standard, Photoshop is a sophisticated and powerful tool for many graphics purposes. Images can be color corrected, scaled, and layered with other images and text. Each layer can be worked on and saved separately, which makes changes and adjustments much easier. Photoshop also includes its own drawing and text creation tools, or files can be imported from word processors or drawing programs and incorporated into a Photoshop image. Photoshop is used for new media projects but also for print and broadcast images. Macromedia's Fireworks is a web graphics production application.

It is important to keep in mind that developers often use multiple software applications to complete a task. A digital photograph can be imported into Photoshop for color correction and layering with text and

Format	Extension	Use
BMP	.bmp	Microsoft format. Generally uncompressed, so file sizes are large.
EPS	.eps	Illustrator format. May include a preview picture.
GIF	.gif	Supports animation. Good for web graphics, but not photographs. Supported by most browsers. Uses lossless compression.
JPEG	.jpg, .jpeg	Good for photographic images. Supported by most browsers. JPEG is both a file format and a type of lossy compression.
PICT	.pict, .pic, .pct	Apple format. Not for print.
PNG	.png	Native to Fireworks. Good for web graphics. Supported by most browsers. Uses lossless compression; can support more compression than GIF.
TIFF	.tif, .tiff	Good for photographs and line art. Flexible. Can be uncompressed or use lossless compression.

Figure 10.6 Common image file formats.

background textures. The result could be used in a website or imported into an animation application for further preparation. There is no one correct method of working with images.

Photoshop originally worked only with raster or **bitmap** graphics. These types of graphics are made up of individual pixels and subject to jagged edges (aliasing) when resized or displayed at a changed computer screen resolution. Bitmaps tend to be images that were captured digitally or scanned. Photoshop now has some **vector** capability. Vector graphics are created from mathematical formulas and tend to be images that have been drawn. They can be rescaled and manipulated while maintaining quality. They also have smaller file sizes than bitmaps, making them appropriate for web use. Adobe Illustrator handles only vector graphics, whereas Fireworks was created as a vector-bitmap hybrid tool for web graphics.

AUDIO AND VIDEO EDITING

Linear audio clips and video clips or movies used in interactive applications are created the same way as audio or video projects distributed in other ways. The sounds and images are captured and edited using nonlinear editing (NLE) systems. If the clips are to remain digital and be distributed through the web or on a DVD, the audio and video must be output to a usable digital file instead of back to tape. If the final file size needs to be smaller, further compression may be involved. Decisions need to be made about the quality of the output sounds and images and, in the case of video, decisions also need to be made about screen size and frame rate. As seems logical, the smaller the image, the smaller the file size. File size can be further reduced by decreasing the frame rate of the video. If you reduce the rate from its normal 30 frames per second (fps) to 15 fps, the file size is decreased, but the playback is not as smooth. These decisions are made based on the desired balance of aesthetics and the practicalities of download time and uninterrupted playback.

The audio and video files need to be stored in a file format that can be decoded by an audio or video player. Audio file formats include AIFF, WAV, MP3, and RealAudio. When saving a file in a particular format, you need to end the file name with a dot and the proper three-letter extension name so it can be identified by the operating system playing it back. Figure 10.7 shows some common audio and video formats and their extensions. Some formats allow more compression than others. MP3, for example, has become very popular because files can be highly compressed without noticeable quality loss. Video formats include QuickTime from Apple, Windows Media Video from Microsoft, and MPEG-4. These formats include audio and can be used for audio-only files. Both are cross-platform. Plug-in players, primarily QuickTime Player and Windows Media Player, play these formats in browsers.

Common Audio File Extensions

AIFF (Audio Interchange File Format)	.aif
WAV (Windows)	.wav
MP3 (Moving Pictures Experts Group)	.mp3
RealAudio (RealNetworks)	.ra

Common Video File Extensions

AVI (Audio Visual Interleave)	.avi
IVF (Indeo Video Files)	.ivf
MPEG-4 or MP4 (Moving Picture Experts Group Level 4)	.mp4
QuickTime Movie	.mov
RealVideo	.rm, .ram
Windows Media	.wmv

Figure 10.7 Common audio and video file formats.

MOTION GRAPHICS AND ANIMATION

The use of motion graphics and compositing for linear film and video is mentioned in Chapter 9. The same type of still and moving images, existing over time and on multiple layers, is an integral part of interactive media. Computer animation is widely used also, both 2D and 3D. The processes for creating these elements are beyond the purview of an introductory text, but desktop motion graphics applications, such as Adobe's AfterEffects, and the animation capabilities of authoring systems, such as Macromedia's Flash, make this realm of media making accessible and relatively affordable.

PUTTING THE PIECES TOGETHER

So far, we have discussed the creation of individual text, sound, and image assets and the structuring of that content in a branching pattern. Combining the pieces into the form you envision with all the desired links requires computer programming. You have the choice of creating unique programming code or using a piece of software designed to structure nonlinear pieces that provides you with "ready-made" pieces of code that can handle most needs.

AUTHORING SOFTWARE

Flash, a software application by Macromedia (acquired by Adobe), is a powerful tool for *authoring* interactive websites, presentations, and mobile content. It allows you to create a graphic, animated interface that is interactive. An authoring program allows you to take different elements or *objects* and link them. Objects can be sections of text, graphics, photographic images, video, audio, or animations. An interactive experience with several of these elements is said to have *rich content*.

In Flash, to animate an object you make it a *symbol* and save it in the *library*. Symbols can be movie clips, buttons, or graphics. Symbols retain all of their original characteristics: sound, motion, interactivity, and so forth. To use a symbol, you drag it onto the *stage*, and it becomes an *instance*. An instance is a pointer file. The same symbol can be dragged to the stage many times and used in different ways. The stage has many layers, like a deck of cards. The layers allow many things to be going on simultaneously—an animation, a button that changes color when you move your mouse over it, a video playing. Each layer has a timeline. The timeline indicates how each layer reacts over time. As with a strip of film, the timeline has frames, and the playing back of those frames in the timeline creates the illusion of movement. The timelines make up a Flash movie (Figure 10.8).

ActionScript is the programming language used in Flash. The Toolbox provides prewritten scripts for common functions. Flash Player is the plug-in that the user's computer must have in order to interpret or play back Flash movies in the browser. This is just a very brief outline of a complex program that is responsible for much of the animation and graphic interface that we experience on the web.

Figure 10.8 Macromedia Flash interface. (Adobe product screen shot reprinted with permission from Adobe Systems Inc.)

HTML

To create a single web-site, programming allows interactivity within the site. Hypertext Markup Language, more commonly known as **HTML**, is the original primary programming language of the Internet. HTML creates *tags*, or messages, attached to the content, which tell the web browser what piece of information should be where; what color, font, and size it should be; and if it is text, image, sound, or video (Figure 10.9). The maker of a website can write her or his own HTML code or use an application that writes the code for her or him. Many of these

Figure 10.9 Most websites are created using HTML. Here is a page from a website entitled *Road Trip Diaries* and the HTML that created it. (Courtesy of the maker, Karla Berry.)

types of applications exist, such as Macromedia's Dreamweaver. Developments in technology, such as Sun Microsystems' Java and Netscape's JavaScript, allowed increased interactivity by building applications directly into the website instead of requiring each Internet user to have all the applications being used within the site on their hard drive. HTML was responsible for the first stage of the Internet, through the 1990s.

CSS

CSS (Cascading Style Sheets) brought much more flexibility to the web. It allowed the separation of content, which would be structured by the HTML and the style elements (font, colors, spacing), which are determined by the CSS coding (Figure 10.10). The advent of CSS means that you can update the content of a site without having to change the code for the visual design. It also means that you can set a style and create many consistent pages or sites by creating a CSS file and linking it to several HTML pages that contain different information but a basic structure. Some older browsers might have difficulty displaying sites using CSS.

XML

XML has been instrumental in the advent of Web 2.0. XML was developed by a working group of the W3C (World Wide Web Consortium). It is not a specific tagging language, like HTML, but a set of guidelines for creating tags that allow information and content to be structured, permitting databases to more easily store and exchange information. It allows content sharing between websites and applications, and it allows powerful search engines to work. It permits you to tag your friend's photo in Facebook and link to other images of her in Flickr. XML is independent of hardware and software applications, so it makes the same information more accessible, including for use on cell phones or PDAs and for use in delivery systems for the blind or deaf communities.

CSS can be used with XML, but the W3C recommends a newer standard called XSL (eXtensible Stylesheet Language).

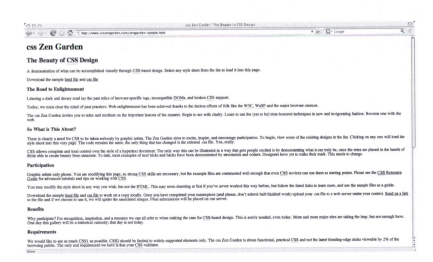

Figure 10.10 Shown here is a web page with its separate HTML file and CSS file. The HTML includes the content and structure. The CSS file contains the style elements. (Courtesy of the designer, Dave Shea, http://www.csszengarden.com.)

(Continued)

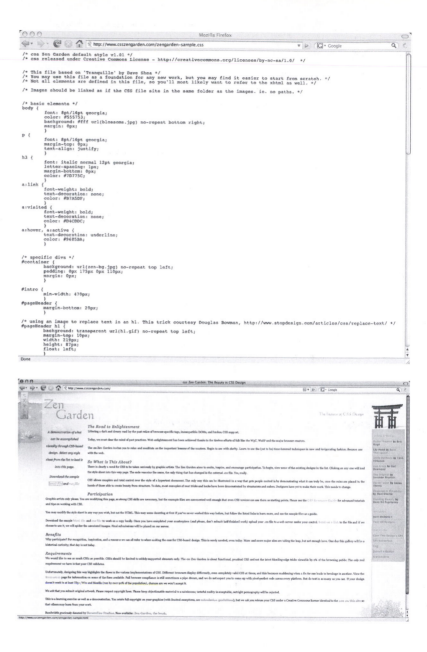

Figure 10.10 *cont'd*

CONCLUSION

It's hard to even touch the surface of all the technical, aesthetic, and ethical issues surrounding the creation and delivery of nonlinear, interactive media. Hardware and software advancements happen daily, and for this reason, technology currently drives the content. The experimenters and innovators are at work. It's an area ripe for creative exploration.

PUTTING IT INTO PRACTICE
WRITING

Create a list of six story ideas (fiction or nonfiction) that would lend themselves to a nonlinear structure. Write a one-paragraph treatment of each and a brief justification as to why they lend themselves to a nonlinear approach.

DOING

Choose one of the six ideas from the "Writing" assignment. Create a flowchart of how the piece would be structured.

KEY CONCEPTS

access	interactivity
artificial intelligence	interface design
assets	menu
bandwidth	navigation design
bitmap	plug-in
branching structure	random access
CSS	software design
database	sound design
file size	tag
flowchart	template
graphic design	URL
hierarchies	user-generated content
HTML	vector
hyperlink	virtual reality
hypertext	web browser
information design	web server
interactive media	XML

CHAPTER 11

Approaches to Production, Exhibition, and Distribution

TRADITIONAL AND CONVERGENT TRENDS AND PREDICTIONS

This book has introduced both the conceptual and practical tools of media production. The attempt has been made to balance the need for appreciation and understanding of how current forms of media are made with the desire to encourage you to challenge the old forms and experiment with alternatives. New forms of media do not tend to make the old forms disappear; new forms tend to make the old forms adapt. Television did not mean the end of radio. It adopted radio's programming, and radio changed to a disc jockey format. Home video did not mean the end of movie theaters. It added another revenue stream to the film industry, and theater attendance actually increased. The Internet has not signaled the end of newspapers or books. Book sales continue to grow. How will the older technologies adapt to the new? What does it mean to add interactivity to television or to a movie through DVD distribution? What does it mean to distribute "TV programming" over a cell phone? Can you tell nonlinear stories that provide the audience with the same level of emotional satisfaction found in linear narrative? What form of media or combinations of forms works best for your concept? Let's review the choices you have in terms of your approaches to production.

DETERMINING YOUR APPROACH

The decisions you make about your production are determined by many factors. Programming type is one. Traditionally a fiction narrative (film or video) is shot with a single camera by a crew guided by the director's vision. An Internet experience is often produced by a team headed by a producer or project manager with individuals working on each task at a computer workstation. Budget is another key factor. A big-budget feature film may employ hundreds of people, be shot on 35 mm film, and be distributed internationally, but a low-budget feature may have only a few people doing several jobs each, be shot on consumer-level digital video, and be screened at a film festival or on an Internet site.

The purpose of the piece may also help define the process. An attempt to educate the elderly on the necessity for early diagnosis of diabetes needs to be produced and distributed in a way that will best get to the target audience. A piece aimed at warning teenagers about the danger of inhalants would most likely demand a different style and outlet than the piece aimed at the elderly. Personal preferences of the maker play a big role as well. One maker may see her ideas best served by a website, another by a video documentary.

PRODUCTION TEAM

The first question to answer is, "Am I producing this piece myself or do I need/want help?" Most media production is a collaborative process, but some makers approach media production as an individual process of expression, such as painting or writing. Recent advancements in digital image making and desktop postproduction make this approach more possible than ever. The benefit of high quality, affordable, and user-friendly digital technologies is the coherence of vision and the ability to eliminate compromises; however, that can be a drawback as well. Collaboration can force you to explain and defend your ideas and can lead to positive changes in your approach.

The scope of most media projects makes collaboration a necessity. There is too much work for one person to do. Collaboration also allows people to specialize in one aspect of media making, which results in greater expertise. Some media projects are made by a process of true collaboration through a process of consensus, but most commercial projects employ a high degree of hierarchy and authority. The executive producer hires and fires and controls the flow of funds. The associate producer answers to the producer. The assistant cameraperson answers to the director of photography who answers to the director. The graphic designer answers to the project manager who answers to the producer. It's not democratic, but it's efficient. This system also assumes that there's a reason that people are in a position of authority—talent and experience. A smart boss, though, is one who will listen to a good idea from anyone, and who encourages the development of those who answer to her or him.

STUDIO VS. LOCATION

Another major decision is where the actual production is going to take place. Will it be in a controlled atmosphere or out in the field in a "real" location? For audio production, video production, and still photography or green screen work for animation and compositing, the controlled space is called a **studio**. For film production, the term **soundstage** is usually used. If sound is being recorded, it's important that the acoustics of the studio or soundstage are correct. You want the space to be free of extraneous background noise, such as traffic or air conditioning. This can be accomplished by careful design and construction of the space. The specific characteristics of the space are determined by the exact use of the space—whether you are recording voice or music dialogue. The "sound" of the room should be different for different purposes.

Most studios in which visuals are captured allow no daylight to enter so all light can be controlled, and you don't have to worry about mixing color temperatures. Also, solid walls block sound better; outside sound is harder to block through glass, but it can be done. Some still photography studios allow daylight as a lighting option, but they have some means of blocking the daylight if desired. Television studios and soundstages tend to have high ceilings and grids from which to hang lighting instruments. The outlets for the lights feed into a dimmer board that allows intensity control of each instrument. Floors in studios are smooth for good camera movement on dollies or pedestals. The studio doorways are widened for the moving of props and sets. Television studios have hidden cabling so the output of video cameras and microphone can be sent to a separate **control room** for switching, audio mixing, and recording. A TV director typically works in the control room; a film director works on the soundstage floor (Figure 11.1).

a. talent

b. floor manager (FM)

c. camera operator

d. production assistant (PA)

e. character generator operator

f. technical director (TD)

g. audio engineer

h. video tape operator

i. director

j. assistant director (AD)

k. microphone outlets

l. character generator

m. switcher

n. audio board

o. video tape recorder (VTR)

p. monitor

Figure 11.1 TV studios generally have at least three cameras, a lighting board, microphone outlets, and a grid for hanging lights. Talent, camera operators, the floor manager, and studio or production assistants work on the studio floor. The cameras and microphones are cabled through the walls and floor, through a master control where the video signals are monitored and adjusted, and on to the control room. The video signals are wired into the switcher, the audio signals into the mixing board. The director, assistant director, technical director, audio engineer, character generator, and tape operators work in the control room.

The advantage of working in a studio or soundstage is control. You can create your own reality and not worry about disturbances from the outside world. The disadvantage is the lack of reality. You can build a set of a busy New York City street in the studio or an outdoor lot, but it's never going to have the realism and immediacy of the actual location.

Working on location offers a world of possibilities but also the unpredictability of that world. Planes fly overhead. Curious onlookers walk through the shot. It rains. You also have the job of securing permission to use both private and public locations. Aside from the immediacy of a location, though, it's often just more practical. It's easier to find a beach to shoot on than to construct one.

It is possible to combine studio work, location shoots, and recording sessions in one project. It's done all the time. Many feature films are shot by traveling to a location to shoot exteriors and "atmosphere" shots and then returning to Los Angeles or elsewhere to shoot the interiors on a soundstage. An audio documentary may include narration recorded in a recording studio and interviews and sound effects recorded in the field.

SINGLE VS. MULTIPLE SOURCES

This is a decision that applies to cameras and microphones. Do you capture several different sources or angles simultaneously, or do you gather one shot or source at a time and combine them later? With electronic sources, such as audio and video signals, you may choose to mix or edit the sources live or record each microphone or camera output separately for postproduction later. We tend to associate multiple-source acquisition with studio production and single-source acquisition with working in the field, but that is not always the case. Multicamera shoots happen in the field, such as sporting events. Single-camera film shooting on a soundstage is a common practice, and the audio recording of narration with one microphone is just one example of a single-microphone audio recording session. Like everything else, there are advantages and disadvantages to working with single vs. multiple sources. You need to look at your particular production, the subject matter, the desired style, and the budget to determine the best approach.

Single Source

The major advantage of single-source production—camera or microphone—is that of *control*. We will make the assumption that single-source production is being done with the intention of editing the elements together later. A disc jockey broadcasting live with a single microphone or a single camera covering the local town meeting to be cablecast by the local access channel obviously does not provide the producer with a high level of control. However, by knowing that the shots or pieces of audio will be polished in postproduction, you can concentrate on making each piece just the way you want it. For visuals, you can place your camera where it will create the strongest composition. You can light just that one image. For sound, you can place your microphone in the optimum position for recording clean sound. Unless you are shooting a long take, you can break your story down into shots. In scripted pieces, you can even do multiple takes of each shot until you are satisfied with the performance and technical aspects.

Because only one camera is being used at a time, the camera can be anywhere on the set, which allows for 360-degree access. Most fiction films and videos, documentaries, and TV commercials are shot this way. Narration, interviews, sound effects, rerecorded dialogue, and other audio elements are usually recorded with a single microphone and combined in a postproduction mix.

This advantage of control continues into the postproduction process in terms of providing *flexibility*. Even though you might go into the shoot or recording session with a clear idea of the editing and transitions, single-source acquisition allows you to fine-tune your editing decisions or completely change your mind in postproduction.

Single-camera shoots may record audio with a single microphone or with multiple microphones fed into a mixer.

Multiple Sources

The major advantage of multiple cameras or multiple-microphone acquisition is that you can capture ongoing sources (camera angles or audio sources) simultaneously. Many documentary or nonfiction situations do not allow the maker to control the action, so if you want more than one visual point of view or more than one audio source recorded cleanly, you need to acquire them all at once. This principle applies to a demonstration on the street, a panel discussion, a live concert, or a volcano erupting. Multicamera production is used for fiction programs because it lets the performance flow uninterrupted, allowing actors to build dramatic or comedic intensity as they do in live theater.

The major disadvantage of multicamera production is the need for compromise. If you're shooting from several angles at the same time, the lighting must work from all the camera angles. Lighting is best done for one particular camera/subject relationship, so lighting the same subject from several angles is a compromise and often results in flatter, less interesting lighting design. Microphone placement can be compromised when talent has to be miked for an ongoing period of time, during which they may move to several positions. In most cases, all of the talent's positions need to be adequately miked while keeping the mikes out of the shot. When multiple cameras are being used, you also need to be careful about camera placement to avoid having a camera in the background of another shot. This challenge encourages a proscenium approach to blocking the cameras, which keeps them on one side of the action, as in a traditional theater setup (Figure 11.2). While this helps with continuity of screen direction because you don't have the opportunity to cross the 180-degree line, it limits your points of view and the camera's mobility.

Multisource acquisition of electronic media—audio and video—can be done in two ways. The first way, as discussed in Chapter 9, is to *switch* (video) or *mix* (audio) *live*, or *live-on-tape*, feeding the multiple sources into a video switcher or audio mixing board. Video switching

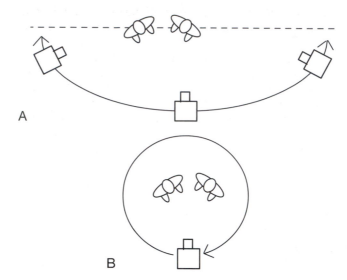

Figure 11.2 **A**, Multiple-camera production usually limits the cameras to one side of the 180-degree line. Otherwise, cameras would get into each other's shots. **B**, Single-camera production generally allows 360-degree access.

is accomplished by having a person, called the *technical director* (TD), push a button on the switcher panel. One of the video sources that has been input to the switcher is chosen to be broadcast live or recorded on a VTR. The TD performs live transitions between sources (cut, dissolves, and wipes) and effects, such as key effects (see Chapter 9). If the switcher is also connected to a character generator, the TD can add titles and credits over video sources, keying them over a solid background, graphics, or live images.

An audio engineer or sound mixer who monitors the incoming signals and sets their volume levels does live audio mixing. He or she wants to make sure the overall audio level is correct (peaking at 0 dB; see Chapter 5), but also that the different sounds are properly balanced, with primary sources louder than background sources. Equalization and other effects can be added as well.

A major advantage of live switching and live mixing is the lack of postproduction. This is a necessity when broadcasting live. The visual output of the switcher and the audio output of the mixing board are being fed to the transmitter for broadcast. If a program is being recorded for later use, little or no postproduction becomes an economic advantage. Sometimes minimal postproduction is done for a switched or mixed program. This can include some *audio sweetening,* which includes the adding of music, sound effects, or a laugh track. Visually, inserts, such as *cutaway shots* (like a close-up of the hand opening a door) or *reaction shots* (someone listening to the speaker), can be added. Even if postproduction is done, the time and cost is far less than with a single-source production or with an iso production (discussed later).

The major disadvantage of switching and live mixing is the lack of control. If the result is being broadcast live or if postproduction is not an option, mistakes can and do occur. Even if a mistake is not obvious, the precision of an edit or the subtleties of an audio mix will not be the same as in a postproduction situation where decisions can be reviewed and adjusted. This lack of control is a fair trade-off for the ability to broadcast programs and events live. The energy and spontaneity of live broadcasting often outweigh minor mistakes. Sometimes, mistakes such as a reporter overcome by emotion or a wild camera pan as the camera searches for the fan who caught the wild pitch add the power of immediacy to your production in a way that no second take or postproduction effect ever could. Live-on-tape productions can benefit from that sense of immediacy, even though they are not really going out live.

Certain types of programming lend themselves to multisource production. Location events, such as sports competitions and major political events, are broadcast live by combining anywhere from 2 or 3 cameras (as in a presidential speech) to 40 or 50 (for an major sporting event). Anytime a radio program has more than one participant—from a studio interview to the broadcast of a 20-participant panel discussion or the in-studio visit of a band—live mixing occurs. As mentioned, a multiple-mike audio mix might accompany a single-camera shoot if there are several actors and positions within a shot. Video is mixed live-on-tape in television studios for news programs, talk shows, game shows, soap operas, and some situation comedies. Usually, shows that are not broadcast live (game shows, sitcoms, and soaps) are taped in sections and assembled later.

The second approach to multicamera production is sometimes called **iso production**, which is short for *isolated,* meaning that more than one camera is recording simultaneously, each camera recording the event or program in its entirety (Figure 11.3). Multisource film shooting is iso by default because film cannot be switched live.

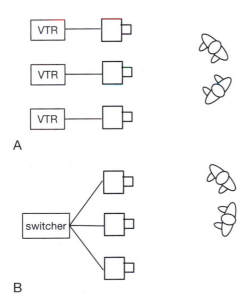

A

B

Figure 11.3 A, Iso production takes the output of each camera and records it in its entirety. **B,** Switched—multicam—production takes the output of each camera and feeds it into a switcher. With video, it's possible to use either or combine the approaches. With film, multiple camera means iso.

Most prime-time situation comedies are shot with multiple cameras on film. This allows an almost live-theater experience for the actors and studio audience along with the image quality of 35 mm film. Iso production allows ongoing action, multiple points of view, and the control of postproduction. Several camera angle options are available for each shot, which can be both a blessing and a curse. The blessing is that for each moment during the shoot, you can choose the very best angle. The curse is that there is so much footage to deal with and so many decisions to make that postproduction takes longer (and thereby costs more). This type of production is done when the budget permits and the situation demands it. Live concerts and other events that cannot be interrupted lend themselves to this approach. Large-scale and expensive stunts, such as blowing up a bridge or a battle scene with a cast of thousands, are usually filmed by several cameras, so you only have to blow up the bridge once.

Often with video, switching and iso are combined. It is possible to output multiple video signals from a camera. One can be recorded directly onto tape; another can be sent to a switcher. In this way, you have the immediacy and cost efficiency of a switched production but the coverage of iso production. Mistakes can be fixed and extra cutaway shots can be added. Both live events and studio programs employ this combination of approaches.

Film cameras can be outfitted with **video assists**, or small video cameras that record a video image of what is also being exposed on the film. These are used in both single-camera film production for immediate playback and multicamera film production, which is fed to a switcher.

Some people assume that single-source production is less expensive because you only need one camera or microphone. On a very low-budget level of production, this might be the case, but generally the old adage, "time is money," applies. The time you spend in postproduction generally makes single-source film or video production more expensive than multi-camera video mixed live. Multiple-camera iso production can be the most expensive, once you factor in increased production costs in equipment and crew and increased postproduction costs because of the time involved logging material and making decisions about the many different options.

A Different Look

Ultimately, single-camera and multicamera productions have a very different look. Think about a prime-time series like *The Office* (NBC) and a situation comedy like *Friends* (NBC). They look very different. Both are comedies. Both are shot mostly in studios, so that's not the difference. *The Office* uses more camera movement and close-ups, and you end up seeing the sets from almost all angles. Watching the series *Friends* is more like watching a play. You hear the audience. Your point of view stays on one side of the action and shots tend to be wide, with the occasional reaction close-up. These are both well-established styles of television (though comedy shows shot with a single camera are a more recent development). The creator's initial decision to produce the show with either a single camera or many cameras determines the look and feel of the final product.

LINEAR OR INTERACTIVE

The choice between single and multiple cameras has been around for a long time. A newer choice for producers is linear, interactive, or both. Should the program be one that the viewer or listener experiences from beginning to end, or should the piece have a branching structure and the opportunity for the user to make decisions? The choice might be made by considering the purpose of the piece. Do want your audience to learn something or access information? An interactive experience might best support learning. Do you want to elicit an emotional response or entertain through creation of suspense and subsequent release? In that case, the control you have over sequence and pacing in a linear piece might be better.

You might want to consider a combination of linear and interactive elements. This linear textbook has an accompanying website that offers interactive learning exercises. A linear documentary on PBS or dramatic TV show has a companion website in which background information about the subjects or characters can be accessed and viewers can chat with each other about their reactions and opinions.

Feature films also have companion websites with interactive games, branching opportunities for additional information, and also short linear teasers presented as Quicktime movies, which create anticipation of the full experience. That same feature film, presented as only a linear experience in the theater, is later released on a DVD that allows you to hear a director's track, see scenes from the film's production, and view outtakes and alternate endings. You may create a video, post it online, and invite viewers to add to it or change it. This line between linear and interactive experiences will continue to blur as the means of media distribution continue to change and expand.

DISTRIBUTION AND EXHIBITION

Distribution is the process of getting a media product from its producers to those who exhibit it. It involves marketing the film or other media project and overseeing its delivery to the *exhibitor* who will actually present the work. A distributor can be a company that distributes a feature film to theaters or cable networks. It can be the film distribution cooperative that helps independent film and video makers submit their work to festivals or sell it to schools and libraries. A distributor is often a middleman, but media makers can act as their own distributors as well.

Strictly speaking, *exhibition* is the actual presentation of media. An exhibitor can be a movie theater, a TV network, a local film society, or a website from which you can download a short video. The term *exhibition*, though, often refers to artwork. It is a term we use more in the context of an installation in a museum or gallery or a screening of films and videos in a festival or film series.

Movies used to be seen only in the movie theater, television only seen on a TV set, and radio programs heard only on a radio. While "convergence of the media" was an overused phrase in the 1990s and is still bandied about today, it is a well-established concept in the history of media. New media have always looked to established media forms for content. Early magazines serialized novels of the day (e.g., Charles Dickens). Radio borrowed from the newspapers—columnists and comics (e.g., Walter Winchell, *Little Orphan Annie*, and many more). Radio replaced vaudeville and hired many of its acts to create radio shows (e.g., George Burns and Gracie Allen). When TV came along, many of its shows came straight from radio, creating situation comedies, anthology drama series, and talk shows. Soon after, Hollywood decided that TV was not a threat but an opportunity and started selling its old films to TV for broadcast.

Now, the overlap of movies, TV, radio, the web, and other interactive media is just a continuation of that established trend. Old media seldom disappear. More are added, and more opportunities for interaction are made. Let's go back and consider the possible distribution outlets or exhibitors for our original means of media production—still images, moving images, and sound. (Still film or digital images are discussed here only in the relationship with motion pictures and electronic media. There are obviously many uses for photography within the field of print media.) As a media maker, it is important not just to understand the status of the media industry at this point, but to see the many possibilities that exist for your creations.

STILL IMAGES

1. Websites and interactive applications on DVD and mobile devices. The small file size of still images compared to moving images makes them a popular choice. Slide shows (series of still images) are used as a low-bandwidth substitution for moving images.
2. Title sequences and composited effects for films and videos. Specially created still images or stills pulled from motion picture film or video are often used as backgrounds for titles or as an asset in a motion graphics program, such as Adobe AfterEffects.

FILM

1. Theatrical distribution
2. Cable TV distribution
3. Public television
4. Network television
5. DVD distribution
6. Film festivals
7. Internet (on an individual's website, through an Internet distributor, or online film festival)
8. Asset for an interactive application or gallery installation (though video is more common)

Entries 2 through 5 can start as theatrical films and be sold for other forms of distribution, or they can be created specifically for that distribution medium, like a TV series or a movie that goes straight to home video release.)

VIDEO

1. Theatrical distribution—HDTV, digital video transferred to film, or exhibited by a high-definition projector (growing development)
2. Cable TV
3. Public television
4. Network television
5. Local television
6. DVD distribution
7. Film and video festivals
8. Gallery installations
9. Corporate and institutional videos
10. Internet (on an individual's website, through an Internet distributor, or online film festival)
11. Asset for interactive applications

AUDIO

1. Music distribution—CDs, MP3s, and so forth
2. Radio programming—broadcast and streamed
3. Podcast
4. Sound for film, video, and interactive presentations

THE FUTURE

Already, visions of the future posed in the first edition of this book—just four years ago—have come to pass. We now have a PC, cell phone, video, and music—all in one handheld device. We're seeing the further integration of television and computers. We watch last night's episode of our favorite show online. Our DVRs *are* PCs. What's next? Will a digital implant in our brains be capable of receiving mediated sound and images in the way our brains receive light and sound vibrations, bypassing a screen and speaker completely?

Which developments will the marketplace adopt? Which new forms of distribution will supplant the old? If history teaches us anything, it shows that technology has always presented more options to the marketplace than it supports. Consider the optical laser disc of the 1980s—*not* a marketplace success. Often, affordability and compatibility outweigh technical quality. Look how long it has taken HDTV to become viable.

To get an idea where the mainstream is headed, you can look to the work of media artists. The work of several are included in the illustrations for this book. The avant-garde has always contributed to (or been appropriated by, depending on your point of view) the mainstream culture. Web art, cell phone art, new media installations, pioneers in 3D cyber-environment—this is where the entertainment industry of tomorrow is being developed. As stated before, new media rarely replace established, successful old media. Portable access to information will not replace our desire to sit back and experience an enlightening and/or entertaining media experience on a large screen. We will just have more media. For you that means there is more media to make.

CONCLUSION

New outlets for media increase the need for media products—that's the good news for media makers. Increased outlets and an unending choice of media products make it harder to have your messages seen and heard by many—that's the challenge for media makers. Advancements in technology and public policy make the means of media production accessible to all voices—that's the promise of media. All of the technological advancements and distribution choices are meaningless without stories told with passion, artistry, and honesty—that's the truth.

PUTTING IT INTO PRACTICE
WRITING AND DOING

The time has come to produce one of your stories, using the production and postproduction means available to you. If possible, consider mixing production methods and/or genres. Combine still images, sound, and moving images. Tell a nonfiction story using continuity. Tell a fiction narrative through montage. Keep it short and sweet.

Write a treatment, script, or storyboard. Don't forget your logs and edit plan. Here are some ideas to get you started.

1. Tell a formative story from your childhood.
2. Create a media portrait of a local person or group that more people should know about.
3. Mediate a recent dream.
4. Create a sound and image "time capsule" of your life now to show your children in 20 years.
5. Tell the history of your birthplace.

KEY CONCEPTS

control room	studio
iso production	video assist
soundstage	

Glossary

180-degree line	Imaginary axis that connects two subjects (guided by their respective gazes) or is defined by directional movement and provides a constriction for camera movement. Remaining on one side of the line maintains consistent continuity of screen direction.

A

ADR	Automatic dialogue replacement; a technique used most commonly in fiction films where inferior audio, recorded in the field, is replaced by having actors come into a studio, watch the film, listen to the field recording, and respeak their lines in a controlled environment. Also called *looping*.
Access	Issue concerning which segments of society your production will reach. Access can be limited by economic and political situations and by physical limitations of the individual user.
Added light	Light created by instruments that are brought to a location to augment the existing light.
Additive color mixing	System of color mixing based on red, green, and blue primaries combined to form white light.
Ambience or ambient sound	Natural sound of a location.
Amplitude	Height of a wave. With sound waves, it determines loudness.
Angle of view	Mathematical angle of a lens' field of view (either normal, wide, or narrow).
Animation	A process that uses a series drawings, paintings, cut-outs, clay or computer images to create the illusion of movement.
Answer print	Print from a conformed negative with a mixed soundtrack.
Aperture	The measurement of the adjustable opening in a lens that allows light to pass through the lens into the camera.

Artificial intelligence	Scientific attempt to have computers or computer-controlled robots perform in ways we think of as human, including learning, reasoning, and finding meaning.
Aspect ratio	Proportions of the frame or the relationship of width to height.
Assemble editing	Form of video editing that reproduces the entire video signal (including audio and control track).
Assets	Building blocks (still images, videos, audio clips, and animations) that make up any particular computer-based media production.
Asymmetrical balance	Approach to creating balanced composition within the frame that can be achieved by balancing a subject on one side of the frame with a subject or other visual element on the other side.
Attenuation	Weakening of an energy wave as it travels.

B

B-roll	Visual footage used to support the soundtrack (narration or interview) in a documentary film or video production.
Backlight	Element of three-point lighting, aimed at the back of the subject, which visually separates the subject from the background.
Bandwidth	Range of frequencies required or available for signal transmission that determines the amount of data that can be transmitted in a given time (usually bits per second). Limited bandwidth can result in slow transmission of data.
Beam splitter	Device inside a video or digital still camera that separates the entering light into three separate colors (red, green, and blue) to be received by the imaging chips or tubes.
Bidirectional microphone	Classification of a microphone pickup pattern that includes the left and right sides of a microphone.
Binaural hearing	Ability of human ears to perceive differences in location, direction, and presence of sound.
Bins	Electronic files that hold groups of media clips in an organized fashion for use in nonlinear editing.
Bit depth	Amount of digital information taken within each individual sample.
Bitmap	A type of computer graphic made up of individual pixels that are subject to jagged edges or aliasing when resized.
Blocking the talent	A part of the production process in which the director makes decisions about talent position and movement relative to camera position.
Branching structure	Information flow of a nonlinear media production that allows multiple paths through the material.
Brightness	Property of a color that references how close it is to either complete reflection or absorption of light.
Broadcasting	Transmission of radio waves from one point of origination to an unlimited number of receivers over a relatively large area.
Budget	Estimation of the costs that will be incurred in the creation of a media production.
Bus	Row of buttons on a switcher used for live editing during a television production.

C

Capturing	The acquisition of sound and image information.
Cardioid microphone	Another name for a unidirectional microphone pickup pattern that describes the pickup's heart-shaped pattern of sensitivity.

CCD Charge-coupled device; a computer chip used as an imaging sensor in a digital still or video camera.

Chromakey Visual effect that electronically cuts a hole in one image and replaces it with another, selecting the part of an image that contains a certain color to create a hole.

Chrominance Color information of light.

Circle of confusion The blurred point that results from light rays traveling through a lens but not quite converging to a single point. Small circles of confusion can appear to be sharp.

Clips Pieces of media material used in the nonlinear video editing process.

Closure Visual phenomenon resulting from the human psychological desire for wholeness. If given the visual clue, a viewer will mentally complete an image. Explains why a human head, framed without showing the shoulder line, appears to be disembodied.

Codec Compressor/decompressor; mathematical model that determines exactly how audio or video compression should take place.

Color temperature Specific proportion of wavelengths (from across the color spectrum) within any source of light, measured in kelvins.

Compression Method of saving digital audio, video, and still images that involves the removal of redundant content or the reorganization of material and results in lower file sizes, increased transmission speeds, and generally reduced quality.

Condenser microphone Type of microphone that uses two charged metal plates (one moving, one fixed) to create an audio signal.

Cones and rods Cells in the retina of the eye that are sensitive to light. Cones are sensitive to brightness and color. Rods are sensitive to dim light.

Conforming Process of cutting and splicing a film negative from which an answer print can be made.

Continuity The result of following stylistic conventions that create a logical, linear story.

Continuity editing 1. Cinematic approach designed to tell a story in a logical, linear fashion based on a set of conventions widely accepted by audiences.

2. Style of film and video editing in which shots are pieced together to create a realistic linear progression through time that remains as seamless and invisible as possible.

Continuous wave End result of the analog recording process based on the direct relationship between the original waves and the recorded signal.

Contrast Comparison of tonal values from white to black.

Control room Room wired to a television production studio that houses equipment for program switching, audio mixing, and recording.

Convergence Trend of "overlapping" between programming, production methods, and distribution taking place in the world of media production.

Counter Device that counts the rotation of heads or the passage of tape or film through the machine.

Crane Long-armed, counterweighted camera mount device that allows sweeping camera moves through space.

Crest Highest point of a wave. With a sound wave, the crest represents the maximum pressure of air molecules.

Crossfade Audio transition, in which one source gradually becomes softer while another becomes louder, that can be used to soften an abrupt change or signal a change in time or place.

CSS Cascading Style Sheets; an approach to designing websites that allows the code that determines the stylistic elements to be separated from the content. It allows for updating of content without having to reprogram the design.

Cut	Instantaneous and complete transition from one source to another.
Cutaway	Cut to a related subject or object that seems a logical part of the story.

D

Daylight film	Daylight film is balanced for approximately 5000 K. The film can be used in other lighting conditions by using the correct colored filter on the lens of the camera.
Database	A collection of digital information that is searchable.
Decibel (dB)	Unit of measurement for the amplitude (loudness) of a sound wave.
Decisive moment	Concept attributed to Henri Cartier-Bresson that describes a frozen moment of time resulting in a powerful photograph.
Deductive reasoning	Method of gathering information that starts with the larger context (i.e., a wide shot) and gradually reveals the details.
Depth of field	A range of acceptable focus along the camera/subject axis.
Dialogue	Lines spoken by subjects or actors that are part of the story.
Diegetic	Existing within the reality of the story.
Diegetic sound	Sound or music that exists within the reality of the story in a film or video production, such as music playing on a radio visible in the scene or the sound of a closing door.
Digital intermediates	The result of importing a piece of digital media into a software application, manipulating it, and exporting it again.
Digitize	To convert an audio and/or video signal to a digital format.
Direct cinema	Approach to documentary that relies on the observation of behavior, as opposed to narration or interviews.
Directed tension	Sense of implied movement created by graphics lines or vectors within the frame or by the inherent tension of certain positions within the frame.
Dissolve	Visual transition in which one source gradually disappears by becoming transparent while another appears by becoming opaque. It can be used to soften an abrupt change or signal a change in time or place.
Documentary	Nonfiction media with a narrative based on real people, places, and events.
Dolly	1. Camera movement along the z-axis 2. Wheeled camera mounts that can roll either on smooth floors or constructed tracks.
Dynamic microphone	Type of microphone that uses a coil and magnet to produce an electric audio signal.

E

Edge number	Markings on film that identify the location of individual frames, as well as manufacturer product information (also called key numbers or footage numbers).
EDL	Edit decision list; a final list of shots used in the video editing process, identified by time code.
Edit plan	Written list of decisions as to which logged shots of video or film footage are going to be used in an edited cut and in what order they will appear.
Edited master	Finished product that is produced by the online editing stage of video production and used to make duplication copies.

Effects bank	Two related buses on a video switcher that can be used to create an electronic effect. The output of the effects bank can be selected on the switcher's program bus.
Electromagnetic energy	Energy traveling along any of the frequencies included in the electromagnetic spectrum that include, from lowest to highest frequency, radio, infrared, visible light, ultraviolet, X-ray, gamma ray, and cosmic ray waves.
Ellipsis of time	Convention of media storytelling that eliminates unnecessary portions of a story but retains continuity.
Envelope	"Shape" of a sound, determined linearly by attack, decay, sustain, and release.
Eyeline	The direction in which a subject or actor is looking.
Existing light	The light naturally existing in a location. Also called *ambient light*.
Exposition	Information needed to understand plot development.
Exposure	The result of light striking a photosensitive material, such as photographic film or a CCD in a video camera.

F

Fade	Dissolve to or from black (or any solid color) or a gradual change in audio volume to or from silence.
Fair use	U.S. legal concept that allows the use of short excerpts of copyrighted work without permission for educational or critique purposes.
Fiction	A construction of words and/or media based on an event or series of events that can include imaginary characters and locations.
Field of view	Amount of a scene included in the frame.
File management	Organization of files associated with a media project software application, including an understanding of the difference between media files and project files, and practicing consistent file backup procedures.
File size	Number of bits or amount of data stored.
Fill light	Element of three-point lighting that softens the shadows cast by the key light.
Filters	Colored pieces of glass or plastic placed in front of a lens to change the color and/or intensity of the light.
Fine cut	Final version of an edited film, ready for release.
Flat lighting	Lighting in which the fill light has the same intensity as the key light, resulting in no modeling or casting of shadows on the subject.
Flowchart	Graphic representation of a nonlinear navigation design that diagrams the elements of the piece and the possible paths through them.
Focal length	Distance from the optical center of the glass elements of the lens to the image plane.
Foley	Creation of sound effects as part of a sound design.
Foot-candle	Unit of measurement for the quantity of light, based on the amount of light produced by one candle at a distance of one foot.
Foreshadowing	Suggested future plot developments through spoken, visual, or aural clues.
Frame	Rectangular shape defining a mediated image.
Frequency	Number of cycles that a wave travels in 1 second.
Frequency response	Sensitivity across a range of frequencies.
F-stop	Incremental settings on a lens that indicate the size of the lens aperture.
Fully scripted	Script (one- or two-column) that includes all dialogue.

G

Generational loss Result of an analog-to-analog signal transfer (or "dub"), which creates an amplification of the noise within the original recorded sound or image and subsequent reduction in quality.

Gestalt Whole image that is more than the sum of its parts; perception of a pattern based on visual information.

Graphic design Planning of the nonphotographic visual elements of a media production, such as text and borders.

H

Handheld microphone Microphone designed for use in proximity to subject. Can be held or placed on a stand.

Hard/direct/ spotted light Light waves traveling in straight lines, producing light energy that covers a limited area with maximum intensity. Results in harsh highlights and dark, hard-edged shadows.

Harmonics Group of similar frequencies that creates a specific sound.

Headroom Space above the subject's head (relative to shot size) that compensates for the magnetism of the frame's edge.

Hertz (Hz) Basic unit of measurement of the frequency of sound.

Hierarchies Prioritizing information in a nonlinear media production.

High key lighting Lighting setups utilizing a 2:1 key/fill ratio, producing an upbeat, daytime effect.

HTML Hypertext Markup Language; the primary programming language used for web page design, based on a system of tags that provide various formatting cues for text and images.

Hue Property of a color that references where it falls within the color spectrum.

Hyperlink Programmed behavior that allows the user to move, or "surf," between different websites.

Hypertext Computer-based telling of nonlinear, interactive text-based stories.

I

Illusion of depth Creation of an appearance of the third dimension within a two-dimensional medium.

Illusion of real time Concept of postproduction in which shots taken out of sequence by a single camera are edited together to create a sense of real-time action.

Image plane The part of the camera where the lens focuses light and the image is created, most often film or a computer chip.

Impedance Amount of resistance to a signal.

Incident light meter Type of light meter that reads the intensity of light emitting from a light source.

Inductive reasoning Method of gathering information that starts with details (i.e., close-ups) and gradually reveals the larger context.

Information design Structuring of content (within the realm of interactive media design).

Input/output Entering and exiting of material or information into and out of a system or device.

Insert editing Form of video editing that allows the separation of the audio and video signals, requiring an unbroken control track to be recorded on the tape first.

Installation A media production that combines any combination of sounds, images, and sculptural elements in a space such as a gallery or museum. Typically, audience members can walk around and sometimes interact with the artwork.

Interactive media Media production in which the user and the program communicate with each other.

Interactivity	Concept of a user and a multimedia program reacting to each other in order to determine the outcome.
Interface design	Determination of how a user will interact with an interactive media program, based on the expectations of and challenges presented to the user.
Interframe	A type of video compression in which several frames are read and then averaged to determine what material is not needed.
Interlaced scanning	The method of recording video in which the rows of pixels that make up one frame of video are separated into two fields. First, odd-numbered rows are scanned, then the even-numbered rows.
Intraframe	A type of video compression that takes place within each frame.
Iris	The adjustable opening in a lens that allows light to pass through the lens into the camera.
Iso production	Short for isolated production; an approach to multicamera production in which all cameras capture the entirety of the action.

J

Jump cut	Edit that breaks the continuity of a film or video production.

K

Kelvin	Unit of measurement for the color temperature of light.
Key light	Element of three-point lighting that provides basic illuminations and creates depth through the casting of shadows.
Key/fill ratio	Brightness relationship between the key and fill lights.

L

Lavaliere microphone	Small microphone designed to attach to a subject.
Leadroom	Extra space in the frame that balances the momentum of movement or implied direction.
LED meter	Mechanism that measures the amount of voltage in an audio signal. The information is displayed by a series of light-emitting diodes (LEDs) on a metered scale.
Letterboxing	Technique of displaying widescreen film or video to video with a 4:3 aspect ratio. Results in reproduction of the full widescreen image with a black band at the top and bottom of the frame.
Linear	1. Having a form that starts at the beginning and progresses to an ending point. 2. An approach to editing that defines the time frame and does not allow for insertions or deletions.
Live mixing	Concept of mixing down and reproducing or broadcasting (and/or recording) a multichannel audio source during its original creation.
Live programming	Programming that is broadcast, cablecast or transmitted via satellite at the time it is produced.
Live switching	Concept of editing "on the fly" during a television production of any live performance or event.
Live-on-tape programming	Method of production that maintains a real-time relationship between production time and replay time but is experienced by the audience sometime later.

Log   Written record of footage, including the order in which each shot appears and its location on the tape or film reel.

Long take   Shot of relatively long duration that relies on camera and subject movement instead of editing.

Lookspace   Extra space allowed in the frame in order to balance a subject's gaze.

Low key lighting   Lighting setup with a key/fill ratio greater than 2:1 (e.g., 4:1, 8:1, 16:1), producing a dramatic or nighttime effect.

Luminance   Brightness information of light.

Luminance key   Visual effect that electronically cuts a hole in one image and replaces it with another, selecting the part of an image that falls below a certain brightness level to create a hole.

M

Mag stock   Audiotape with sprocket holes that match that of film stock.

Matched cut   Edit of two shots that matches one point in the action from two different angles or shot sizes to create the sense of continuous action.

Mechanical rights   Permission to use a specific recording of a musical composition for a media production that involves only aural elements.

Menu   Screen page or section with a series of buttons that allows the user to navigate to and between various sections within an interactive media program.

Monitoring   Process of listening to an audio signal during recording to ensure proper levels and sound quality.

Montage   Editing technique used in film and video production that allows the viewer to create interpretive meaning by contrasting and comparing the content of adjacent shots or the relationship between the sound and image.

Motion capture   Creating a pattern of movement and inputting it into a computer. For computer animation, sensors are placed on a human body and read to create the pattern.

Motion graphics   Computer-animated text and other graphics that are often used for title sequences.

Motivated edit   Edit justified by the action or content of a scene.

Motivated lighting   Technique used to promote representational lighting, creating the illusion that every source of light in the frame is natural or realistic.

N

Narration   Lines spoken that describe or reflect on the action but are not a part of it.

Narrative   A story or series of events.

Navigation design   Process of deciding all the different possible routes a user can take within an interactive media production.

Needle drop fee   Monetary fee paid to a sound studio or postproduction company for one time use of an audio recording in a media production.

Negative film   Type of photographic film in which the film that is exposed in the camera creates an opposite image. A positive print must be made from the camera negative.

Neutral density   Gray filters or gels that decrease the intensity of light without affecting color temperature.

Nondiegetic sound   Sound or music that exists outside the reality of the story in a film or video production, such as background music or a voice-over narration.

Nonfiction   A construction of words and/or media based on actual events and situations and subjects representing themselves.

Nonlinear	1. Having a form that allows for multiple paths through the information, having a branching structure.
	2. Approach to editing (analog and digital) that allows for redefining the overall time frame through the insertion and deletion of material.
Nonlinear editing	System in which sound and/or image is digitized and edited with random access capabilities and the ability to insert and delete material.
Nonnarrative	Describing a work of art or media that does not tell a story, often relying on abstraction.
Nonsynchronous sound	Sound that is recorded separately from the film or video image.

O

Off-line editing	First stage of the video editing process, with more emphasis placed on structure and content than image quality.
Omnidirectional microphone	Classification of microphone pick-up pattern that includes the entire surrounding area, eliminating only the area directly behind the microphone.
On-axis	Proper location of the subject within the pick-up pattern of a microphone for optimum audio recording quality.
On-line editing	Final stage of the video editing process, with an emphasis on image and sound quality, effects, and transitions.
Overmodulation	Point at which the peak of an audio signal exceeds the maximum safe recording range and risks the possibility of distortion.

P

Pan	Camera movement in which the camera pivots right or left.
Pan and scan	Technique of transferring widescreen film or video to video with a 4:3 aspect ratio. Results in an image that is cropped so as to fill the whole frame. Cropping varies according to the specific composition of the shot, so as to retain vital visual info.
Peak	Highest point of voltage within an audio signal.
Pedestal	1. Camera movement up and down through space. 2. Heavy, wheeled camera mount used in studio productions.
Persistence of vision	Perceptual occurrence in which the human brain fills in the gaps between rapidly-projected individual frames of an action that has been broken down into a series of still images.
Perspective	Perception of depth and distance from a particular point of view. Linear perspective represents three-dimensional space in two dimensions by having parallel lines converge at the horizon line.
Phantom power	Externally-provided power circuit used for pre-amplification in condenser microphones.
Phi phenomenon	Perceptual occurrence in which the human eye perceives two closely-proximate lights flashing in quick succession as movement.
Pick-up pattern	The area around the microphone in which sound will be clearly reproduced.
Pillarboxing	The technique of displaying a full, undistorted 4:3 image on a 16:9 monitor. Results in black bars on either side of the image.
Pitch	Aural manifestation of a sound wave directly proportional to its frequency.
Pixel	Short for picture element; the smallest unit that makes up an image on a computer screen, TV monitor, or digital display, usually a colored dot.

Plug-in	Piece of software that sits on the hard drive of your computer and talks to the web browser, extending its functionality and ability to view rich media content.
Podcast	A term derived from the Apple iPod referring to an audio production (radio program or audio blog) that can be downloaded or streamed to a personal computer.
Pointer	Type of file within a nonlinear editing project (such as a clip or bin) that serves as a reference to the location of an actual media file.
Postproduction	Stage of creating a media production where the acquired sound and images are chosen, sequenced, corrected, and manipulated, resulting in a form ready for distribution.
Preproduction	Stage of creating a media production that occurs prior to acquisition of sound and images.
Presentational lighting	Lighting design specifically constructed for the camera that directly acknowledges the presence of the viewer, such as a newscast.
Producer	Person responsible for overseeing the production process. The specific duties vary by production type.
Production	Stage of creating a media production in which sound and image acquisition occurs.
Progressive scanning	The method of recording video or a digital image in which all the rows of pixels are scanned in order, from the top row of the frame down to the bottom row.
Proposal	Written description of a media production that is created as part of preproduction.
Public domain	Copyright status of a published work 70 years after its creator's death (determined by U.S. government).

Q

Quantization	Conversion of a sampled signal to mathematical units.

R

Rack focus	Camera technique in which the focal plane is shifted, changing the focus from one subject on a plane of action to another on a different plane of action.
Radio frequency	Part of the electromagnetic spectrum that is used for wireless broadcasting communication.
Random access	Ability to jump quickly and easily from one piece of data to another.
Real time	Temporal concept of media production in which the duration of the replayed action is the same as when it was captured.
Reflected light meter	Type of light meter that reads the intensity of light bouncing off a surface.
Reflexivity	Acknowledging the maker's biases and inherent manipulation of the media-making process.
Representational lighting	Lighting design constructed in an attempt to recreate a real-life situation, ignoring the presence of the viewer.
Resolution	Clarity or sharpness of a reproduced image.
Reverberation	Multiple reflections of a sound off of all the surfaces surrounding its initial source.
Reversal film	Type of photographic film in which the film exposed in the camera is processed twice, creating a positive image.
Reverse angle	Shot taken from the opposite side of the action from a first shot that does not cross the 180-degree line.
Ride the gain	To adjust a level while recording or taping.
Rods	See *Cones and rods*.
Rough cut	First edit of a film, generally consisting of synch sound and straight cuts.

Rule of thirds	Aesthetic concept describing the division of the rectangular frame into thirds, both horizontally and vertically. The placement of subjects at the points of intersection creates dynamic and visually pleasing compositions.
Run-down sheet	Script format that outlines the content and timing of a program but does not include dialogue.
Running time	Elapsed time of a piece of exposed film or recorded tape.

S

Sampling	Measurements of an analog signal that allow the creation of a digital stream of binary data (ones and zeroes).
Sampling rate	Number of digital samples taken per second.
Saturation	Property of a color that references the intensity (boldness) of its hue.
Scanning	Process that takes place inside a video in which an electron beam reads the image reproduced on the image plane. Scanning occurs left to right and top to bottom of the frame.
Scoring	Composition of music to complement visual elements and heighten mood in a media production.
Screenplay	Script used for fiction narrative productions, such as feature films or TV dramas, that has a prescribed format.
Script outline	Plan for how a program will be structured and what content will be included prior to shooting a program that cannot be scripted, such as an interview-based documentary.
Segue	Audio transition that involves a rapid level drop of the original source and a quick fade in of the second source.
Sensitivity	Trait of film stock and video CCDs that is based on the amount of light necessary to create a properly exposed image. With film, it relates to film speed; with video, to gain. Used in conjunction with aperture and shutter speed to determine exposure.
Sequence	Series of still images or individual shots that require a specific order for the message to be clear.
Series	Linear-based order of media pieces that possess individual characteristics and can stand alone.
Shooting ratio	Ratio between the amount of film or video footage acquired and the amount that ends up in the edited version.
Shooting script	Script marked with shot numbers and shooting instructions.
Shot	A continuous piece of film or video, captured from the time the camera is turned on until it stops.
Shot sizes	Range of options regarding how much of a subject to include in the frame (usually pertaining to human subjects).
Shotgun microphone	Microphone with a narrow pick-up pattern (unidirectional) designed for recording audio at a distance from the source, usually as a method of removing the microphone from the frame of the image.
Shutter	Mechanical or electronic functioning of a lens that allows light to strike the image plane for a set period of time in order to create a frame of visual media.
Shutter speed	The length of time that each frame of media receives light through the lens aperture.
Signal flow	Path taken by a signal.
Signal-to-noise ratio	Relative proportions of desired information and interference.
Slate	Device used to synchronize the simultaneous shooting of film and recording of sound. Slates can be manual or digital.
Soft/diffused/ flooded light	Light waves bent through or bounced off a surface, producing light energy that covers a broad area. Results in less intense highlights and lighter, softer-edged shadows than direct light.

Software design — Planning of the actual computer programming or coding that makes an interactive media program and allows a structured approach to the process of building interactivity.

Sound bite — Short piece of interview footage.

Sound design — Technical and aesthetic plan to combine sound elements to work together as a whole or in combination with image.

Sound effects — Sounds created to emphasize or add to the action.

Sound perspective — Concept of matching of sound presence and shot size and establishing a sense of where the sound source is coming from.

Sound presence — Subjective sense of sound proximity. A sound that seems close to the listener has a lot of sound presence.

Soundstage — Production environment, free from extraneous background noise, with the specific characteristics determined by its intended use.

Source/record deck — Equipment for linear electronic editing in which material is copied from the original tape (source) onto another tape (record).

Spatial — Space-occupation aspect of art and media experiences.

Split screen — Partially completed wipe, most often used to divide the screen and show two separate locations simultaneously at full opacity.

Stereo — Method of recording, mixing, and playing back audio on two separate channels or tracks.

Storyboard — Hand-sketched or computer-generated visualization of a story that breaks down the action shot by shot.

Streaming audio — Media presentation technique that allows simultaneous viewing or listening while downloading rich media from the Internet onto a computer.

Studio — Production space with a controlled environment.

Subject — The talent appearing as himself or herself in documentary media.

Subtractive color mixing — System of color mixing based on cyan, magenta, and yellow primaries that, when combined together, form black.

Superimposition — Partially completed dissolve, appearing as a ghosted images of two different sources, both filling the whole screen.

Symmetrical balance — Approach to creating balanced composition within the frame in which the left half of the frame is identical to the right. One example is a subject centered in the frame.

Synchronization rights — Permission to use a specific recording of a musical composition for a media production that involves both aural and visual elements.

Synchronous sound — Sound that matches the action—recorded as the film or video image is acquired.

T

Tag — Piece of code in HTML that provides a certain formatting parameter for either text or images on a website.

Talent release — Form granting a producer the right to reproduce a person's voice or image in a media production.

Telephoto — Lens with a long focal length that selects a small segment of what is in front of the lens and makes it seem closer and larger than it would to the eye.

Template — A piece of prewritten programming code that allows the user to input content using the format or functionality provided.

Temporal — Time-based aspect of art and media experiences.

Three-point lighting	Approach to lighting in which a key light casts shadows, a fill light softens shadows, and a backlight creates separation between the subject and the background.
Tilt	Camera movement in which the camera pivots up and down.
Timbre	Distinctive tonal quality of a sound.
Timecode	Electronic signal that provides a discrete numerical reference for each frame of video.
Timeline	Graphical representation of the "linear" edited sequence being constructed within a non-linear editing program.
Track	1. Camera moving through space on a dolly track. 2. Single audio or video signal.
Transcription	Written log of a subject's spoken words.
Transducer	Device that converts one form of energy into another.
Transduction	Conversion of energy from one form to another.
Transitions	Ways of getting from one piece of visual or aural material to another.
Tripod	Adjustable three-legged stand used to stabilize a camera.
Trough	Lowest point of a wave. With a sound wave, the trough represents the maximum release of air molecules.
Truck	Camera movement through space to the right or the left on a wheeled dolly on the studio floor.
Tungsten film	Tungsten film is balanced for light with a color temperature of 3200 to 3400 K. The film can be used in other lighting conditions by using the correct colored filter on the lens of the camera.

U

Unidirectional microphone	Classification of microphone pickup pattern that includes a limited area in front of, to the sides of, and behind the microphone.
URL	Uniform resource locator; provides the information that allows the server to find the document you wish to view through your web browser.
User-generated content (USG)	Information shared and uploaded to a website by Internet users.

V

Vector(s)	1. Strong diagonal line either implied or existing within the frame that suggests movement. 2. A type of computer graphics created from a mathematical formula that can be rescaled while maintaining quality.
Velocity	Speed of a wave in relation to time.
Verbally driven structure	Approach to creating a media production where the primary story or information is provided by narration.
Video assist	Small video cameras attached to film cameras, designed to record a video image of what is being exposed simultaneously on the film.
Virtual reality	Any application that allows a user, typically wearing goggles or a headset and gloves or a body suit, to interact with a three-dimensional sensory environment.
Voiceover	Narration for a film or video that can be written and spoken in either the first or third person.
Voltage	Electric energy.
VU meter	Mechanism that measures the amount of voltage in an audio signal. A needle indicates volume units or percentage of signal on a linear scale, or LEDs display the strength of the signal.

W

Wavelength	Measurement of one full cycle of a wave, from crest to crest.
Waves	Undulations of traveling energy.
Web browser	Software application that allows users access to web documents through the Internet.
Web server	System of hardware and operating software that provides physical housing for documents accessible across the globe via the Internet.
Whitebalancing	Process within a video or digital still camera that electronically adjusts the color of the light entering the lens so that white will be neutral and therefore all other colors accurately reproduced.
Wide angle	Type of lens with a short focal length that takes in a wide field of view, making objects in that scene appear farther away than they would to the eye.
Windowboxing	Technique used when displaying an image with a 4:3 aspect ratio on a 16:9 monitor without cropping or distortion. Results in reproduction of the full frame with a black band running down both sides of the frame.
Wipe	Visual transition that starts in one portion of the frame and replaces one image with another in a variety of directions.
Workprint	Straight print of a camera negative used to complete a rough cut.

X

x-axis	Geometrical concept used to describe the width of an image frame.
XML	Extensible markup language; guidelines for creating programming tags that allow search engines to easily access information.

Y

y-axis	Geometrical concept used to describe the height of an image frame.

Z

z-axis	Geometrical concept used to describe the implied depth within a two-dimensional image frame.
Zoom	Changing of focal length and resulting field of view through movement of lens elements.

Works Consulted

Alten, Stanley R. *Audio in Media*. Belmont, CA: Wadsworth, 2002.

Arnheim, Rudolf. *Art and Visual Perception: A Psychology of the Creative Eye*. Berkeley and Los Angeles: University of California Press, 1974.

Arnheim, Rudolph. *Film as Art*. Berkeley and Los Angeles: University of California Press, 1974.

Association of Independent Video and Filmmakers et al. *Documentary Filmmakers' Statement of Best Practices in Fair Use*. Center for Social Media, 2005. Accessed January 2007. < www.centerforsocialmedia.org/ fairuse.htm >

Bazin, André. *What Is Cinema? Vol. II*. Berkeley: University of California Press, 1972.

Behrens, Roy R. "Rudolph Arnheim: The Little Owl on the Shoulder of Athene." July 1997. *Leonardo On-Line*. Accessed January 2002. < http://mitpress.mit.edu/e-journals/Leonardo/osart/articles/arnheim. html >

Brodel, Max, Franz Frohse, and Leon Schlossberg. *Atlas of Human Anatomy*. New York: Barnes and Noble, 1961.

Butcher, S. H. *Aristotle's Theory of Poetry and Fine Art With a Critical Text and Translation of the Poetics*. New York: Dover, 1951.

Cage, John. *Silence*. Hanover: Wesleyan University Press, 1961.

"Cartier-Bresson, Henri." *Encyclopedia Britannica*. 2007. Encyclopedia Britannica Online. Accessed April 2007. < www.britannica.com/eb/ article-9020555 >

Case, Dominic. *Motion Picture Film Processing*. London: Focal Press, 1985.

Dancyger, Ken. *The World of Film and Video Production: Aesthetics and Practices*. Orlando: Harcourt, 1999.

Donaldson, Michael C. *Clearance & Copyright: Everything the Independent Filmmaker Needs to Know*. Los Angeles: Silman-James Press, 2003.

Eisenstein, Sergei. *Film Form: Essays in Film Theory*. Orlando: Harcourt, 1977.

Eisenstein, Sergei. *The Film Sense*. Orlando: Harcourt, 1975.

"Glossary of Photographic Terms." *Kodak/Motion Picture Imaging*. 2007. Accessed May 2007. < www.kodak.com/US/en/motion/support/glossary/glossary.jhtml >

Happé, L. Bernard. *Your Film and the Lab*. London: Focal Press, 1983.

Hilliard, Robert. *Writing for Television and Radio*. Belmont, CA: Wadsworth, 1997.

Jackson, Earl Jr. "Persistence of Vision." *Cinema and Subjectivity*. Winter 2001/January 2002. < www.anotherscene.com/cinema/pov/pov1.html >

James, Jack. *Digital Intermediates for Film and Video*. Boston: Focal Press, 2006.

"John Cage." *Encyclopedia Britannica*. 2002. Encyclopedia Britannica Online. April 2002. < www.britannica.com/eb/article-9018542 >

Kingslake, Rudolf. *Lenses in Photography: The Practical Guide to Optics for Photographers*. New York: Barnes, 1963.

Lipton, Lenny. *Independent Filmmaking*. San Francisco: Simon and Schuster, 1972.

LeTourneau, Tom. *Lighting Techniques for Video Production: The Art of Casting Shadows*. Boston: Focal Press, 2000.

Lowell, Ross. *Matters of Light & Depth*. New York: Lowell-Light, 1992.

Newhall, Beaumont. *The History of Photography*. New York: Museum of Modern Art, 1978.

O'Reilly, Tim. "What Is Web 2.0?" September 30, 2005. *O'Reilly Network*. Accessed April 2007. < www.oreillynet.com/pub/a/oreilly/tim/news/2005/09/30/what-is-web-20.html >

Pizlo, F. J., Z. Pizlo, and R. M. Steinmen. "Phi Is Not Beta." May 1, 2000. *Magni-phi and Related Phenomena*. Accessed June 2001. < http://psych.purdue.edu/Magniphi/ >

Rabiger, Michael. *Developing Story Ideas*. Boston: Focal Press, 2000.

Rundrum, David. "From Narrative Representation to Narrative Use." *Narrative*, Vol 13, No. 2 (2005), pp. 195–204.

"Sergei Eisenstein." *Encyclopedia Britannica*. 2002. Encyclopedia Britannica Online. Accessed April 2002. < www.britannica.com/eb/article-9032166 >

Sontag, Susan. *On Photography*. New York: Farrar, Straus and Giroux, 1978.

Spalter, Anne Morgan. *The Computer in the Visual Arts*. Reading, MA: Addison, 1999.

"Technical Information." *Kodak Cinema and Television*. 2007. Accessed May 2007. < www.kodak.com/US/en/motion/support/ >

Utz, Peter. "High Definition Video Recording Formats." Accessed March 2007. < http://videoexpert.home.att.net/artic3/262 >

Wilt, Adam. "HD Numerology." *DV Magazine*. 2006. Accessed March 2007. < www.dv.com/columns/columns_item.php?articleId = 55301757 >

Whittaker, Ron. *Television Production*. Mountain View, CA: Mayfield, 1993.

Zettl, Herbert, *Sight Sound Motion*. Belmont, CA: Wadsworth, 1998.

Zettl, Herbert, *Television Production Handbook*. Belmont, CA: Wadsworth, 2000.

Index

180-degree Line, 176–179, 182, 257

A

Above the line positions, 9
A/B-roll editing, 202–203
Acceptable focus, 47
Access, 234, 257
Action, 170–173
AD (assistant directors), 247
Added light, 257
Additive color mixing, 101, 257
ADR (automatic dialogue replacement), 144–145, 257
Advanced Television Systems Committee (ATSC), 63
AI (artificial intelligence), 226–227, 258
Ambience (ambient sound), 123, 134, 144, 257
Ambient light, 99, 104–105, 261
Ambient light meters, 87–88, 94–95
Ambient sound (ambience), 123, 134, 144, 257
American Society of Composers, Authors and Publishers (ASCAP), 16–17
American Standards Association (ASA), 52
Amplitude, 117, 119, 257
Analog linear editing
    audio, 205
    drawbacks, 205
    edit decision lists (EDL), 207
    versus nonlinear, 197–198
    on-line edit, 207–208
    overview, 203–208
    video, 205–206

Analog nonlinear editing
    audio, 199–200
    film, 200–201
    versus linear, 197–198
    rough cuts, 201–202
Analog reproduction, 51–52.
    See also Film
Analog sound recording
    versus digital, 127–129
    formats, 135–136
Analog video, 59–60
Anamorphic lenses, 57
Angle of view, 39, 257
Animation
    defined, 257
    movement, 82–83
    software applications for, 239
Answer prints, 203, 257
Aperture, 44, 48–49, 86, 257
Arc lamps (HMI), 106–107
Arc shots, 77–78
Aristotle, 6
Arnheim, Rudolf, 69
A-roll editing, 202–203
Art and Visual Perception: A Psychology of the Creative Eye, 69
Artificial intelligence (AI), 226–227, 258
Artificial light
    added, 105–107
    color temperature, 102
    existing, 105
As American as Apple Pie (CD-ROM), 231
ASA (American Standards Association), 52
ASCAP (American Society of Composers, Authors and Publishers), 16–17

Aspect ratios
defined, 258
motion picture film, 57–58
overview, 25–26
still images, 56
Assemblages, 201
Assemble editing, 206, 258
Assets, 232, 258
Assistant directors (AD), 247
Asymmetrical balance, 33–35, 258
ATSC (Advanced Television Systems Committee), 63
Attack, 131–132
Attenuation
defined, 258
light, 86–87
sound, 118
Audience research, 2–4
Audio
See also Sound
distribution, 255
editing
analog linear, 205
analog nonlinear, 199–200
overview, 148
exhibition, 255
file formats, 238
Audio cartridges (carts), 135–136
Audio cassettes, 136
Audio continuity, 184
Audio engineers, 247, 250
Audio-based media, 149–150
Audiotape, 135
Authoring software, 239–240
Automatic dialogue replacement (ADR), 144–145, 257

B

Backlights, 92, 97–98, 258
Balance, 33–37
Balanced audio analog connections, 205
Bandwidth, 234, 258
Barrel distortion, 41
Batch digitizing, 212
Bazin, André, 80
Beam splitters, 111–112, 258
Below the line positions, 9
Bidirectional microphones, 122–123, 258
Binaural hearing, 132, 258
Bins, 201, 212–213, 258
Birth of a Nation, 169

Bit depth, 129, 258
Bitmaps, 237, 258
Blocking talent, 73, 258
BMI (Broadcast Music Inc.), 16–17
Booms, 127
Branching structure, 225, 258
Brightness, 100, 258
Broadcast Music Inc. (BMI), 16–17
Broadcasting, 138, 258
B-rolls
defined, 258
editing, 202–203
footage, 181
Browser-based editing, 222
Budgets
above the line positions, 9
below the line positions, 9
defined, 258
long takes, 81–82
need for, 8
Burn-ins, 206–207
Burns, Ken, 167
Buses, 192, 258
Business, 80

C

Cage, John, 140
Camera movement
overview, 75–79
types of, 77–79
Camera operators, 247
Camera-axis key lights, 94
Capacitor microphones, 121–122
Capturing
defined, 258
digital nonlinear editing, 211–212
Cardioid microphones, 123–125, 258
Cartier-Bresson, Henri, 154–155
Carts (audio cartridges), 135–136
Cascading Style Sheets (CSS), 241–242, 259
Casting shadows, 92
Cathode-ray tubes (CRT), 59–60, 89
CCDs (charge-coupled devices), 39, 54, 60, 111–112, 259
CD-Rs (recordable CDs), 137
CD-RWs (rewritable CDs), 137
CDs (compact discs), 137, 156
Cel animation, 82
Center for Social Media, 16
CG (character generation), 218, 247

Character development, 6
Character generation (CG), 218, 247
Charge-coupled devices (CCDs), 39, 54,
　　60, 111–112, 259
Chromakeys, 193, 259
Chrominance, 112, 259
Cilia, 119
Cinema verité, 81
Circles of confusion, 46, 48, 259
Civil War, The, 167
Clappers, 147
Clapsticks, 147
Clips, 201, 212–213, 259
Close-up media, 28–29
Close-ups (CU), 30
Closure, 30–32, 259
Cochlea, 119
Codecs, 215–216, 259
Collaboration, 246
Color
　　overview, 99–100
　　reproducing, 100–101
　　temperature, 101–104, 259
Color negative film, 109–110
Color of Money, The, 80
Color reversal film, 109
Color temperature, 101–104, 259
Compact discs (CDs), 137, 156
Compilation approach, 180–181
Component analog connections, 205
Composite analog connections, 205
Compression
　　defined, 259
　　digital reproduction, 56
　　file, 150, 215–217
Computer animation, 82–83
Computer-based media, 149–150
Computers
　　See also Software applications
　　Windows versus Macintosh, 221
Condenser microphones, 121–122, 259
Cones, 100, 259
Conforming negatives, 203, 259
Content
　　See also Preproduction
　　developing story ideas
　　　　audience research, 2–3
　　　　classifying content, 4–6
　　　　linear versus nonlinear, 6–7
　　　　matching medium to message, 3–4
　　　　overview, 1–2
　　ethical responsibilities, 15–16

fictional, 5
　　legal issues
　　　　copyrights, 16–17
　　　　location releases, 19
　　　　talent releases, 17–19
　　primacy of, 1
Content relationship, 165
Continuity
　　action, 170–173
　　costumes, 174
　　defined, 259
　　eyeline match, 174
　　hair, 174
　　lighting, 174–176
　　maintaining in production, 179
　　makeup, 174
　　props, 174
　　screen direction, 176–179
　　shot size sequencing, 173–174
　　sound, 174–176
Continuity editing, 159, 259
Continuous waves, 51, 128, 259
Contrast, 88–89, 259
Contrast ratios, 88
Control rooms, 247, 259
Control tracks, 206
Controllers, 204–205
Controlling shadows, 92
Convergence, 3, 259
Converter boxes, 212
Copyrights, 16–17
Cores, 202
Costumes, 174
Counters, 195, 259
Crane shots, 78
Cranes, 75–76, 259
Crests, sound wave, 116, 259
Cropping, 26
Crossfades, 189, 259
CRT (cathode-ray tubes), 59–60, 89
Crystal synch, 147
CSS (Cascading Style Sheets), 241–242,
　　259
CU (close-ups), 30
Cue sheets, 203–204
Cutaways, 182, 250, 260
Cuts, 189, 260

D

Daguerreotypes, 24
Dailies, 200

DAT (digital audiotape), 136–137
Databases, 231, 260
Daylight, 104–105
Daylight film, 109, 260
DBs (decibels), 117, 260
Dead space, 132
Decay, 131–132
Decibels (dBs), 117, 260
Decisive moments, 154–155, 260
Deductive reasoning, 173, 260
Deep focus, 47–48, 50, 68
Defying time, 161–162
Depth
    focus, 68–69
    lens choice, 68–69
    placement, 66–68
Depth of field, 47–48, 50, 68, 260
Developing story ideas
    audience research, 2–3
    classifying content, 4–6
    linear versus nonlinear, 6–7
    matching medium to message, 3–4
    overview, 1–2
Diagetic (diegetic) sound, 146, 260
Dialogue, 144, 260
Diction, 6
Diegetic (diagetic) sound, 146, 260
Diffused light, 89–91, 267
Diffusion material, 91–92
Digital audio recorders, 137–138
Digital audiotape (DAT), 136–137
Digital images
    accurate color, 112–113
    color reproduction, 111–112
Digital intermediates, 220–221, 260
Digital nonlinear editing
    advantages, 209–210
    capturing, 211–212
    file management, 212–217
    logging, 211
    overview, 208–209
    random access, 210–211
    sequencing, 217–219
Digital nonlinear editing (NLE) systems,
    210
Digital reproduction
    versus analog, 51–52
    still images, 54–56
Digital sound recording
    versus analog, 127–129
    digital audio recorders, 137–138
    formats, 136–137

Digital television (DTV), 59
Digital versatile discs (DVDs), 137
Digital video, 60–61
Digital Video Broadcasting (DVB), 62
Digitizing, 211, 260
DIN standard, 52
Direct cinema, 81, 260
Direct light, 89–91, 262
Directed tension, 69, 260
Directors, 247
Dissolves, 189, 260
Distance, 48–49
Distribution
    audio, 255
    film, 254
    means of, 3
    overview, 253–254
    still images, 254
    video, 255
Documentaries
    defined, 5, 260
    long takes in, 80–81
    montage within, 185
    preproduction, 167
    verbally driven structure, 185–186
Documentary Filmmakers' Statement of
    Best Practices in Fair Use, 16
Dollies, 75, 260
Dolly shots, 77–79
Drag, 77
Dropouts, 129
DTV (digital television), 59
Dubbing, 51
Duration, 166
DVB (Digital Video Broadcasting), 62
DVDs (digital versatile discs), 137
Dynamic microphones, 121, 260

E

Ears, 118–119
Eastgate, 233
ECU (extreme close-ups), 30
Edge numbers, 195–196, 260
Edison, Thomas, 72
Edit decision lists (EDL), 207–208, 217,
    260
Edit plans, 196, 260
Edited masters, 208, 260
Editing
    A/B-roll, 202–203
    analog linear, 197–198, 203–208

analog nonlinear, 197–198, 199–202

audio, 148, 199–200, 205

browser-based, 222

digital nonlinear, 208–219

live, 191–193

movement through, 79

postproduction, 194–208

software applications for, 237–238

EDL (edit decision lists), 207–208, 217, 260

Effects banks, 192–193, 261

EI (exposure index), 52

Eisenstein, Sergei, 180

Electret microphones, 122

Electromagnetic energy, 100, 261

Ellipses of time, 160–161, 170, 261

Envelope, sound, 131, 261

EPS format, 237

Ethical responsibilities, 15–16

Executive producers, 9, 246

Exhibition
  audio, 255
  film, 254
  overview, 253–254
  still images, 254
  video, 255

Existing light, 99, 104–105, 261

Exposition, 7, 261

Exposure, 44, 86–88, 261

Exposure index (EI), 52

EXtensible Markup Language (XML), 241, 270

Extreme close-ups (ECU), 30

Eyeline, 174–175, 261

F

Faceplates, 59

Fade ins/outs, 189, 261

Fader bars, 192

Fair use, 16, 261

Federal Communications Commission (FCC), 59

Fictional content
  defined, 261
  long takes in, 80
  overview, 5

Field of view, 39, 261

Fields, 59

File formats
  audio, 238
  image, 56, 237
  video, 150, 216–217, 238

File management
  compression, 215–217
  defined, 261
  overview, 212–213
  storage, 214

File size, 234, 261

Fill lights, 92, 94–95, 98, 261

Film
  analog nonlinear editing, 200–201
  color reproduction, 109
  color temperature, 109–111
  conversion to video, 220–221
  daylight, 109, 260
  distribution, 254
  exhibition, 254
  light, 107–111
  motion picture, 57–58
  negative
    color, 109–110
    defined, 264
    nonlinear editing, 200
    overview, 52–53
  resolution, 52
  reversal
    color, 109
    defined, 266
    nonlinear editing, 201
    overview, 52, 54
  sound, 146–148
  still image, 52–54

Filters, 109, 111, 261

Fine cuts, 199, 261

FireWire connections, 212–213

Fixing, 24

Flash, 105–106

Flash memory, 137

Flat lighting, 94, 261

Flatbed editors, 148, 201

Flooded light, 89–91, 267

Floor managers (FM), 247

Flowcharts
  alternatives to, 14–15
  branching structure, 14–15
  defined, 261
  interactive media, 233
  navigation design, 227–228

Fluorescent lights, 106–108

FM (floor managers), 247

Focal length, 39–42, 48–49, 261
Focal plane, 47
Focal points, 46
Focus, 46–50, 68–69
Foley artists, 144, 261
Foot-candles, 86–87, 261
Foreshadowing, 7, 261
Formal relationship, 165
Frames
  animation, 82–83
  controlling, 24–37
  defined, 20, 261
  depth, 65–69
  media considerations, 51–62
  motion graphics, 82
  movement, 69–80
  reproducing, 37–50
  still images, 23–24
Frequency, 117, 261
Frequency response, 122, 261
Fresnels, 106
Friction, 77
Friends, 252
Frozen time, 154
F-stops, 44, 50, 261
Fully scripted programs,
  11, 261

G

Gaffer's tape, 106–107
GB (gigabytes), 214
Gels, 104
Generational loss
  analog editing, 205
  analog reproduction, 51, 60
  audio, 129
  defined, 262
Gestalt theory, 36, 180, 262
GIF format, 236–237
Gigabytes (GB), 214
Glass masters, 219
Golden Section (Golden Mean), 34
GOPs (groups of pictures), 216
Grain, 52
Graphic design, 227, 262
Graphics tablets, 235–236
Gray cards, 100
Grayscale, 88–89
Griffith, D. W., 168–169
Groups of pictures (GOPs),
  216

H

Hair, 174
Handheld cameras, 75, 77
Handheld microphones, 124–125, 262
Hard light, 89–91, 262
Harmonics, 131, 262
HD. *See* High definition
Headroom, 34–35, 38, 262
Helical scanning, 136
Hertz (Hz), 117, 262
Hierarchies, 227, 262
High definition (HD)
  lighting, 111
  versus standard definition, 61–62
High key lighting, 95–96, 262
Hill Street Blues, 77
HMI (arc lamps), 106–107
Hollywood narrative style, 169
Homicide, 183
Horozontal resolution, 61
HTML (Hypertext Markup Language),
  240–241, 262
Hue, 100, 262
Hypercardioid microphones, 123–124
Hyperlinks, 231, 262
Hypertext, 233, 262
Hypertext Markup Language (HTML),
  240–241, 262
Hz (hertz), 117, 262

I

IDSB (Integrated Services Digital
  Broadcasting), 62
Illusion of depth, 65, 92, 262
Illusion of real time, 159–160, 170, 262
Image file formats, 236–237
Image plane, 37, 39–40, 46–47, 262
Images. *See* Digital images; Sound/image
  combinations; Still images; Video
  images
IMAX™, 58
Impedance, 134, 262
Incident light meters, 87–88, 94–95, 262
Inductive reasoning, 173–174, 262
Information design, 227, 262
Informed consent, 19
Initial decay, 131–132
Input, 262
Insert editing, 206, 262
Installations, 6, 262

Instances, 239

Institute of Radio Engineers (IRE) units, 89

Insurance, 8

Integrated Services Digital Broadcasting (IDSB), 62

Interactive media
   accessibility, 234
   defined, 262
   process of creating, 232–234
   technical concerns, 234
   types of, 229–232

Interactivity
   defined, 226, 263
   versus linear production, 253

Interface design, 227, 263

Interframe (temporal) compression, 216, 263

Interlaced scanning, 60–61, 263

Internal keys, 193

International Organization for Standardization (ISO), 52

Internet
   downloaded music, 139
   interactive media, 231
   radio, 138–139
   streaming audio, 150

Intraframe (spatial) compression, 216, 263

IRE (Institute of Radio Engineers) units, 89

Iris, 44, 263

ISO (International Organization for Standardization), 52

Iso production, 251, 263

J

Jam synch, 147

JPEG format, 56, 236, 237

Jump cuts, 170, 263

Jungle Fever, 80

K

KB (kilobytes), 214

Kelvin (K), 101, 263

Key lights, 92–94, 98, 263

Key/fill ratio, 94–97, 108, 263

Keyframes, 82

Keys, 192–193

KHz (kilohertz), 117

Kickers, 98

Kilobytes (KB), 214

Kilohertz (kHz), 117

Kinescopes, 220

L

Lavaliere microphones (lavs), 125–126, 135, 263

Law of proximity, 35–36, 38

Leader, 201–202

Leadroom, 34, 37, 263

LED (light-emitting diode) meters, 130–131, 263

Legal issues
   copyrights, 16–17
   location releases, 19
   talent releases, 17–19

Lenses
   anamorphic, 57
   aperture, 44
   depth, 68–69
   focal length, 39–42
   normal, 41
   prime, 40
   sensitivity, 46
   shutter speed, 44–45
   telephoto
      defined, 268
      focus, 68–69
      overview, 40–44
      zooming, 78
   variable focal length, 40
   wide angle
      defined, 270
      focus, 68–69
      overview, 40–43
      zooming, 78
   zoom, 40, 270

Letterboxing, 26, 263

Libel, 17

Light
   color, 99–104
   continuity, 174–176
   direction, 91–99
   importance of, 85
   media considerations, 107–113
   quality, 89–91
   quantity, 86–89
   safety issues, 107
   sources of, 104–107

Light meters, 87–88

Light-emitting diode (LED) meters, 130–131, 263

Line producers, 9
Linear structure
    defined, 263
    versus interactivity, 253
    versus nonlinear, 6–7
    practice of
        browser-based editing, 222
        digital nonlinear editing, 208–219
        live editing, 191–193
        media compatibility, 220–221
        postproduction editing, 194–208
        tapeless cameras, 221–222
        transitions, 189–190
    programming, 153–154
    theory of
        audio continuity, 184
        continuity style, 168
        montage, 179–180, 184–185
        multicamera video, 182–183
        observational documentaries,
            183–184
        overview, 165–166
        preproduction, 166–167
        verbally driven structure, 180–181,
            185–186
Live editing, 191–193
Live mixing, 191, 250–251, 263
Live programming, 157–158, 263
Live rooms, 132
Live switching, 191, 250–251, 263
Live-on-tape programming, 157, 159,
    191, 249, 263
Location releases, 19, 20
Logging
    defined, 264
    digital nonlinear editing, 211
    edit plans, 197
    postproduction, 194
Long shots (LS), 30
Long takes
    budget considerations, 81–82
    defined, 264
    in documentaries, 80–81
    versus editing shots, 80–82, 191
    in fiction narratives, 80
Lookspace, 34, 36, 264
Looping, 144–145
Lossless compression, 215
Lossy compression, 215
Low key lighting, 95–96, 264
LS (long shots), 30
Lumière, Louis and Auguste, 72

Luminance, 88, 112, 264
Luminance keys, 193, 264

M

Macintosh operating system, 221
Magnetic (mag) stock, 148, 201, 264
Magnetism, 69, 71
Makeup, 174
Mashups, 231
Matched cuts, 172, 264
MB (megabytes), 214
MCU (medium close-ups), 30
MDs (mini discs), 137
Mechanical rights, 17, 264
Media
    See also Media formats by type
    analog versus digital, 51–52
    audio-based, 149–150
    close-up, 28–29
    compatibility, 220–221
    computer-based, 149–150
    convergence, 3
    interactive, 229–234
    light, 107–113
    matching to message, 3–4
    motion picture film, 57–58
    movement, 80–82
    sensitivity, 46, 52, 267
    sound, 138–140
    sound/image combinations, 146–150
    still images, 52–56
    video motion pictures, 59–62
Media activists, 2
Media advertisers, 2
Media artists, 2
Media files, 213
Medium close-ups (MCU), 30
Medium long shots (MLS), 30
Medium shots (MS), 30
Megabytes (MB or megs), 214
Megapixels, 54
Menus, 232–233, 264
Metatags, 231
Microphones
    bidirectional, 122–123, 258
    capacitor, 121–122
    cardioid, 123–125, 258
    condenser, 121–122, 259
    dynamic, 121, 260
    electret, 122
    handheld, 124–125, 262

hypercardioid, 123–124
lavaliere (lavs), 125–126, 135, 263
omnidirectional, 122–123, 125–126, 265
pick-up patterns, 122–124
ribbon, 121
ribbon handheld, 124
shotgun, 126–127, 135, 267
supercardioid, 123–124
transducers, 121–122
transduction, 119
unidirectional, 122–124, 269
usage types, 124–127
using, 121
Mini discs (MDs), 137
Mixdowns, 211, 219
Mixing
consoles, 119–120
live, 191–192
sound, 145, 203
MLS (medium long shots), 30
Mockumentaries, 5
Monaural playback, 133
Monitoring, 130–131, 134, 264
Monitors, 56
Monopods, 75
Montage
continuity, 179–180
defined, 264
within documentaries, 185
within narratives, 185
uses of, 184
Motion capture, 82, 264
Motion graphics
defined, 264
movement, 82
software applications for, 239
Motion Picture Experts Group (MPEG)
formats, 150, 216–217
Motion pictures
See also Video
film, 57–58
video, 59–62
Motivated edits, 172, 264
Motivated lighting, 99, 264
Mounted cameras, 75, 77
Movement
camera, 75–79
media, 80–82
moving images, 71–72
within still frames, 69–71
subject, 72–75
through editing, 79

MP3, 140
MPEG (Motion Picture Experts Group)
formats, 150, 216–217
MS (medium shots), 30
Multicamera shooting, 182–183,
248–249
Multiple-source production, 249–252
Music
See also Audio; Sound
downloaded, 139
libraries, 17
recording, 139–140
sound design, 145
Myst, 233–234

N

Nagra recorders, 148
Narration, 144, 264
Narrative structure
defined, 264
example, 169–170
long takes, 80
montage within, 185
nonfiction, 5
National Television System Committee
(NTSC), 60
Native (untouched) editing, 217
Navigation design, 227, 264
ND (neutral density) filters, 113, 264
Needle drop fees, 17, 264
Negative film
color, 109–110
defined, 264
nonlinear editing, 200
overview, 52–53
Networks, 214
Neutral density (ND) filters, 113, 264
NHK system, 61
NLE. *See* Nonlinear editing
NLE (digital nonlinear editing) systems,
210
Noise, 51, 111, 210
Nondiegetic sound, 146, 264
Nonfictional content, 5, 264
Nonlinear editing (NLE)
defined, 265
software applications, 217–219
systems, 210, 238
Nonlinear structure
authoring software, 239–240
CSS, 241

Nonlinear structure (*Continued*)
    defined, 265
    design, 226–228
    HTML, 240–241
    interactive media, 228–234
    interactivity, 226
    versus linear, 6–7
    programming, 154
    random access, 225–226
    software applications, 235–239
    XML, 241
Nonlinearity
    defined, 210–211
    overview, 225
Nonnarrative structure, 5–6, 265
Nonsynchronous (nonsynch) sound,
        145–146, 265
Normal lenses, 41
NTSC (National Television System
        Committee), 60
NYPD Blue, 183

O

Objects, 239
Observational documentaries,
        183–184
Office, The, 252
Off-line editing, 199, 206, 265
Omnidirectional microphones, 122–123,
        125–126, 265
On location production, 246–248
On-axis range, 123, 265
One-channel playback, 133
One-light workprints, 200
On-line editing, 199, 207–208, 265
Open reel audiotape, 135,
        199–200
Order, 165
Ossicles, 119
Out-of-synch sound, 147
Output, 211, 219, 262
Overexposure, 86–87
Overlapping, 67–68
Overmodulation, 130, 265

P

PA (production assistants), 247
PAL, 59–60
Pan and scan technique,
        26–27, 265

Panning
    audio, 133
    defined, 77, 265
Peak, 265
Pedestal shots, 78
Pedestals, 75–76, 265
Permissions, 8
Persistence of vision, 71–72, 265
Personnel
    assistant directors (AD), 247
    camera operators, 247
    executive producers, 9, 246
    floor managers (FM), 247
    foley artists, 144, 261
    overview, 9
    producers, 9, 266
    production assistants (PA), 247
    production team, 246
    technical directors (TD), 192–193,
        247, 250
Perspective, 65, 265
Phantom power, 122, 265
Phi phenomenon, 71–72, 265
Photography, 23–24. *See also* Still
        images
Pick-up patterns, 122–124, 265
PICT format, 237
Picture elements (pixels), 54, 55, 265
Pillarboxing, 26–27, 265
Pitch, 117, 119, 265
Pixels (picture elements),
        54, 55, 265
Placement, 66–68
Plot, 6
Plug-ins, 231, 266
PNG format, 237
Podcasts, 139, 266
Poetics, 6
Pointers, 213, 266
Police Tapes, 77
Postproduction
    defined, 266
    editing, 194–208
        A/B-roll, 202–203
        analog linear, 203–208
        analog nonlinear, 199–202
        preparation, 194–197
        sound mix, 203
        stages of, 198–199
    overview, 7
Preamplification, 121–122
Premixing, 203

Preproduction
    See also Content
    defined, 266
    developing story ideas
        audience research, 2–3
        classifying content, 4–6
        linear versus nonlinear, 6–7
        matching medium to message, 3–4
        overview, 1–2
    ethical responsibilities, 15–16
    legal issues
        copyrights, 16–17
        location releases, 19
        talent releases, 17–19
    linear structure, 166–167
    process of
        alternatives, 14–15
        budgets, 8
        flowcharts, 14
        insurance, 8
        overview, 7–8
        permissions, 8
        personnel, 9
        scripts, 9–14
Pre-roll, 205
Presence, 132
Presentational lighting, 97, 266
Prime lenses, 40
Printers, 55
Producers, 9, 266
Production
    defined, 7, 266
    linear versus interactive, 253
    methods of, 3
    multiple-source, 249–252
    overview, 245–246
    production team, 246
    single-source, 248–249, 252
    studio versus on location,
        246–248
Production assistants (PA), 247
Production team, 246
Profiles, 73
Progressive scanning, 61, 266
Project managers, 9
Proposals, 8, 266
Props, 174
Protection masters, 208, 219
Psychological closure, 30–32
Public domain, 16, 266
Pulldowns, 220
Pulling the focus, 79

Q
Quantization, 129, 266
Quartz lights, 102–103, 106–107

R
Rack focus, 69–70, 266
Radio, 138–139
Radio frequency, 120–121, 266
Random access, 154, 210–211,
        225–226, 266
Reaction shots, 250
Real time
    defined, 266
    illusion of, 159–160
    overview, 157
    recorded, 157–159
Reality TV, 5
Record decks, 204–205, 268
Recordable CDs (CD-Rs), 137
Recorded real time, 157–159
Reel-to-reel tape, 135–136, 199–200
Reference black, 89
Reference white, 89
Reflected light meters, 87–88, 266
Reflectors, 92, 94
Reflexivity, 81, 266
Releases
    location, 19
    talent, 17–19
Representational lighting, 99, 266
Reproduction
    color, 100–101, 109, 111–112
    sound, 119–129
Rerecording mixes, 203
Resolution
    defined, 266
    digital imaging, 54–55
    digital reproduction, 54–56
    film, 52
    overview, 50
Reverberation, 132, 266
Reversal film
    color, 109
    defined, 266
    nonlinear editing, 201
    overview, 52, 54
Reverse angle shots, 177, 266
Rewritable CDs (CD-RWs), 137
Ribbon handheld microphones, 124
Ribbon microphones, 121

Rich content, 239
Ride gain, 131, 266
Rods, 100, 259, 266
Room tone, 134
Rope, 80
Rough cuts
    analog nonlinear editing, 201–202
    defined, 266
    editing, 199
RSS, 139
Rule of thirds, 34, 267
Run-down sheets, 11, 267
Running time, 195, 267

S

Sampling, 51, 129, 267
Saturation, 100, 267
Scanners, 235
Scanning, 59–60, 267
Scoring, 145, 267
Screen direction, 176–179
Screenplay format, 9–10, 267
Scripts
    alternatives to, 14–15
    outlines of, 11, 267
    shooting, 9, 267
    two-column, 11–13
    visualizing, 11–14
SD. *See* Standard definition
SDI (Serial Digital Interface) connections,
    212
Second Life, 229–230
Segues, 189, 267
Self-expression, 2–3
Semiscripted programs, 11
Sensitivity, media, 46, 52, 267
Sequences, 156, 267
Sequencing, 211, 217–219
Serial Digital Interface (SDI) connections,
    212
Series, 154–156, 267
SESAC, 16–17
Shallow depth of field, 68–69
Shallow focus, 47–48, 50
Shape, frame, 24–29
Shooting ratios, 81–82, 267
Shooting scripts, 9, 267
Shot sizes, 29–32, 173–174, 267
Shotgun microphones, 126–127, 135,
    267
Shots, 156, 267

Shoulder mounts, 75
Show runners, 9
Shutter speed, 44–45, 86, 267
Shutters, 44, 267
Sibilance, 134
Signal flow, 191, 267
Signal-to-noise ratio, 131, 267
Silence, 140
Sims, The (game), 234
Single-source production, 248–249, 252
Skylight, 101–102
Slander, 19
Slates, 147, 267
Slugs, 202–203
Soft boxes, 91–92
Soft light, 89–91, 267
Software applications
    animation, 82, 239
    authoring software, 239–240
    digital imaging, 56
    digital nonlinear editing, 209
    editing, 237–238
    image creation, 235–236
    image manipulation, 236–237
    motion graphics, 82, 239
    nonlinear editing (NLE) systems,
        217–219
Software design, 227, 268
Sound
    See also Audio; Sound/image
        combinations
    continuity, 174–176
    direction of, 132–134
    ears, 118–119
    importance of, 115–116
    media, 138–140
    microphones, 121–127
    quality of, 131–132
    quantity of, 130–131
    recording clean, 134–138
    reproducing, 119–129
Sound bites, 181, 268
Sound design, 227, 268
Sound effects, 144–145, 268
Sound mixing, 145, 203
Sound perspective, 132, 268
Sound presence, 132, 268
Sound waves, 116–118
Sound/image combinations
    media
        audio-based media, 149–150
        computer-based media, 149–150

film sound, 146–148

video sound, 149

time

defying, 161–162

ellipsis of, 160–161

illusion of real, 159–160

real, 157

recorded real, 157–159

Soundstages, 246–247, 268

Source decks, 204–205, 268

Spatial (intraframe) compression, 216, 263

Spatial aspects, 153, 268

Spectacle, 6

Split screens, 190, 268

Spot meters, 88

Spotted light, 89–91, 262

Spreaders, 75

Standard definition (SD)

versus high definition, 61–62

video, 60, 62

Steadicam, 75, 77

Stereo recording, 133, 268

Still images

digital, 54–56

distribution, 254

exhibition, 254

film, 52–54

frame, 23–24

history of, 23–24

media, 52–56

movement within, 69–71

Stop-motion animation, 82

Storage, file, 214, 221

Story

defined, 1

development of ideas

audience research, 2–3

classifying content, 4–6

linear versus nonlinear, 6–7

matching medium to message, 3–4

Storyboards, 11, 14, 166–167, 268

Streaming audio, 150, 268

Studios

defined, 268

versus production on location, 246–248

Subjects

defined, 268

movement of, 72–75

Subtractive color mixing, 101, 268

Sunlight, 101–102

Supercardioid microphones, 123–124

Superimposition, 189–190, 268

Surround sound, 133–134

Sustain, 131–132

S-Video (Y/C) analog connections, 205

Sweetening, 203, 250

Symbols, 239

Symmetrical balance, 33, 35, 268

Synching rushes, 201

Synchronization rights, 17, 268

Synchronous (synch) sound, 145, 268

T

Tags, 231, 240, 268

Talent blocking, 73, 258

Talent releases, 17–19, 268

Tapeless cameras, 221–222

TD (technical directors), 192–193, 247, 250

Technical directors (TD), 192–193, 247, 250

Telecines, 212

Telephoto lenses

defined, 268

focus, 68–69

overview, 40–44

zooming, 78

Temperature, color

defined, 259

film stocks, 109–111

overview, 101–104

Templates, 235, 268

Temporal (interframe) compression, 216, 263

Temporal aspects, 153, 268

Thought, 6

Three-point lighting, 92, 97, 269

TIFF format, 56, 237

Tilted lines, 36–37, 39

Tilting, 77, 269

Timbre, 131, 269

Time

frozen, 154

overview, 153–154

sequences, 156

series, 154–156

sound/image combinations, 157–162

defying time, 161–162

ellipsis of time, 160–161

illusion of real time, 159–160

real time, 157

recorded real time, 157–159

Timecode synchronization, 147
Timecodes, 195–196, 198, 269
Timed workprints, 200
Timelines, 211, 217, 269
Tracking, 77–78, 269
Transcriptions, 194–195, 269
Transducers, 59, 121–122, 269
Transduction, 119–120, 269
Transitions, 189–190, 269
Transparencies, 52, 54, 109
Trims, 202
Tripods, 75–76, 269
Troughs, sound wave, 116, 269
Trucking, 77–78, 269
Tungsten film, 109, 269
Tweening, 82
Two-column scripts, 11–13
Tympanic membrane, 119

U

Unbalanced audio analog connections,
    205
Underexposure, 86–87
Unidirectional microphones, 122–124, 269
Uniform resource locators (URLs),
    231, 269
Unit production managers, 9
Universal Serial Bus (USB) connections,
    212
Untouched (native) editing, 217
Upright film editors, 148, 201
URLs (uniform resource locators),
    231, 269
USB (Universal Serial Bus) connections,
    212
User-generated content (USG),
    231–232, 269

V

Vanishing points, 66
Vantage points, 66–68, 79, 81
Variable focal length lenses, 40
Vector graphics, 237
Vectors
    defined, 269
    diagonal, 71
    movement, 69
Velocity
    defined, 269
    of sound, 116–117

Verbally driven structure
    defined, 180–181
    documentaries, 185–186
    overview, 269
Vertical lines of resolution, 59, 61
Video
    See also Motion pictures
    analog linear, 205–206
    distribution, 255
    exhibition, 255
    film conversion to, 220–221
Video assists, 252, 269
Video file formats, 238
Video images
    accurate color, 112–113
    color reproduction, 111–112
Video motion pictures
    analog, 59–60
    digital, 60–61
    standard definition versus high
        definition, 61–62
Video sound, 149
Video tape operators, 247
Virtual reality (VR), 226, 269
Visualizing scripts, 11–14
Voiceover (VO), 144, 185–186, 269
Voltage, 269
Volume unit (VU) meters, 130, 269
VR (virtual reality), 226, 269
VU (volume unit) meters, 130, 269

W

Water Music, 140
Waveforms, 89
Wavelengths
    light, 99–100
    sound, 116–117, 270
Waves, 270
Web
    See also Internet
    browsers, 231, 270
    interactive media, 231
    servers, 231, 270
Wet plates, 24
White light, 99
Whitebalancing, 112–113, 270
Wide angle lenses
    defined, 270
    focus, 68–69
    overview, 40–43
    zooming, 78

Wide shots (WS), 30
Wikipedia, 232
Wild sound, 146
Window dubs, 206–207
Windowboxing, 26, 270
Windows operating system, 221
Wipes, 190, 270
Workprints, 200, 270
WS (wide shots), 30

X-axis, 65, 73, 270
XML (eXtensible Markup Language),
    241, 270

Y-axis, 65, 270
Y/C (S-Video) analog connections,
    205
YouTube, 232

Z-axis
    defined, 270
    depth, 65–69
    subject movement, 73–74
Zoom lenses, 40, 270
Zooming, 78